中国—东盟法律研究中心

重庆市人文社会科学重点研究基地

最高人民法院东盟国家法律研究基地

本书是中国—东盟法律研究中心规划课题成果

中国—东盟法律评论

CHINA-ASEAN LAW REVIEW

【第十四辑】

■ 主　　编: 张晓君
■ 执行编辑: 徐忆斌　罗媛媛

■ Chief Editor: Zhang Xiaojun
■ Executive Editors: Xu Yibin　Luo Yuanyuan

厦门大学出版社 XIAMEN UNIVERSITY PRESS | 国家一级出版社 全国百佳图书出版单位

中國—东盟法律评论

Journal Undang Undang Asean-China

越南—中国—东盟法律信息咨询中心主任陈大兴用越南文字为《中国—东盟法律评论》题写刊名

冯正仁

马来西亚联邦法院前大法官、第五届“中国—东盟法律合作与发展高层论坛”组委会主席冯正仁先生以马来语为《中国—东盟法律评论》题写刊名。

柬埔寨司法部大臣昂翁 •瓦塔纳用高棉语为《中国—东盟法律评论》题写刊名

China-ASEAN Legal Research Centre plays vital role in legal communication and cooperation between China and Myanmar

17.12.16

H.E. Mr. Win Myint
Deputy Attorney General
Union Attorney General's Office
Republic of the Union of Myanmar

前缅甸联邦最高检察院副检察长吴温敏为中心题词

Many thanks for China-ASEAN Legal Research Center to provide the strengthening legal cooperation between Indonesia and China

Nanning. China
6th. Dec. 2017
Indonesia Attorney General
H.M PRASETYO

前印尼最高检总检察长 穆罕默德·普拉赛特为中心题词

中国—东盟法律研究中心：

法学之花盛开！

佟晓玲
驻东盟大使
二〇一六年十二月七日

Advisory Committee

目 录

Research on Legal Issues of Sino-Myanmar Cooperation under the Lancang-Mekong Cooperation Mechanism

Chit Aye Aye Kyi*

Abstract: The Lancang-Mekong Cooperation (LMC) is based on the agreements of the governments of the member countries. The LMC identifies three cooperation pillars of political and security issues, economic and sustainable development, and social, cultural and people-to-people exchanges as well as five key priority areas, namely, connectivity, production capacity, cross-border economic cooperation, water resources, agriculture and poverty reduction. This article expresses the feature of the LMC mechanism, the legal issue of Sino-Myanmar cooperation, and analyzes the impact of Sino-Myanmar cooperation under the LMC.

Keywords: the Lancang-Mekong Cooperation, the Belt and Road Initiative, China-Myanmar Relations, China-Myanmar Economic Corridor

Introduction

The Lancang-Mekong area is one of the regions with the greatest development potential in Asia and beyond. Lancang and Mekong differ in name, but refer to the same river—an important river running across China and the Indo-China Peninsula. Originating from China's Qinghai-Tibet Plateau, the river has its source in Yushu of Qinghai Province. It is called Lancang River in China, while in its downstream after flowing out of Yunnan Province, it

---

* Second-year doctoral candidate of the School of International Law, Southwest University of Political Science and Law (SWUPL) and deputy director of the Constitutional Tribunal of the Union of Myanmar.

is called the Mekong River, running across Myanmar, Laos, Thailand, Cambodia, and Vietnam, measuring 4,880 kilometers in length, covering an area of 795,000 square kilometers, and feeding altogether 326 million people. The five Mekong River countries are home to 230 million people and boast a combined GDP over $600 billion and an average annual growth rate of nearly 7%. Linked by mountains and rivers, the six LMC countries feature cultural similarities, and enjoy profound traditional good neighborliness and friendship, and share closely inter-connected security and development interests. This article explores the LMC mechanism with the practical cooperation and the legal issue of Sino-Myanmar cooperation, and analyzes the official attitude of the Myanmar government relating to the Belt and Road Initiative under the LMC and the specific plan between China and Myanmar. In addition, it analyzes the impact of Sino-Myanmar cooperation under the LMC from the perspectives of the United States government and Indian government on the LMC, finds the impact on Myanmar's political economy and society, and provides suggestions.

1. The Lancang-Mekong Cooperation Mechanism

The Greater Mekong Basin (GMB), covering an area of 795,000 square kilometers, is one of the most biologically and geologically diverse regions on Earth. The Lancang-Mekong River, with an average annual discharge of 475 cubic kilometers, flows roughly 4,900 kilometers from the Qinghai-Tibet Plateau to the ocean through the Mekong Delta in Vietnam. The basin has been rapidly transformed, particularly over the past four decades as each country in the GMB has focused on boosting national income, output, exports, and employment by exploiting what each of their governments sees as an abundant supply of "cheap" natural resources. The resulting expansion of irrigation, hydro-power facilities, plantations, logging, wild-capture fishing, aquaculture, and the intensification of crop and livestock production have degraded the basin's natural resources, and urban growth and industrialization have compounded the damage. Much of the environmental transformation is irreversible. With current policies, these trends will continue, and they will

most likely be accentuated by climate change. This part explores the background and objective of the LMC and the practical cooperation of the LMC.

1.1 Background and Objective of Lancang-Mekong River Cooperation

Since the early 1990s, the sub-regional cooperation that centered on Lancang-Mekong sprang up. Many cooperation mechanisms formed gradually, such as the Greater Mekong Sub-region Cooperation (GMS), the Mekong River Commission (MRC), ASEAN-Mekong Basin Development Cooperation (AMBDC), Golden Quadrangle or the Quadripartite Economic Cooperation (QEC), the Lower Mekong Initiative (LMI), the Summit Meeting between Japan and the Mekong River Basin Countries, the China-Laos-Myanmar-Thailand Joint Patrol Law Enforcement and Security Cooperation on the Mekong River Basin. Thus, a diversified and multilevel cooperation pattern was set up.

Among them, the GMS and MRC attracted more attention. The GMS was initiated by the Asian Development Bank (ADB) and launched in 1992 to enhance cooperation among six countries, namely China, Myanmar, Laos, Thailand, Cambodia and Vietnam. All the countries carried out extensive cooperation in fields such as transportation, energy, agriculture and tourism; and made great progress in promoting the regional economic integration. The MRC was established on the basis of the Committee for Coordination on the Lower Mekong Basin(the former MRC) founded in 1957. In April 1995, Thailand, Vietnam, Laos, Cambodia signed the Agreement on the Cooperation for the Sustainable Development of the Mekong River Basin in Chiang Rai, Thailand and announced the establishment of the new MRC. In 1996, China and Myanmar became the MRC's dialogue partners, but China has not formally joined the MRC. China has been seeking to upgrade the GMS cooperation since the Belt and Road Initiative was put forward in 2013.

In 2012, Thailand proposed the initiative of sustainable development of the Lancang-Mekong Sub-region, which got positive response from the Chinese side. At the 17th China-ASEAN Summit held in November 2014, Chinese Premier Li Keqiang proposed the establishment of the Lancang-Mekong Cooperation Framework, which was warmly welcomed by the five Mekong

River countries. On 23 March, 2016, the First LMC Leaders' Meeting was successfully held in Sanya of China's Hainan Province, which brought together Chinese Premier Li Keqiang, Thai Prime Minister Prayut Chan-o-cha, Cambodian Prime Minister Hun Sen, Lao Prime Minister Thongsing Thammavong, Vice President of Myanmar Sai Mauk Kham, and Vietnamese Deputy Prime Minister Pham Binh Minh. The meeting, with "Shared river, shared future" as its theme, released the Sanya Declaration of the First LMC Leaders' Meeting for a Community of Shared Future of Peace and Prosperity Among Lancang-Mekong Countries, and officially launched the LMC mechanism.

The LMC has identifies three cooperation pillars of political and security issues, economic and sustainable development, and social, cultural and people-to-people exchanges as well as five key priority areas, namely connectivity, production capacity, cross-border economic cooperation, water resources, agriculture and poverty reduction. By synergizing China's Belt and Road Initiative and the ASEAN Community Vision 2025 as well as the Master Plan on ASEAN Connectivity 2025 and visions of other Mekong sub-regional cooperation mechanisms, the LMC is moving towards a new sub-regional cooperation mechanism with unique features driven by internal strength and inspired by South-South cooperation, which will support the ASEAN Community building and regional integration process, as well as promote the implementation of the UN 2030 Agenda for Sustainable Development.①

LMC aims at bolstering the economic and social development of the sub-regional countries, enhancing the wellbeing of their people, narrowing the development gap among regional countries, and supporting ASEAN Community building as well as promoting the implementation of the UN 2030 Agenda for Sustainable Development and advancing South-South cooperation. LMC will be conducted within a framework featuring leaders' guidance, all-round cooperation and broad participation, and follow a government-guided,

---

① Jingyi Zhu, Rui Wang and Li Zhu, The Study on the Current Situations, Problems and Countermeasures in Economic and Trade Exchanges Between China and Lancang-Mekong Countries, *Advances in Economics, Business and Management Research*, 2021, Vol. 146.

multiple-participation and project-oriented model, aimed at building a community of shared future of peace and prosperity among Lancang-Mekong countries and establishing the LMC as an example of a new form of international relations featuring win-win cooperation.①

1.2 Three Cooperation Pillars of Political and Security Issues, Economic and Sustainable Development, Social, Cultural and People-to-People Exchanges

There are four fundamental documents relating to LMC which provide the framework of LMC. They are the Sanya Declaration, the Phnom Penh Declaration, the Five-Year Plan of Action on LMC (2018—2022) and the Vientiane Declaration. These documents are the commitment of the member countries. The Sanya Declaration② includes 26 articles for cooperation among the six member countries, and it is the foundation, the framework, and aims of the LMC. In this declaration, the member countries agree to carry out the practical cooperation of LMC through the three cooperation pillars, which are political and security issues, economic and sustainable development, and social, cultural and people-to-people exchanges.

Regarding the first pillar, the leaders of the member countries have agreed to promote high-level exchanges, dialogue and cooperation in order to enhance trust and understanding in the sub-region and to strengthen sustainable security. It encourages the stakeholders of the members to promote exchanges and cooperation. They have also agreed to deepen law enforcement and security cooperation through information exchange, capacity building and coordination of joint operations according to their rules, regulations and procedures. In addition, they have also agreed to enhance cooperation on non-traditional security threats including terrorism, transnational crimes and

---

① A Breif Introduction of Lancang-Mekong Cooperation, http://www.lmcchina.org/eng/n3/2020/0904/c416294-9755278.html, last visited on Dec.13,2017.

② The Sanya Declaration was Adopted by the First LMC Leaders' Meeting in Sanya, China, https://www.fmprc.gov.cn/mfa_eng/zxxx_662805/t1350039.shtml, last visted on Mar.23,2016.

natural disasters and promote cooperation in addressing climate change impacts, humanitarian assistance, ensuring food, water and energy security.

The 2nd LMC Leaders' Meeting was held on 10 January, 2018 in Phnom Penh. At this meeting, the leaders haveadopted the Phnom Penh Declaration. The LMC leaders have declared to promote high-level exchanges and to strengthen cooperation to safeguard sub-regional peace and stability in the Phnom Penh Declaration. In addition, they also endorsed the Five-Year Plan of Action on the LMC (2018-2022) as a guiding document for LMC development in this declaration. This Plan of Action mentions the detailed activities for the first pillar such as maintaining high-level exchanges, strengthening political dialogues and cooperation, and exchanges among political parties and non-traditional security cooperation. In addition, the leaders of the member countries mentioned "the political and security pillar is of crucial importance to the LMC cooperation" in the Vientiane Declaration.

Regarding the second pillar, the leaders of member countries have agreed to step up both hardware and software connectivity among them. They have agreed to implement trade facilitation measures, promote trade and investment, facilitate business travel, support enhanced economic and technological cooperation and the development of economic zones in border areas, industrial zones and sci-tech parks, and enhance cooperation in sustainable water resources management. The Phnom Penh Declaration reaffirms to enhance hard and soft infrastructure connectivity and facilities. The 5-Year Plan of Action on the LMC (2018-2022) mentions the detailed activities for the second pillar such as production capacity, economy and trade, finance, water resources, agriculture, poverty reduction, forestry, environmental protection and customs and quality inspection. The leaders of member countries recognized that the economic and sustainable development pillars reflects an essential component and the main driving force for the cooperation toward regional development and economic growth in the Vientiane Declaration.

Regarding the third pillar, the leaders of member countries have agreed to strengthen cultural exchanges among member countries, advance cooperation and experience sharing in science and technology, expand cooperation in public health, increase tourism exchanges and cooperation as well as encour-

age exchanges among the mass media, think tanks, women and the youth. The MLC countries agreed to promote cooperation and support engagement from relevant stakeholders in people-to-people connectivity initiatives such as exchanges related to human resource development, education and culture in the Phnom Penh Declaration.① The 5-Year Plan of Action on the LMC (2018-2022) mentions the detail activities for the third pillar such as culture, tourism, education, health, media, people-to-people exchanges and local or regional government cooperation. In the Vientiane Declaration, the leaders have declared to enhance greater people-to-people connectivity through education, intellectual, tourism cooperation, media cooperation and culture exchanges.

1.3 The Cooperation on Five Key Priority Areas of Connectivity, Production Capacity, Cross-Border Economic Cooperation, Water resources, Agriculture and Poverty Reduction

In the Sanya Declaration, the leaders of the member countries have agreed to carry out the practical cooperation of the LMC through the three pillars. In addition, they have endorsed the view that the practical cooperation will be started with five key priority areas during the initial stage of the LMC. These five key priority areas are connectivity, production capacity, cross-border economic cooperation, water resources, agriculture and poverty reduction. They have also emphasized these five key priority areas to start the practical cooperation of the LMC in the Phnom Penh Declaration, the Five-Year Plan of Action on LMC (2018-2022) and the Vientiane Declaration.

Regarding connectivity, the leaders agreed to step up both hardware and software connectivity. They agreed to push forward key infrastructure projects to build a comprehensive connectivity network of highways, railways, and waterways in the Lancang-Mekong region, expedite the construction of network of power grids, telecommunication and the Internet, implement trade facilitation measures, promote trade and investment, and facilitate business travel.

Regarding the second priority, they have agreed to support economic

① Pich Charadine, Cambodia in the Context of Mekong-Lancang Cooperation (MLC): Progress and Ways Forward, *Working Paper*, December 2018, p.9.

and technological cooperation and the development of economic zones in border areas, industrial zones and sci-tech parks.

Regarding the third priority area, the leaders of the member countries have declared to promote cross-border economic cooperation and trade facilitation.

Regarding the fourth priority area, they have agreed to enhance the water resources cooperation, strengthen comprehensive cooperation in technical exchanges, capacity building, drought and flood management, data and information sharing, and conduct joint research and analysis related to Lancang-Mekong River resources.

Regarding the last area, they have also agreed to carry out technical exchanges and capacity building cooperation in agriculture, strengthen cooperation in fishery, animal husbandry and food security as well as elevate the level of agricultural development. They have also agreed to establish poverty reduction model bases.

2. Legal Issues of Sino-Myanmar Cooperation

In 2016, China founded the LMC as an intergovernmental organization for promoting regional water cooperation, which is funded under the auspices of the Belt and Road Initiative (BRI).① The LMC is a new subregional cooperation mechanism tailored by the six countries according to their common needs. Although the six countries have different national conditions, they have common cooperation needs in industrialization, infrastructure construction, upgrading industrial structure, accelerating agricultural modernization, and developing tourism, and have strong complementary advantages. The LMC is a platform discussed, constructed and shared by the six countries. All countries are equal and uphold principles of consensus, equality, mutual benefit and others. The countries jointly plan cooperation according to the actual situation and needs. The LMC is a common responsible farmland for all countries.

① Grunwald, Lancang-Mekong Cooperation: Present and Future of the Mekong River Basin, *Political Sciences*, 2020, Vol. 23, No. 2, p.70.

The LMC adheres to the pragmatic cooperation orientation, adopting government guidance, multi-participation and project-based models to fully mobilize all resources of governments, industries and people, and jointly promote the implementation. In the first foreign ministers' meeting, all parties put forward a number of cooperation projects on water resources, environmental protection, information communication, sanitation, poverty relief and others. The projects have been seriously discussed by related departments of all countries, and are believed to be practical and people-oriented. Some projects are implemented or under implementation, and others are stepping up its consultation and planning. As long as the conditions are ripe, the projects will be immediately launched, and strive for results and benefit the people at an early date.①

The LMC mechanism does not conflict with the existing Great Mekong Sub-region Cooperation (GMS), ASEAN-Mekong Basin Development Cooperation (AMBDC) and the Mekong River Commission (MRC), but promotes and complements these cooperation mechanisms. The greatest superiority of the LMC is the direct promotion of national governments, which will give full play to the advantages of national talent policies and infrastructure, as well as better coordinate and realize the comprehensive development and management of the entire basin.

The LMC is based on the agreements of the governments of the member countries and the memorandum of understanding of the relevant ministries of the member countries, such as Agreement on Commercial Navigation on Lancang-Mekong River among the governments of the People's Republic of China, the Lao People's Democratic Republic, the Union of Myanmar and the Kingdom of Thailand. It is also based on the bilateral agreements and the memorandum of understanding of China and the other member countries, such as the agreement on the transfer of funds for Lancang-Mekong Cooperation Special Fund between China and Myanmar. However, there is no spe-

① Ministry of Foreign Affairs of the People's Republic of China, Five Features of Lancang-Mekong River Cooperation, https://www.fmprc.gov.cn/mfa_eng/zxxx_662805/t1349239.shtml, last visited on Mar.17, 2017.

cific mechanism to solve the disputes between the member countries relating to water management. This part mentions the official attitude of the Myanmar's government towards the Belt and Road Initiative(BRI) and the specific initiative or plan released by the central governments to deepen the political, economic relations between Myanmar and China.

2.1 Official Attitude of the Myanmar's Government towards the Belt and Road Initiative under Lancang-Mekong Cooperation

China is currently the largest investor and trading partner of Myanmar, while Myanmar forms only a small portion of China's total economic input. In the past, China's ambition for fast economic growth took precedence over all other issues, but in recent years China has also started to pay attention to its international reputation as was demonstrated during the 32th Olympic Games. The leaders of both countries always say that they think highly of the "pauk-phaw" friendship between them.

In 2013, China's President Xi Jinping proposed this initiative and it aims to create the world's largest platform for economic cooperation. This project will build a network of roads, railroads and shipping lanes linking nearly 70 countries from China to Europe passing through Central Asia, the Middle East and Russia. It will allow for a more efficient and productive free flow of trade as well as further integration of international markets both physically and digitally.① There are five major goals for BRI such as policy coordination, facilities connectivity, unrestricted trade, financial integration and people-to-people bonds.

It has two main components: the Silk Road Economic Belt and the 21st Century Maritime Silk Road. The BRI also includes the six east-west or north-south trans-regional economic corridors: China-Mongolia-Russia Corridor, New Eurasian Land Bridge, China-Central Asia-WestAsia Corridor, China-Pakistan Corridor, Bangladesh-China-India-Myanmar (BCIM) Economic

---

① Mi Mi Gyi, The Belt and Road Initiative and Its Implication on *Myanmar*, *Mandalay University of Foreign Languages Research Journal*, 2019, Vol. 10, No. 1, p.106.

Corridor and Indochina Peninsula Corridor.[①] Myanmar takes part in the BCIM economic corridor.

Myanmar has geostrategic advantages from which It could play either active diplomacy in multilateral relations or economic benefits. Regarding the proposed 21st Century Maritime Silk Road, Myanmar considered that the route can play an important role in the development of the country by bringing new economic opportunities for Myanmar and its people.

Since 2013, both countries, China and Myanmar, have made significant achievements in taking forward the BRI. Myanmar is regarded as a newly emerging destination for businesses on account of its strategic geographical location. It is located on the cross road of China's "Go West" campaign on the one hand and India's Look East Policy on the other. Similarly, Myanmar is important for the market access of China's landlocked southwestern provinces to Bangladesh and India through transit trade instead of China's eastern coast. Myanmar is always aware of changes and development in China that brings both positive and negative implications. Although Myanmar is a unique case with the longest military administration in the history of modern states, the year 2011 was a new era of developing democracy in Myanmar.

Myanmar-China relations went sour after Myanmar's democratization and reforms were undertaken in 2011 because President U Thein Sein suspended the Myitsone hydropower dam project in his official term, and local people have been against the Chinese investment projects nationwide. However, after the 2015 election, China-Myanmar relations were restructured with the State Counselor's visit to China in August 2016. This visit paved the way for signing two infrastructure development projects: one for electrification in Myingyan Township of Mandalay Region and the other for highway project that runs from Shwe Li-Mandalay-Nay Pyi Taw-Mon State, which is under the framework of Asia Infrastructure Investment Bank. China and Myanmar also reached an agreement to open a cross-border pipeline into

---

① Tian Jinchen, One Belt and One Road: Connecting China and the World, Mckinesey & Company, http://www.mckinsey.com/industries/capitalprojectsandinfrastructure/ourinsights/onebeltandoneroadconnectingchinaandtheworld, last visited on Mar.37,2016.

southeast China during the state visit of President U Htin Kyaw to China in April 2017. Myanmar's position in China's BRI can also be observed from the State Counselor's visit to Beijing to attend the Belt and Road Forum for International Cooperation in May 2017. She laid emphasis on closer people-to-people bond, and held that peaceful and stable neighborhood based on mutual understanding and respects is the basis for the success of the BRI. Even though the Myanmar government is willing to embrace the BRI, there remains the question of local people's anxieties on Chinese investments.

The President of Myanmar has formed a steering committee for the implementation of tasks relating to the BRI. This committee is chaired by the State Counselor Daw Aung San Su Kyi. Vice President U Myint Swe is the vice chairman and other ministers and regional chief ministers are the members.[①] The committee is tasked to implement works relating to the establishment of the CMEC and Myanmar-China border economic cooperation zone under the Belt and Road Initiative.[②] This committee is responsible to coordinate the ministries, governmental organizations and region or state governments in collective operating regarding the BRI projects between China and Myanmar. It is also responsible to pass the policy relating to the BRI projects. So the government of Myanmar has prepared to implement the BRI projects.

The Lancang-Mekong River is the sixth largest river in the world, the third largest river in Asia and the largest river in Southeast Asia.[③] There are more than four regional initiatives such as the GMS, the Mekong River Commission, the LMC, the Lower Mekong Initiative.[④] Among them the LMC is the sub-regional cooperation. In the LMC, China is the main supporter for other

---

① President Office's Notification No. 16/2019, last visited on Jan.25,2019.

② Mizzima news from Myanmar, Myanmar Forms Steering Committee for Implementation of Belt and Road Projects, https://www.mizzima.com/article/myanmar-forms-steering-committee-implementation-belt-and-road-projects, last visited on Jan. 25,2019.

③ Yuanshuai Niu, Analysis on the Dilemma and Coping Strategies of the People-to-People Bond in Lancang-Mekong Basin, Advance in Economics, *Business and Management Research*, 2019, Vol. 110, p.779.

④ Thearith Leng, Mekong Countries in the Context of the Connectivity Competition, *SWP Working Paper*, Session 6, November 2019, p.1.

member countries. The LMC is also meant to promote synergy with the BRI.①

In March 2020, the signing ceremony of the agreement on the transfer of funds for Lancang-Mekong Cooperation (LMC) Special Fund was held in Nay Pyi Taw, the capital of Myanmar. According to the agreement, China will provide over $6.7 million to Myanmar, which will be spent on 22 projects in areas of agriculture, education, and ICT (information and communications technology), among others. In this ceremony, Chinese ambassador said that since the launch of Lancang-Mekong Cooperation, they have put in place an LMC framework guided by leaders and underpinned by all-round cooperation and broad participation. In addition, cooperation has always been enriched through a "3 + 5+ × cooperation framework". The LMC Special Fund has supported more than 410 projects proposed by five countries for the benefit of people's livelihood, and the LMC has transitioned from the nurture phase into a phase of growth. China will continue to work hand in hand with Lancang-Mekong countries, including Myanmar, to solidly promote the LMC. This cooperation is characterized by pragmatism and efficiency so as to make substantial progress and achieve the goal of building a community with a shared future for mankind.② U Soe Han, Permanent Secretary of the Ministry of Foreign Affairs of Myanmar, said that Myanmar is the country with the largest number of projects supported by the LMC Special Fund this year.

Former President U Win Myint participated in the 3rd LMC Leaders' Video Conference Meeting. Myanmar takes over LMC co-chairmanship for the next two years. During the meeting, the leaders of member countries reviewed the work and progress made under the LMC, and cordially exchanged views on the future development of cooperation framework. In his

---

① Sebastian Biba, China's "old" and "new" Mekong River Politics: the Lancang-Mekong Cooperation from a Comparative Benefit-Sharing Perspective, *Water International*, 2018, Vol. 43, No. 5, p.633.

② China and Myanmar Sign Agreement on LMC Special Fund for Projects in Myanmar, http://www.lmcchina.org/eng/2020-03/27/content_41450280.html, last visited on Mar.27, 2020.

statement, U Win Myint expressed his condolences and sympathies for the loss of lives and hardships caused by the COVID-19 throughout the world, and congratulated the governments of China and the Mekong-Lancang countries on their able management to bring the pandemic under control. He also expressed his gratitude to the People's Republic of China for the generous assistance rendered to Myanmar in its fight against the COVID-19.

U Win Myint stated that the LMC has contributed to the socio-economic development of the peoples of the Mekong region, narrowing development gaps and complements to ASEAN Community building and implementation of United Nations' Sustainable Development Goals 2030. He also stressed the importance of LMC's collective strength in promotion of peace and prosperity in the region and in addressing non-traditional security challenges such as climate change, natural disasters, illicit drug trafficking, human trafficking, terrorism and trafficking of firearms and ammunition.

Furthermore, he welcomed the timely expansion of new cooperation areas, in particular health sector, in order to cope with current and future global challenges. He added that the LMC needs to enhance cooperation in research and development of the vaccine for the COVID-19, and formulation of a mechanism to provide equitable access without discrimination. Enhancement of regional connectivity and economic integration in facilitation of a smooth flow of trade, investment, tourism and people-to-people contact were some of the points he stressed in his statement for the consideration of the LMC's future work plan. The government of Myanmar recognizes the Government of China for its generous contribution to the LMC Special Fund which enables the implementation of the projects by the Mekong countries in synergy with respective national sustainable development strategies. So the government of Myanmar's attitude regarding the LMC will be seen as positive.

2.2 The Specific Initiative or Plan Released by the Central Governments to Deepen the Political, Economic Relations between Myanmar and China

There are many plans or projects which have been implemented between China and Myanmar such as the CMEC, Myitsone hydropower dam project,

Yangon "new city" plan, the gas pipeline project, the copper mine project in Monywa, Kyaukpyu Special Economic Zone. Among them the CMEC is the most popular project. The CMEC is the signature project of China's ambitious BRI in Myanmar.[①] The CMEC may be a "Y" shape corridor. It will start from Kunming City, Yunnan Province, China and head toward Mandalay in Myanmar, and then it will extend from Mandalay towards Yangon, Myanmar in the east and Kyaukpyu Special Economic Zone, Rakhine State, Myanmar in the west. The CMEC will further develop the China-Myanmar cooperation under the BRI. As Myanmar locates in the area between China and Southeast Asia, it serves as an important intersection for China's BRI. When both countries implement the CMEC, this corridor will allow China to access the Indian Ocean more conveniently. China and Myanmar agreed to start operating a $ 1.5 billion pipeline in April 2017 under the CMEC project, which allows China to import oil through the Bay of Bengal and has an estimated capacity of 22 million tons of crude oil per year.

The CMEC is based on the long-term interests of the people of both countries, especially those living in the rural areas with lower living standards. This corridor is a great project that gives the benefits highly corresponding to the development plan of both countries. When China and Myanmar can successfully construct the CMEC, not only will it connect the BCIM economic corridor, facilitating China's trade link with Myanmar, Bangladesh, India and even with Middle East and African countries, but also it will represent a model cooperating project of the BRI. The CMEC will make the improvement for the economic relation between China and Myanmar.

There has been fraternal relationship between China and Myanmar for over 70 years. As China stands ready to benefit its neighborhood and Asia at large with its own development regarding BRI, Myanmar considers that the BRI shall play an important role in the development of the country by bringing new economic opportunities for its people. The Myanmar leaders have

---

① Khin Khin Kyaw Kyee, Finding Peace along the China-Myanmar Economic Corridor: Between Short-Term Interests and Long-Lasting Peace, Institute for Strategy and Policy-Myanmar China Research Project, *Working Paper*, 2019, No.3, p.18.

shown their strong support for the BRI. Therefore, in the official visit of Myanmar State Counselor Daw Aung San Suu Kyi to China in August 2016, she announced in the joint press release that Myanmar welcomed China's BRI and the initiative of Bangladesh-China-India-Myanmar (BCIM) Economic Corridor. Moreover, in the two days of the Belt and Road Forum for International Cooperation in Beijing, Myanmar State Counselor said that the BRI would bring peace, reconciliation and prosperity to the region and the world at large and Myanmar was willing to work with China on peace and stability.

The CMEC is very important and beneficial for both China and Myanmar in the cooperation and coordination of economic, social and political affairs. China will have the chance to connect with the Indian Ocean under this corridor. This corridor will accelerate the transfer of China's industries to Myanmar. In addition, the CMEC is one part of the BCIM Economic Corridor, whose core objectives are development of regional transport infrastructure, accelerated exploitation of the resource-rich region, expansion of regional trade and border crossings, and establishment of industrial growth zones. The CMEC is also very important in implementing China's Belt and Road Initiative (BRI), which is a great strategy for China to connect Eurasia, South east Asia, South Asia and Africa through roads, railway lines, maritime routes and energy infrastructure.①

The BRI consists of two paths, which are the Silk Road Economic Belt, a Eurasian overland trading road modeled on its ancient prototype, running across Central Asia and Russia and linking China with Europe, and the 21st Century Maritime Silk Road, a trading route connecting China and Europe via Southeast Asia, India and Africa, and building among others on China's maritime bases in the Indian Ocean. Regarding this BRI, China's President Xi Jinping introduced in Kazakhstan the "Belt" originally targeted only at Central Asia in 2013. Later in this year, he also presented in Indonesia the "Road"

① Sai Ur Rahman and Zhao Shurong, Analysis of Chinese Economic and National Security Interests in China-Pakistan Economic Corridor (CPEC) under the Framework of One Belt One Road (OBOR) Initiative, *Arts and Social Sciences Journal*, 2017, Vol.8, No.4, p.1.

mainly directed at the Association of South east Asian Nations (ASEAN).[①]

The six economic corridors under the BRI run parallel to or link the "Belt and Road" and differ largely in size, and are at various stages of planning and implementation, with some relying on existing infrastructure or projects integrated into the BRI. Among the six economic corridors, the Bangladesh-China-India-Myanmar (BCIM) Economic Corridor has been under consideration for several years. In addition, in Myanmar, the most strategic project under the BRI is centered on the port of Kyaukpyu in the Rakhine State, from where twin gas and oil pipelines run across the country to Kunming in China's Yunnan Province. This oil pipeline is of strategic importance for China as an alternative import route beside the Malacca Straits. Kyaukpyu is also a designated special economic zone, where China's state-owned CITIC Group has a majority of stakes in its development, but its key role as a production and connectivity hub requires new rail or upgraded road infrastructure.[②]

The BCIM Economic Corridor is one of the corridors of the BRI, and the CMEC is one part of the BCIM Economic Corridor. If China and Myanmar can implement the CMEC projects well, this corridor will effectively help implement the projects of the BCIM Economic Corridor as well as the BRI. The CMEC will create many other opportunities and benefits for economic cooperation between China and Myanmar. On one hand, this corridor will bring development opportunities and benefits to China's economically backward southwestern provinces, in particular, Yunnan and Sichuan. On the other hand, it will reduce Myanmar's dependence on Thailand in foreign direct investment and its gas exports as the corridor will provide Myanmar with an alternative export market for its natural gas and other commercial goods.[③]

---

① Gisela Grieger, One Belt, One Road (OBOR): China's Regional Integration Initiative, *European Parliamentary Research Service*, 2016, Vol. 6, p.3

② Henrik Hallgren and Richard Ghiasy, Security and Economy on the Belt and Road: Three Country Case Studies, *SIPRI Insights on Peace and Security*, 2017, No. p.6

③ Zhao Hong, Yang Mu, China-Myanmar Economic Corridor: Opportunities and Challenges, *EAI Background Brief*, No. 670.

Although the CMEC may bring many opportunities and benefits in economic cooperation for both countries, there are many potential risks and challenges regarding the legal protection for this project. The bilateral cooperation for CMEC grounded on the projects inevitably involves the policy support and coordination between China and Myanmar. It also requires the participation of enterprises and individuals.

In implementing the CMEC project, both countries shall enact the necessary laws, rules, regulations and policies of the countries concerned. The coordination between the laws, rules, regulations and policies of both countries is also unavoidable. In such case, the laws, rules and regulations of both countries concerning trade, investment, finance and banking, protection of intellectual property rights, product inspection and safety standards, as well as the labor law, environmental law, tax law and anti-unfair competition law of the host country shall be taken into consideration.

3. Analysis of the Impact of Sino-Myanmar Cooperation under the Lancang-Mekong Cooperation Mechanism

The Lancang-Mekong Cooperation is a new sub-regional cooperation platform jointly initiated and established by China, Cambodia, Laos, Myanmar, Thailand, and Vietnam.① Currently, the LMC is not only beginning with the principles and goals of the BRI but also holding an international prominent position which may eventually reformulate concerns of Southeast Asian countries about China's all-round cooperation with the BRI's funds. In addition, it has become one of the most successful cooperation mechanisms in Asia. Actually, it focuses on priority areas of cooperation among its member countries such as connectivity, production capacity, cross-border economic cooperation, and water resource management.

Under the Vientiane Declaration of the 3rd MLC Leaders' Meeting, one

① China and Myanmar Sign Agreement on LMC Special Fund for Projects in Myanmar, http://www.lmcchina.org/eng/2020-03/27/content_41450280.html, last visited on Mar.27,2020.

expresses their common aspiration and collective commitment to advance the MLC development to realize the enormous and untapped development potentials through creating conducive environment of lasting peace, stability, solidarity and harmony, which will contribute to sustainable development and shared prosperity in the Lancang-Mekong region as well as jointly addressing socio-economic and environmental challenges faced by the region. In these situations, the LMC's aim is not only to cooperate in the economic and social sectors but also to upgrade its security sectors. In addition, as China is the main support to LMC's fund, China has more influence on other member countries. Considering this, the United States, Japan, South Korea, India, Australia, the European Union and Russia have stepped in and coopted sub-regional countries to add to their geopolitical and geo-economic weight.① This part emphasizes the perspectives of the United States and India because China and the United States are two powers in the world, and China and India are the neighbouring countries of Myanmar. In addition, it also mentions the impact on Myanmar's political economy and society.

3.1 The Ways Adopted by the U.S. Government and the India Government to Watch the Cooperation between China and Myanmar

The United States, after the cold war, aimed its policy toward the Mekong River Basin's countries by focusing on strengthening its strategic position in order to balance the emerging power of China and to help regional economics integrate into global value chains. On the one hand, China leads the LMC; on the other hand, the United States initiates the Lower Mekong Initiative (LMI). The LMI was launched by former President Obama in his first year in office in 2009. It is a multinational partnership among the LMC's member countries, that is, Cambodia, Laos, Myanmar, Thailand and Vietnam, except China and the United States. The framework of the LMI is a detailed roadmap that strengthens cooperation between member

① Li Jiacheng, Li Zengtaozi, Constraints on Poverty Reduction Cooperation under the Lancang-Mekong Cooperation Mechanism, *China Quarterly of International Strategic Studies*, 2019, Vol. 5, No. 3, p.441.

countries in the areas of energy, agriculture, environment, water management and food security.[①] In addition, the LMI may be the frontline for the United States relating to "Indo-Pacific strategy."[②]

At present, China and American are the biggest power states. One always watches the other's actions because they always counterbalance each other. For example, as China leads the LMC, the U.S. leads the LMI project; as China leads the RCEP, the U.S leads the TPP; as China works together with ASEAN, American also works together with ASEAN. So the United States emphasizes the LMC projects because the LMC is led by China and it wants to reduce the influence of China over member countries of the LMC.

China and Myanmar are close neighbors and their diplomatic relations began in 1950. Myanmar and China share a border of nearly 2200 kilometers. Myanmar also plays a very important role in the diplomacy of China. In addition, Myanmar would be strategically important for China to direct access to the Pacific Ocean and the Indian Ocean.[③] Myanmar has experienced a political transition in the process of nine to ten years since 2010 with two successive governments. Before 2010, the Chinese government had a good relationship with the successive governments of Myanmar. However, most of people in Myanmar disliked the Chinese government and Chinese businessmen because they thought that the Chinese government and Chinese businessmen did not pay due attention to them.

After the general election of Myanmar in 2010, the President U Thein Sein, former General, initiated a series of political and economic reforms, which resulted in a substantial opening of the long-isolated country. He had also done that the National League for Democracy (NLD), which was led by

---

① Li Jiacheng, Li Zengtaozi, Constraints on Poverty Reduction Cooperation under the Lancang-Mekong Cooperation Mechanism, *China Quarterly of International Strategic Studies*, Vol. 5, No. 3, 2019, p.443.

② Pongphisoot Busbarat, Re-enmeshment in the Mekong: External Powers' *Turn*, *Iseas Yusof Ishak Institute*, 2020, No. 88, p.7.

③ Poon Kim Shee, The Political Economy of China-Myanmar Relations: Strategic and Economic Dimensions, *The International Studies Association of Ritsumeikan University: Ritsumeikan Annual Review of International Studies*, 2002, Vol.1, p.36

Daw Aung San Suu Kyi, could enter the election in 2012. The distance between Myanmar and the United States is very long and they are not neighbors. In terms of the past history, we can't say that the relationship between them is good. The United States has imposed sanctions on Myanmar's military government. However, the United States supports the peaceful, prosperous and democratic sectors in Myanmar.① The United States also recognized the political transition of Myanmar in 2011. In addition, after the NLD government took over the state in 2016, the relation between the United States and Myanmar is in good progress.

Although the United States is not much interested in Myanmar, it is interested in the relation between China and Myanmar in order to check the Chinese power. At present, the government of China is striving to implement the BRI, which is a great strategy for China to connect Eurasia, Southeast Asia, South Asia and Africa through roads, railway lines, maritime routes and energy infrastructure.② The United States always criticizes the BRI project and is worried that China's power will be overwhelmed. The Myanmar government has agreed to cooperate in the BRI. In addition, China and Myanmar have agreed to build the CMEC. Regarding the CMEC project, the United States also emphasizes it because it thinks that China will direct access to the Pacific Ocean and the Indian Ocean via CMEC. Although we don't know the consent of the United States relating the China-Myanmar's relation, the philosophers relating to strategic in the United States thinks to change the economic sanction, which was imposed on Myanmar because this sanction will be more closely to Myanmar with China.

India, one of the most neighbors of Myanmar, also initiated the Mekong-Ganga Cooperation Initiative (MGC) in 2000. It included six members:

---

① U.S. Relations with Burma, http://www.state.gov/u-s-relations-with-burma/, last visited on Jan.12,2020.

② Sai Ur Rahman and Zhao Shurong, Analysis of Chinese Economic and National Security Interests in China-Pakistan Economic Corridor (CPEC) under the Framework of One Belt One Road (OBOR) Initiative, *Arts and Social Sciences Journal*, 2017, Vol.8, No.4, p.1

Myanmar, Laos, Thailand, Cambodia, Vietnam and India. All the countries except India are the members of the LMC. The MGC aims to cooperate in tourism, culture, education, transport and communications.① It also aims to facilitate closer contacts among the people inhabiting these two major river basins.

In 2019, the member states of the MGC issued the MGC Plan of Action (2019-2022). This plan includes the detailed activities to carry out the cultural cooperation, tourism cooperation, cooperation in education, cooperation in public health and traditional medicine, cooperation in agriculture and allied sectors, cooperation in water resources management, cooperation in science and technology, cooperation in transport and communications, cooperation in micro-, small- and medium-sized enterprises, skill development and capacity building, and quick impact projects scheme.②

As China has been implementing the LMC project, India has also been implementing the MGC Initiative. In addition, India, after practicing the Look East Policy, promoted the construction of economic corridors in the Mekong River Basin and tried to build an economic network connecting the Mekong River Basin and the Ganges River Basin. Promoting the implementation of the MGC shows India's perspective on the LMC that India deeply emphasizes the members of the LMC except China, because it wants to constrain the power of China in Asia.

Myanmar and India were the British colonials and have gained their independence after World War Ⅱ. India's Look East Policy and its interest in Myanmar reflects growing international interest in Asia as an engine of economic growth in the 21st century. Myanmar supports India's quest for a place in the sun and is comfortable with India's increasing engagement with its immediate and extended neighborhood. Moreover, India's move to engage Myan-

---

① http://www. newsonair. com/News? title=12th-Mekong-Ganga-Cooperation-Senior-Officials %26%2339%3B-Meeting-reviews-progress-made-since-Aug-last-year&id = 399028, last visited on Jan.12,2020.

② Mekong Ganga Cooperation (MGC) Plan of Action (2019-2022), https://mea.gov.in/bilateral-documents.htm? dtl/31712/Mekong+Ganga+Cooperation+MGC+Plan+of+Action+20192022, last visited on Jan.12,2020.

mar closely reflects its growing concern over Myanmar's jettisoning its policy of neutrality toward India and China and gradually tilting toward China.①

India always emphasizes the China-Myanmar relation because India wants to constrain the emerging power of China in Asia and in the world. In addition, Myanmar is situated at the junction of East, South, and Southeast Asia and functions as a land bridge to Southeast and East Asia. Myanmar is the second-largest of India's neighbors, and they share a land border of 1,640 kilometers. Myanmar has a role in the Bay of Bengal littoral region and shares a maritime boundary with India. Myanmar shares a 2,185-kilometer border with China, and is located next to the disputed section of the India-China border.

China has also built an all-weather road from Kunming in Southern China to Mandalay in central Myanmar. Trade between the two has increased by multiples, so much so that China is now Myanmar's third largest trading partner (after Thailand and Singapore). Plans have also been formalized for the transportation of oil and gas through a 1,100-kilometer pipeline from Kyaukpyu Port in Myanmar to Kunming, the capital of Yunnan Province. After the completion and activation of this pipeline, China's dependence on the Malacca Straits will be reduced considerably.

3.2 Impact on Myanmar's Political Economy and Society

Myanmar is an important neighbor and partner in the implementation of BRI for China. The Chinese government always attaches great importance to developing its relations with Myanmar.② Regarding the China-Myanmar relations, China and Myanmar are close neighbors and their diplomatic relations started in 1950. Myanmar and China share a border of nearly 2,200 kilometers. Myanmar also plays a very important role in the diplomacy of China. In addition, Myanmar would be strategically important for China to direct access to the Pacific Ocean and the Indian Ocean. We have seen that

① Gurmeet Kanwal, A Strategic Perspective on India-Myanmar Relations, https://www.researchgate.net/publication/292667167, last visited on Jan.12,2020.

② Li Chenyang, From Comprehensive Strategic Cooperative Partnership to the Community with a Shared Future, *Myanmar Affairs*, 2020, No. 15, p.236.

although the China-Myanmar relations are good mostly, the relationship of the Chinese government and the Myanmar people is not so. This part explores the impacts on Myanmar's political economy and society under the China-Myanmar relations with the suggestions for a good China-Myanmar relationship.

As China and Myanmar are close neighbors, one country is always aware of changes and development of the other that bring both positive and negative implications for them. Although, before 2011, China-Myanmar relations seemed good, it can be seen that it was only limited to the leaders of both countries. The Chinese government only built the good relations with the government of Myanmar but not the Myanmar's people. Their relations went sour after Myanmar's democratization and reforms were undertaken in 2011. There are several factors which have been crucial matters to their relations, such as suspension of China's state-owned investment of State Power Investment Corporation(SPIC) in the Myitsone hydropower dam project, local people's opinion on the gas pipeline project which runs from Rakhine to Yunnan, severe environmental degradation in the copper mine project in Monywa, illegal trading of jade in northern Kachin and Chinese people's influx into Mandalay areas. Besides, the railway project linking Kunming to Myanmar's Rakhine coast was cancelled in 2014 by Myanmar Railway Ministry due to the strategic reasons, for example, this railway will give China access to the Indian Ocean.

The Chinese investors have faced difficulties since 2011 such as the suspension of the Myitsone Power Plant project.① President U Thein Sein suspended the Myitsone dam project during his tenure because this project was against the will of the people.② However, after the 2015 election, China-Myanmar relations have been restructured with the State Counselor's visit to China in August 2016.

---

① Chen Yang Li, James Char, China-Myanmar Relations since NayPyiDaw's Political Transition: How Beijing can balance short-term interests and long-term values, *RSIS Working Paper*, 2015, No. 288, p.5.

② David I. Steinberg, Hongwei Fan, *Modern China-Myanmar Relations: Dilemmas of Mutual Dependence*, NIAS Press,2012, p.354.

In February 2021, there was political change in Myanmar. The Acting President of the State declared the State of Emergency in accord with Section 417 of the Constitution (2008) and handed over legislative, executive and judicial powers of the State to the Commander-in-Chief of Defence Services in accordance with Section 418 (a). The Commander-in-Chief of Defence Services pledged to practise the genuine and discipline-flourishing multiparty democratic system in a fair manner. Upon completion of the tasks in accord with the provisions of the State of Emergency, the free and fair general election will be held, and assigned duty of the State will be handed over to the political party which won in the election.

In the current situation of Myanmar, most people in Myanmar are dissatisfied with the military government, the policy and the standing of the Chinese government relating to the performance of Myanmar's military. They think that the Chinese government has stood by the State Administration Council, Military Government of Myanmar, and neglected their feelings and opinions. In addition, they assume that western countries including the United States will only help them regarding their Summer revolution. So it is clear that China-Myanmar relationship is very important for Myanmar's political economy and may impact Myanmar's political society.

At present, although we can say that the government of China and the government of Myanmar have built deep relations, the relations between the government of China and the people of Myanmar remain to be improved. In order to promote good relations not only between both governments but also between Chinese government and the people of Myanmar, the government of China should pay attention to the opinions of the people of Myanmar. Regarding Chinese investment in Myanmar, the Chinese investors should get the consent of local people where the investment projects are located, create job opportunities for them, and promote the development of the area. On the other hand, if Myanmar's government can't create a good environment for Chinese investors and businessmen, Myanmar's economy and investment will fall behind because the top foreign investment of Myanmar is Chinese investment and Myanmar's economy mainly depends on China-Myanmar border trade. Therefore, the Myanmar government should create related policy and legal framework for foreign investors transparently.

4. Conclusion

The LMC is a platform discussed, constructed and shared by six countries. All countries are equal and uphold principles of consensus, equality, mutual benefits and others. The countries jointly plan cooperation according to the actual situation and needs. The LMC is a common responsible farmland for all countries.

The LMC is based on the agreements of the governments of the member countries and the memorandum of understanding of the relevant ministries of the member countries, such as Agreement on Commercial Navigation on Lancang-Mekong River among the governments of the People's Republic of China, the Lao People's Democratic Republic, the Union of Myanmar and the Kingdom of Thailand. It is also based on the bilateral agreements and the memorandum of understanding of China and the other member countries, such as the agreement on the transfer of funds for LMC Special Fund between China and Myanmar. In order to implement strongly the LMC, the member countries should create a legal framework. The United States government and the India government also pay much attention to the LMC and China-Myanmar relations to constrain China's power.

Although Myanmar has built deep relations with China under the LMC, the relations between the government of China and the people of Myanmar remain to be improved. In order to promote good relations not only between both governments but also between the Chinese government and the people of Myanmar, the government of China should pay attention to the opinions of the people of Myanmar. Regarding Chinese investment in Myanmar, the Chinese investors should get the consent of local people where the investment projects are located, create job opportunities for them, and promote the development of the area.

The Substantive Issues Combating Transnational Organized Crimes in the Lancang-Mekong Region and Suggestions

Cho Nge Nge Thein*

Abstract: Socio-economic vulnerabilities increase and accelerate in the Lancang-Mekong regional population, and these incidents are caused by threat of transnational organized crimes (TOC). Governments in the region have adopted national policies and legal frameworks to fight those crimes even though they are vulnerable countries affected by TOC issues in the Lancang-Mekong region. However, policy gap and weak enforcement are challenges in cooperation among countries in the region. This article mainly focuses on examining the cooperation system in handling TOC in the Lancang-Mekong region, discussing international legal instruments against TOC, and exploring appropriate cooperation mechanism for effective collaboration on combating TOC issues among the Lancang-Mekong countries, by reviewing and analyzing literatures regarding current cooperation mechanism and response to fight TOC in the Lancang-Mekong area. Recommendations and suggestions are also put forward to support the combating mechanism for TOC issues and to conduct additional research.

Keywords: Lancang-Mekong Cooperation (LMC), Transnational Organized Crimes (TOC), Human Trafficking, Drug Trafficking, Terrorism

1. Introduction

A river is named Lancang River in China and it is also called Mekong River that determines the boundary line for Myanmar, Cambodia, Laos, Thailand and Vietnam. Depending on the great Mekong River, those six riparian countries

* Ph. D, Candidate of SWUPL, Officer of MOLA, Myanmar.

are connected in several areas such as trade, investment, tourism, water resources, water transportation, agriculture, security and culture. Therefore, the LMC countries agreed to set up a cooperation mechanism in 2016 by proposing and initiating of Thailand to become strong collaboration in the political, economic and social pillars and to promote peace and prosperity in the region.[①]"Shared river, shared future" is the theme of the LMC, and the LMC aims to improve people's livelihood in the area. Government authorities agreed to cooperate in trade connectivity, public health, water resources, etc., and to promote agriculture cooperation and security cooperation for peace and tranquillity in the border area. However, transnational crimes threaten those countries, and according to data from United Nations Office on Drugs and Crime (UNODC), drug trafficking, manufacturing and trading the precursor chemicals, human trafficking and other crimes are increasing year by year in the Mekong sub-region. [②]

2. Cooperation Mechanism for Combating TOC in the Mekong Region

According to a summary report from DT Institute, transnational organized crimes (TOC), especially human trafficking and drug trafficking issues, encompass the Mekong region including the southwestern part of China. Perpetrators commit transnational crimes such as money laundering, human trafficking, exploitation of migrant workers, and they doesn't settle in one country when committing such offences. Therefore, the government departments and central authorities of respective countries must cooperate with each other. However, there will be difficulties in cooperating due to the dif-

① Busbarat, Pongphisoot, Grabbing the Forgotten: China's Leadership Consolidation in Mainland Southeast Asia through the Mekong-Lancang Cooperation, *Research Gate*. Issue 2018, No. 17.

② H. T. Luong, Transnational Crime and its Trends in Southeast Asia: A Detailed Narrative in Vietnam. *International Journal for Crime, Justice and Social Democracy*, 2020, Vol.9, No.2, pp.88-101.

ferent legal systems. Therefore, this part will overview the status of TOC in the Mekong Region and examine the cooperation mechanism among the LMC countries to handle this issue.

2.1 A Brief Study of the Current Status of Each TOC Issue in the Mekong Region

(a) Drug Trafficking

Illegal production and trading of drug and opium has a long history in the Mekong region. Significantly, heroin is transported from East Asian counties such as Afghanistan to the Golden Triangle area, and then it is imported crossing Myanmar and Yunnan Province of China and flows into other countries in the region. Heroin was majority seizure of 8.5 tons in 2000 in the Greater Mekong Sub-region (GMS). Methamphetamine trade was also estimated to be over 40 million a year in the region and the total seizure in 2018 in the region was 116 tons. ① The Mekong MoU on Drug Control was concluded between China, Lao PDR, Myanmar, Thailand and the United Nations International Drug Control Programme (now UNODC) in 1993 to address the problem of using, trafficking and producing drug in the Mekong region. The Sub-regional Action Plan (SPA) on Drug Control was established through the Mekong MoU and the SAP is a framework to address the difficulty in law enforcement, international judicial cooperation and drug reduction. According to the UNODC report, cross-border security, economic liberalization, reduced border control and travel restrictions in the region pose some challenges in a law enforcement mechanism. Some MoU countries partially perform international legal instruments on TOC in their national legal framework. This situation may have some gaps for international legal cooperation in judicial matters.

(b) Human Trafficking and Smuggling

According to the UNODC, migrants from Myanmar, Lao PDR and

---

① H.T. Luong, Transnational Crime and its Trends in Southeast Asia: A Detailed Narrative in Vietnam. *International Journal for Crime, Justice and Social Democracy*, 2020, vol.9, No.2, pp.88-101.

Cambodia are smuggled to Thailand after paying service fees to illegal smugglers, and these migrants are also trafficked to be victims of sexual exploitation and labour exploitation. Thailand is also a destination country for human smuggling from Myanmar to Malaysia.

According to the "Report on the Ninth Mekong Regional Workshop Towards Well-Knit Net of Assistance for Victims of Trafficking in the Grater Mekong Sub-region", the number of victims of trafficking (VOT) to China was increasing, and the Myanmar government strived to raise the number of border liaison offices to identify and protect the victims and to enhance border cooperation with China. Vietnam also suffered from the same issue that the human traffickers sent Vietnamese women and children to China for adoption, reproduction and traded new-born babies. So Vietnam proposed imporving the Memorandum of Understanding, Standard Operation Procedure (SOP) for anti-TIP and that regular meetings should be held among the GMS countries for enhancing the cooperation.

The Coordinated Mekong Ministerial Initiative against Trafficking (COMMIT) signed the Memorandum of Understanding (MoU) in 2004 to combat trafficking in person especially in women and children. The cooperation mechanism between the GMS countries is started by the COMMIT and these intergovernmental organizations continue their good cooperation by formulating bilateral agreements to eradicate the TIP issue in countries such as Laos and Thailand, Vietnam and China. The COMMIT has been successfully continued by signing declarations in 2007, 2012 and 2015, and the subregional action plan was also adopted to address the TIP issue. The COMMIT also established the Transnational Referral Mechanism including assessment and development of institutional design, capacity building and adoption of indicator guidelines for victims' identification.①

---

① Japan International Cooperation Agency (JICA), Report on the Ninth Mekong Regional Workshop towards Well-Kint net of Assistance for Victims of Trafficking in the Grater Mekong Sub-region: Learning From the Bilateral and Regional Cooperation Experiences, JICA Office Thailand, 2019. pp. 1-45.

(c) Wildlife and Forest Crime

Custom authorities of Australia, Bangladesh, Brunei, Cambodia, China's mainland, Hong Kong SAR, India, Lao PDR, Mongolia, Myanmar, Nepal, New Zealand, Singapore, Thailand, Vietnam cooperate in the Mekong Dragon Operation II from May to September 2019 to combat the drug trafficking, wildlife products trading and forest crime in those countries. The operation reported that 1,892 kg of 1,567 endangered wildlife products, 82 live wild animals, 145 tons of protected timber were seized during the four months' operation period.①

According to a report of the Wildlife Justice Commission (WJC), raw ivory and pangolin scales are being trafficked in Cambodia, Lao PDR, and Vietnam. WJC reports that border control and travel restrictions reduce illegal transport and trafficking of the wildlife products and species. World Wildlife Fund (WWF) implements the Provisional Wildlife Enforcement Networks in the Golden Triangle area (a connected border area of Myanmar, Laos and Thailand) to conduct joint enforcement action to deter trafficking of wildlife and their products and to support national law for protection of wildlife in the Mekong region.

(d) Cultural Property Smuggling

Cultural properties are the treasure of a country, including temples and ancient pagodas, which are also the landmark and tourist attraction of the country. These properties need to be protected and maintained without destroying their original objects. Cultural properties in the Mekong region are being stolen, transported, trafficked and removed from their original place. UNESCO and the Thai National Commission for UNESCO co-hosted the "Greater Mekong Sub-regional Symposium for International Cooperation to Protect Cultural Properties" in July, 2019 to strengthen regional cooperation within law enforcement agencies in the Mekong region, and an operation-level workshop titled "Countering Trafficking of Cultural Objects in the Containerised Supply Chain" was also held as a special training for capacity

---

① UNODC, *Wildlife and Forest Crime Analytic Toolkit*, United Nations, New York, 2012, pp.1-212.

building of customs officers to seize, store and handle cultural properties. Improvement in coordination at operation level for cultural objects came out as a result of the discussion of the Symposium.

(e) Anti-money Laundering

Trade-based money laundering related with drug trafficking, casinos, illegal trading of antiquities, wildlife species and products is increasing in Mekong region countries like Thailand and Lao PDR. According to their global survey in 2017, UNODC estimated that there were only 26 percent of investigation, prosecution and jurisdiction set up upon wildlife and money laundering crimes in the region, which shows inadequate cooperation and institutional arrangements, weak law enforcement and legal framework in the region regarding money laundering crimes.①

(f) Terrorism and Financing Terrorism

Foreign terrorist fighters continue their movements in the Middle East, Southeast Asia and the Mekong region. During last three years, investigating officers and prosecutors from the Mekong region have participated in several workshops and seminars for policy dialogue and practical training for cooperation and fighting against terrorism and issues of border security, immigration and customs. The workshops and seminars had positive outcomes for the participant countries such as accelerating effective cooperation, strengthening capacity building, welcoming and accepting technical assistance from international and regional organizations, and accessing more legal and general information regarding terrorism and foreign terrorist fighters. The Mekong region component of the Global Programme against Money Laundering (GPML) operated in Vietnam, Lao PDR, Myanmar and Cambodia from 2011 to 2016. According to the report of UNODC, the project was addressed to the countries to strengthen national legislation on money laundering and financing terrorism, and to have a deeper knowledge among relevant stake-

---

① Navin Beekarry, The International Anti-Money Laundering and Combating the Financing of Terrorism Regulatory Strategy: A Critical Analysis of Compliance Determinants in International Law, *North-western Journal of International Law and Business*, 2011, Vol.37, p.137.

holders and better cooperation in regional and international areas.

2.2 Current Cooperation System for Combating TOC in the Mekong Region

After studying the status of TOC issues in the region, the article examines the cooperation and collaboration mechanism of LMC countries to fight against TOC and also identifies the strengths and weaknesses of the mechanism.

Governments of the six riparian states have adopted many cooperation arrangements both to fight TOC issues and to develop common interest among the countries. The Mekong-Lancang Water Resources Cooperation Centre adopted the Five year Action Plan (2018-2022) for sharing knowledge and information, doing joint research, providing technical assistance and enhancing capacity building in five areas such as connectivity, production capacity, cross-border economic cooperation, water resources and poverty reduction. The Action Plan aims to cooperate in water resource, and it does not address the TOC issue.

In 1995, the Mekong Agreement was adopted between the six Mekong countries (China, Myanmar, Lao PDR, Cambodia, Thailand and Vietnam) to foster the cooperation for sustainable development in the region. The Mekong River Commission (MRC) was also established for the purpose of regional cooperation to enhance the socio-economic role in the Mekong River Basin. The Commission has priority in three areas as follows: to develop rules and regulations for using water under the Water Utilization Programme, to cooperate in and facilitate sustainable development in the Mekong Basin, and to monitor the protection of environment and water-related resources.① Myanmar has the status as a dialogue partner in the MRC.

The GMS, the MRC, the Mekong-Lancang Water Resources Cooperation Centre are the regional organizations and programs in the Mekong region, and they mainly focus on cooperating in and enhancing the economic and so-

---

① Rémy Kinna and Alistair Rieu-Clarke, *The Governance Regime of the Mekong River Basin: Can the Global Water Conventions Strengthen the* 1995 *Mekong Agreement?* Brill Publishing House, 2017.

cial development of the region, and one of the weaknesses is not addressing the TOC issue.

China, Lao PDR, Myanmar and Thailand established the Mekong River Basin joint law enforcement and security cooperation mechanism in 2011 to promote law enforcement, security cooperation and to control organized crimes in the Mekong River sub-region. In 2015, the Ministerial Meeting on Law Enforcement and Security Cooperation for Mekong River announced a joint statement that included the following points: to hold the Ministerial Meeting once every two years and to hold the senior-level meeting for law enforcement and security cooperation once a year; to establish the Lancang-Mekong River Comprehensive Law Enforcement and Security Cooperation Centre; and to cooperate and fight against organized crimes including drug trafficking, human trafficking and terrorism. Cambodia and Vietnam are observers in this cooperation mechanism. The joint statement is not legally binding to member countries and it is just an understandable cooperation mechanism for communication, information exchange and the setup of a combined operation centre.

Senior officials met and discussed the Lancang-Mekong Cooperation, and the Third Lancang-Mekong Cooperation Leaders' Meeting was held in 2020 by way of virtual meeting. State leaders and president participated in this video conferencing meeting and stated their honourable speeches where they appealed to work together for a new international Land-Sea Trade Corridor, water resources cooperation, the promotion of peace and cooperation to combat security issues in the Mekong region, for example, transnational organized crimes including drug trafficking, human trafficking and smuggling, terrorism and financial terrorism.

The Grater Mekong Sub-region countries have implemented the Border Liaison Office Mechanism in the last two decades, and the mechanism has expanded under the Partnership against Transnational Crime through Regional Organized Law Enforcement Project (PATROL project) to strengthen cross-border cooperation against migrant smuggling, human trafficking, illicit cross-border movement of wildlife, drug and timber. According to the UNDOC's report, the Border Liaison Office and border posts need to

provide sufficient infrastructure such as office space, communication equipment, internet and vehicles. Database establishment and maintenance system are also required. Furthermore, government departments and agencies such as customs, police forces, immigration and border trade department need to improve themselves to facilitate effective cooperation in the Border Liaison Mechanism. Border officials also need capacity building and awareness regarding law enforcement and all forms of transnational organized crimes. Therefore, the report indicates that the cooperation mechanism may face challenges and weaknesses in practice.

According to the Convention against Transnational Organized Crime, mutual legal assistance (MLA) and extradition are important matters for the state parties in combating TOC. Regarding mutual legal assistance in criminal matters in ASEAN, the Model Treaty on Mutual Legal Assistance in Criminal Matters (MLAT) entered into force in 2013 and the ASEAN Ministers/Attorneys-General Meeting of the Central Authorities of Mutual Legal Assistance in Criminal Matters (AMAG-MLAT) and the Senior Officials Meeting of the Central Authorities of Mutual Legal Assistance in Criminal Matters (SOM-MLAT) are included into Annex 1 of the ASEAN Charter. Currently, senior officials of respective government departments from ASEAN countries actively participate in the meetings of SOM-MLAT. China has bilateral agreements with some ASEAN countries for cooperating in the MLA issue.

The author of this article attended the ASEAN Regional Conference on Promoting Criminal Justice Cooperation that was held on 26 March, 2019 in Bangkok, Thailand. According to the discussing and information sharing in the conference, in practice, there have been some challenges in mutual legal assistance in criminal matters, for example, delaying replying the MLA request, inadequacy or lack of focal person or focal organization to contact for the MLA request in the requesting state, technical and language barriers, human resources. Therefore, this article also points out that a specific guideline or standard operation procedure is required to facilitate the MLA process in regional countries.

3. International Legal Framework for TOC and International Cooperation

After studying the current status of TOC and cooperation mechanisms of countries in the region against TOC, the Article presents the international legal framework to fight against TOC and discusses the status and intervention of LMC countries in the international treaties.

Furthermore, international conventions or treaties encourage state parties to enhance international cooperation by concluding bilateral or multilateral agreements. For example, the Model Treaty on Mutual Legal Assistance in Criminal Matters develops tools to conclude agreements in legal and judicial cooperation. The United Nations (UN) Security Council further called upon in its 2019 Resolution to review, amend national legislation and to implement the law compliance with international instruments. Therefore, this article explores the existing international legal framework for TOC and the role of international cooperation for the TOC issue in the Mekong region and analyses the status of the LMC countries in international legal instruments.

3.1 International Legal Framework for TOC

Transnational organized crimes include drug trafficking, human trafficking and smuggling, terrorism and financial terrorism, wildlife and forest crime, cultural property smuggling, illegal gambling, anti-money laundering and cyber-crime. A group of people commit these serious crimes in one or more countries including cross-border areas. The United Nations Convention against Transnational Organized Crime is an international legal framework for combating transnational crimes, including adopting new respective local laws, formulating effective cooperation mechanisms and implementing law enforcement measures for state parties. The United Nations Convention against Corruption (2003) is a related international convention for the TOC issue. This article briefly introduces the existing international legal framework for TOC and international intervention or supporting for each TOC issue in the Mekong region.

(a) Drug Trafficking

Drug and psychotropic substance trafficking, producing and manufacturing are criminal activities for all mankind and they threaten the economy, society, culture of a country and affect the health of human beings. The Single Convention on Narcotic Drugs of 1961, the Convention on Psychotropic Substances of 1971 and the United Nations Convention against Illicit Traffic in Narcotic Drugs and Psychotropic Substances of 1988 are the major treaties for eliminating illicit drugs and psychotropic substances. The Single Convention on Narcotic Drugs of 1961 aims to control using, trading, manufacturing, producing and possession of drugs in illegal ways, and to enhance international cooperation for combating drug trafficking. The Convention on Psychotropic Substances of 1971 mainly concerns public health in using the substances for medical and scientific purposes, and aims to control abusing psychotropic substances such as ephedrine, ketamine. The United Nations Convention against Illicit Traffic in Narcotic Drugs and Psychotropic Substances of 1988 is a comprehensive international convention to combat illicit trading of narcotic drugs and psychotropic substances and it provides room for international cooperation against drug and precursor chemicals trafficking, money laundering and extradition.①

(b) Human Trafficking and Smuggling

Human beings are not for sale, trade, abduction, and cannot be forced to do work or marry without their free consent. All these actions are exploitation upon them. Surrogacy and newborn trafficking (baby trading) emerged as new types of trafficking in persons.

The United Nations Protocol to Prevent, Suppress and Punish Trafficking in Persons, Especially Women and Children is a fundamental international legal instrument to combat human trafficking. Article 3 of the Protocol defines "trafficking in persons" as (a) the recruitment, transportation, transfer, harbouring or receipt of persons, by means of the threat or use of force or other forms of coercion, of abduction, of fraud, of deception,

① E. Jensema, N. P. Ei Kham, *The Impact of Drug Law Enforcement Practices in Myanmar*, 2016, Transnational Institute (TNI), The Netherlands.

of the abuse of power or of a position of vulnerability or of the giving or receiving of payments or benefits to achieve the consent of a person having control over another person, for the purpose of exploitation. Exploitation shall include, at a minimum, the exploitation of the prostitution of others or other forms of sexual exploitation, forced labour or services, slavery or practices similar to slavery, servitude or the removal of organs; (b) the consent of a victim of trafficking in persons to the intended exploitation set forth in subparagraph (a) of this article shall be irrelevant where any of the means set forth in subparagraph (a) have been used; (c) the recruitment, transportation, transfer, harbouring or receipt of a child for the purpose of exploitation shall be considered "trafficking in persons" even if this does not involve any of the means set forth in subparagraph (a) of this article; (d) "child" shall mean any person under eighteen years of age.①

International Labor Organization (ILO) Convention No. 29 on forced labour also determines the meaning of "forced labour": all kinds of workers or employees who do not consent voluntarily to do the work. Forced labour is also included in TIPs and those kinds of workers need to be protected in accordance with national and international law from exploitation. ILO Convention No. 182 is also a related international convention to prevent children from exploitation and doing worst forms of forced labour.

(c) Wildlife and Forest Crime

Wildlife and forest crime are also involved as one of the transnational crimes in the Asia and Pacific region. According to the data from UNODC, USD 19.5 billion are earned per year in the region from illegal trading and trafficking timber. UNODC has established the Global Programme for Combating Wildlife and Forest Crime for four years' term with the aims to link the regional to global system and improve capacity building and law enforcement regarding wildlife and forest crime at the regional and sub-regional levels. United Nations Convention against Transnational Organized Crime (UNTOC) convention is a global legal instrument for wildlife and forest

---

① ILO, *The Mekong Challenge—Human Trafficking: Redefining Demand*, International Labour Organization, Bangkok Office, 2005, pp. 1-91.

crime and state parties put those international legal standards into their national legal framework to prohibit the killing, trading, selling, importing, and exporting, and exploiting of wildlife, natural resources, and forest products. Convention on International Trade in Endangered Species of Wild Fauna and Flora—CITES (1973), the International Convention on the Simplification and Harmonization of Customs Procedures (1973), WTO Agreement on the Application of Sanitary and Phytosanitary Measures (1995), Convention on Biological Diversity (1992), Convention concerning the Protection of the World Cultural and Natural Heritage (1972) and Convention on the Prohibition of the Development, Production and Stockpiling of Bacteriological (Biological) and Toxin Weapons and on their Destruction (1972) are the related legal instruments for wildlife and forest crime. The United Nations Economic and Social Council (ECOSOC) adopted Resolution 2013/40, which encourages state parties to conduct bilateral or regional cooperation for protection of wildlife species and products from illegal trade and trafficking.[①]

For the regional cooperation, governments from Australia, China, India, Japan, South Korea, New Zealand, Russia, United States and ASEAN adopted Declaration on Combating Wildlife Trafficking in East Asia Summit in 2014. The Declaration recognizes the protection of wildlife from illegal trafficking and promotion of cooperation in wildlife law enforcement among respective agencies such as Customs, Forestry, Police, Judicial and Attorney.

(d) Cultural Property Smuggling

Trafficking, selling, importing, exporting and transferring the cultural properties are transnational crimes and the Hague Convention for the Protection of Cultural Property in the Event of Armed Conflict (1954) and its two protocols of 1954 and 1999, the UNESCO Convention on the Means of Prohibiting and Preventing the Illicit Import, Export and Transfer of Ownership of Cultural Property (1970) and the International Institute for the Unification of Private Laws (UNIDROIT) Convention on Stolen or Illegally Exported Cultural Objects (1995) are fundamental international legal frameworks for

---

① UNODC and Freeland, Legal Framework to Address Wildlife and Timber Trafficking in the ASEAN Region: A Rapid Assessment, *Working Paper*, April, 2015, Bangkok.

preventing illegal trafficking of culture property. The 1954 convention and its protocols are the first international legal instruments for cultural property and they aim to protect cultural properties and objects from attacking and damaging, and prevent using the objects of reprisals, misusing of the distinctive emblem during armed conflicts. The obvious case regarding the protection of cultural property during war was the Iraq and Kuwait case. In 1991, United Nations Security Council adopted the Resolution 686/ 1991 that required Iraq to return Kuwait's cultural properties that were seized by Iraq during the First Gulf War. Both countries are members of the 1954 Hague Convention and its first protocol, and Iraq paid a compensation of USD 19 million for occupying Kuwait's cultural objects.①

The 1970 UNESCO Convention addresses state parties to ensure the security level around national museums and capacity building, to raise awareness of the public, to improve national legislation and law enforcement, to cooperate with other countries and international organizations for preventing illegal trade, transfer of ownership, import and export of cultural property. The 1995 UNIDROIT Convention declares that the act of stolen or illegally exported cultural objects is an action against the contracting sate and those kinds of objects need to be returned to the belonging state.

(e) Anti-money Laundering

Money laundering is one of the organized crimes and it threatens every country in the Mekong region. Offenders usually launder the illegal money that comes from drug trading, human trafficking and corruption.

The United Nations introduced the provisions that determine the money laundering as a criminal offence in their Convention against Illicit Traffic in Narcotic Drugs and Psychotropic Substances of 1988 and then the Palermo Convention was a comprehensive and fundamental legal instrument for combating money laundering and organized crimes. International Convention for the Suppression of the Financing Terrorism (1999) is also a related international instrument on combating financing terrorism. The Financial Action

---

① UNESCO, *Fighting the Illicit Trafficking of Cultural Property: A Toolkit for European Judiciary and Law Enforcement*. UNESCO, France, pp. 1-122.

Task Force (FATF) was founded by G-7 in 1989 and the Force indicates and monitors mutual evaluation and recommends to countries regarding their activities on money laundering crimes such as legislation, prosecution and conviction of the money laundering offenders. The FATF makes the Non-Cooperative Countries and Territories List for non-compliant countries and places them on a blacklist until they comply with and fulfil 40 recommendations of the FATF.[①]

(f) Terrorism and Financing Terrorism

Terrorism is threat or use of violence to coerce or to intimidate civilians with the intention of influence in political, economic and religious affairs on a particular state or government and society. Terrorism is a serious crime and every country needs to undertake counter-terrorism measures in international cooperation.

Now, the number of terrorist acts is increasing in many countries and these violent acts threaten the world peace and security. The United Nations Security Council Resolution 1373 (2001) called for cooperation among UN members to fight against terrorism through the effective implementation of regional and international conventions on terrorism. 19 universal legal instruments against terrorism adopted in international community are as follows: 1963 Tokyo Convention; 2014 Montreal Protocol; 1970 Hague Hijacking Convention; 2010 Beijing Protocol; 1971 Montreal Sabotage Convention; 1988 Montreal Protocol; 2010 Beijing SUA Civil Aviation Convention; 1988 Rome SUA Maritime Navigation Convention; 1988 Rome SUA Fixed Platforms Protocol; 2005 London SUA Maritime Navigation Protocol; 2005 London SUA Fixed Platforms Protocol; 1980 Vienna Nuclear Material Convention; 2005 Vienna Nuclear Material Amendments; 2005 New York Nuclear Terrorism Convention; 1973 New York Protection of Diplomats Convention; 1979 New York Hostages Convention; 1991 Montreal Plastic Explosives Convention; 1997 New York Terrorist Bombings Convention and 1999 New York Terrorist Financing Convention. ASEAN Convention on

① UNODC and Freeland, Legal Framework to Address Wildlife and Timber Trafficking in the ASEAN Region: A Rapid Assessment, *Working Paper*, April, 2015, Bangkok.

Counter Terrorism and the Treaty on Mutual Legal Assistance in Criminal Matters are regional instruments for countering terrorism issues.

The following table shows clear information about international legal instruments of TOC and the respective status of the LMC countries in them:

Table 3.1

Conventions	China	Myanmar	Thailand	Vietnam	Cambodia	Lao PDR
The United Nations Convention against Transnational Organized Crime	√	√	√	√	√	√
The Single Convention on Narcotic Drugs of 1961	√	√	√	√	√	√
The Convention on Psychotropic Substances of 1971	√	√	√	√	√	√
The United Nations Convertion against Illicit Traffic in Narcotic Drugs and Psychotropic Substances of 1988	√	√	√	√	√	√
The United Nations Protocol to Prevent, Suppress and Punish Trafficking in Persons, Especially Women and Children	√	√	√	√	√	√
Convention on International Trade in Endangered Species of Wild Fauna and Flora—CITES (1973)	√	√	√	√	√	√
the International Convention on the Simplification and Harmonization of Customs Procedures (1973) and Revised Kyoto Convention	√	√	√	√	√	√

Continued

Conventions	China	Myanmar	Thailand	Vietnam	Cambodia	Lao PDR
Convention concerning the Protection of the World Cultural and Natural Heritage (1972)	√	√	√	√	√	√
WTO Agreement on the Application of Sanitary and Phytosanitary Measures (1995)	√	√	√	√	√	√
Convention on Biological Diversity (1992)	√	√	√	√	√	√
Convention on the Prohibition of the Development, Production and Stockpiling of Bacteriological (Biological) and Toxin Weapons and on their Destruction (1972)	√	√	√	√	√	√
The Hague Convention for the Protection of Cultural Property in the Event of Armed Conflict (1954)	√	√	√	×	√	×
The UNESCO Convention on the Means of Prohibiting and Preventing the Illicit Import, Export and Transfer of Ownership of Cultural Property (1970)	√	√	×	√	×	×
The UNIDROIT Convention on Stolen or Illegally Exported Cultural Objects (1995)	√	×	×	×	√	√

Continued

Conventions	China	Myanmar	Thailand	Vietnam	Cambodia	Lao PDR
International Convention for the Suppression of the Financing Terrorism (1999)	√	√	√	√	√	×
1963 Tokyo Convention and 2014 Montreal Protocol	√	√	√	√	√	√
1970 Hague Hijacking Convention and 2010 Beijing Protocol	√	√	√	√	√	√
1971 Montreal Sabotage Convention	√	√	√	√	√	√
1988 Montreal Protocol	√	√	√	√	√	√
2010 Beijing SUA Civil Aviation Convention	√	√	√	×	×	×
1988 Rome SUA Maritime Navigation Convention	√	×	×	×	×	×
1988 Rome SUA Fixed Platforms Protocol	√	×	×	×	×	×
2005 London SUA Maritime Navigation Protocol	×	×	×	×	×	×
2005 London SUA Fixed Platforms Protocol	×	×	×	×	×	×
1980 Vienna Nuclear Material Convention and 2005 Vienna Nuclear Material Amendments	√	√	√	√	√	√
2005 New York Nuclear Terrorism Convention	√	×	√	√	√	×

Continued

Conventions	China	Myanmar	Thailand	Vietnam	Cambodia	Lao PDR
1973 New York Protection of Diplomats Convention	√	√	√	√	√	√
1979 New York Hostages Convention	√	√	√	√	√	√
1991 Montreal Plastic Explosives Convention	×	√	√	×	×	√
1997 New York Terrorist Bombings Convention	√	√	√	√	√	√
1999 New York Terrorist Financing Convention	√	√	√	√	√	√

Notes: √ Ratification, accession or signatory status
× Non-Ratification, accession or signatory status

According to the table, some states have not yet ratified or signed relevant international instruments for transnational organized crimes.

3.2 International Cooperation

International cooperation is also important for LMC countries because these states should encourage cooperation mechanisms in combating TOC issues in the region through exchange of technical and legal assistance and sharing of knowledge and information with each other. In 2019 Resolutions, the UN Security Council called upon member states to strengthen regional and international cooperation and to promote border cooperation for combating and countering transnational organized crime.

For international intervention and cooperation in TOC in the Mekong region, Australian Government established the Mekong-Australia Program on Transnational Crime in 2019 for coordinating with Mekong countries to promote cross-border cooperation, to link with law enforcement organizations from Mekong countries, to exchange information and to mix policy and strengthen address at national and regional level to combat transnational crime. Australian

Government funded this regional program with AUD 30 million.

Japan International Cooperation Agency (JICA) provides technical assistance for anti-trafficking in the Mekong region and the JICA gives assistance to draft and publish the Repatriation Handbook for Foreign Victims of Trafficking in Cambodian, Laotian and Vietnamese and the handbook offers guidance on the repatriation procedure to treat the victims. JICA also supports technical cooperation projects of Myanmar and Vietnam to combat human trafficking in the region and to strengthen the regional cooperation network.①

The Greater Mekong Sub-region Program was established in 1992 provides the financial and technical assistance from the Asian Development Bank to promote economic cooperation among the six Mekong countries. The GMS Program focuses to enhance cross-border trade and transport, tourism, investment, telecommunication, agriculture and develop human resources in the region.②

The Mekong-Ganga Cooperation (MGC) was founded in 2000 by India, Myanmar, Cambodia, Lao PDR, Thailand and Vietnam to cooperate in tourism, culture, health, agriculture, education and connectivity. India has funded the MGC with USD 1 million for the annual budget for promoting the cooperation areas.

The Japanese government initiated the Japan-Mekong Region Partnership Program in 2007 to support the industrial infrastructure development, human resources development, institutional, economic and people-to-people connectivity, and sustainable development. Furthermore, South Korean government engaged in the collaboration with Mekong countries in 2011 and they set up the Mekong-Korea Plan of Action (2014-2017) for mutual eco-

---

① Japan International Cooperation Agency (JICA), Report on the Ninth Mekong Regional Workshop towards Well-kint Net of Assistance for Victims of Trafficking in the Grater Mekong Sub-region: Learning from the Bilateral and Regional Cooperation Experiences, JICA Office Thailand, 2019, pp: 1-45.

② Vannarith Chheang, *The Mekong Region: From a Divided to a Connected Region*, Konrad-Adenauer-Stiftung Cambodia, 2017, pp.1-8.

nomic cooperation. The United States also started the Lower Mekong Initiative (LMI) in 2009 to connect regional economic cooperation in the Mekong region and to strengthen cooperation in education, food security, water security, environmental and public health issues.

4. Findings, Suggestions, Recommendations and Conclusion

Every nation directly or indirectly follows international and regional legal standards when they implement and enforce them in their national legal framework, even though they have different legal systems. Sometimes, a gap can arise in international or regional cooperation if there is no appropriate legal mechanism or national policy in respective countries. Therefore, countries need to develop effective and strong policy and strategy in operating their national legal provisions to participate in the regional cooperation mechanism.

Aiming to promote and improve sustainable development and to eliminate TOC in the region, the implementation of agreed international norms and polices and the strengthening of the capacity of those engaged in promoting the implementation and enforcement of national law are cornerstones. The UN Security Council, in its 2019 Resolutions, called upon Member States to consider ratifying and implementing global instruments. Moreover, the article finds that the LMC countries have not yet signed, ratified or acceded some relevant international legal instruments against TOC. Therefore, this article suggests that the LMC countries should ratify or accede the required international conventions or treaties for each TOC issue if they have not been a member of those international conventions, for example, conventions relating to the protection of culture property, conventions relating to the prevention of wildlife and forest crime.

After ratifying the international conventions, countries need to transform their national legal framework to fulfil the obligations of those international legal instruments. To prevent crimes and protect the victims, each country should create an efficient and effective prosecuting and enforcing mechanism under its own legal system. Therefore, the article suggests national laws should be reviewed and updated in accordance with inter-

national standards.

Myanmar Vice President U Henry Van Thio attended the Greater Mekong Sub-region (GMS) Summit in VietNam in 2018 and in the meeting, he said that climate change, natural disasters, cross-border migration, geo-political instability and terrorism issues remain challenges and threat to rule of law and security in the Mekong region. He also pointed out that to review new strategy for regional cooperation is a top priority to solve these problems and challenges in the region. Therefore, the article suggests that LMC countries should establish plans or strategies in regional frameworks to combat transnational organized crimes.

After setting up the regional framework or regional action plan, each country should implement national action plan or strategic plan in them terrorises for each TOC issue should raise and develop among key and relevant government ministries.To become effective collaboration and implementation mechanism, Therefore, the article also suggests that an umbrella strategic plan against TOC issues should be set up among the LMC countries and then national strategy should follow this umbrella regional framework.

For national mechanism, each country needs to set up a new and effective national action plan (if there is no action plan established before) and work plan for relevant sectors, monitor policies, programs and projects for each area, need to give awareness and campaign for both law enforcement bodies and the public, cooperate with civil societies actively to support the national plan. Furthermore, the government needs to upgrade the existing national action plan. Therefore, the article suggests that national and regional workshops should be organized and convened to review and exchange national policies and legal frameworks against each TOC issue and to raise the legal awareness of stakeholders in the region.

We all understand that Lancang-Mekong Cooperation Mechanism is not a regional association or organization like ASEAN, which was established by ASEAN Charter. Therefore, it is not legally binding for LMC countries to conclude, follow and implement the regional legal framework for TOC issues like ASEAN Convention on Counter Terrorism (ACCT), etc. However, bilateral or multilateral agreements for mutual legal assistance and ex-

tradition should be established among the LMC countries for an effective cooperation mechanism in TOC issues. If LMC countries consent to make legally binding agreements to eliminate transnational organized crimes in the Mekong region, they should conclude specific agreements in each area of transnational organized crimes to set up an effective regional cooperation mechanism for TOC in the Lancang-Mekong area.

For example, arrange and conclude particular regional cooperation MoU or agreement for some areas such as wildlife and forest crimes, and enhance and improve the implementation of MoU or agreements in some areas such as human trafficking, drug trafficking, and terrorism. Furthermore, this article also recommends that the member countries should review their existing agreement or MoU and that they should consider signing new MoU or renewing the current MoU if these agreements have inappropriate or insufficient mechanisms that deter effective cooperation.

There is no doubt that China takes a leading role in LMC cooperation mechanism for LMC countries. The other countries should collaborate with each other in providing legal and technical assistance, sharing information regarding TOC matters, creating regional action plans to combat transnational organized crimes in the region. This article finds that several ministerial meetings or senior official meetings were held for sharing information, learning and discussing to solve the problem and to promote international and regional cooperation mechanisms against TOC issues. However, an effective implementation and enforcement mechanism also needs to be established. Therefore, the article suggests that more dialogue meetings among LMC countries should be convened to discuss substantive issues and effective joint mechanisms should be impleneted.

At present, the global pandemic is still threatening the world and people want to avoid face-to-face meeting in their communication. Therefore, the article suggests that the above dialogue meetings should be held through any convenient ways such as the internet and online platform.

The article finds that the establishment of Border Liaison Office is a key mechanism but the lack of capacity building and insufficient infrastructure can be a weakness in cooperation. Therefore, the article recommends that governments should offer required training, organize seminars or workshops to provide capacity building opportunities to Border Liaison Officials and relevant government officials, raise their awareness, and also supplement required infrastructure and communication tools or devices for the Border Liaison Office to improve the cooperation in Border Liaison Mechanism.

Expert groups or working groups should be set up to facilitate cooperation in data sharing and exchange, to offer technical assistance among LMC countries, to promote capacity building, to raise the legal awareness of the public, border control officers, and government officers, to strengthen monitoring and review the implementation of national policy and legislation.

The article finds that there are several challenges in mutual legal assistance in criminal matters especially the language barriers and lack of standard operation procedure (SOP). Therefore, a systematic and clear communication pathway should be established among respective government agencies of LMC countries to enhance cooperation mechanism and to encourage close connection in these countries. Relevant committees, working groups and relevant focal points should be established to help start the above communication pathway. English should be determined as a main language when contacting for the MLA process or cooperation mechanism among LMC countries to terminate language barriers. The relevant ministries should formulatea a specific guideline or standard operation procedure to facilitate the MLA process.

The article finds that many countries support and cooperate with Mekong countries not only in combating TOC but also in the economic field. They provide technical and financial assistance in several areas. China has a leader role in the cooperation mechanism with Mekong states and the Chinese government provides a special fund of USD 300 million to LMC countries to implement a sustainable development plan in the Mekong-Lancang region in 2016. For example, Chinese and Myanmar officials signed the Agreement on the Cooperation Projects of the Mekong-Lancang Cooperation Special Fund for Myanmar in 2018. Thus, Myanmar was provided by the Fund with USD 16.3 million to undertake 51 projects under the National

Sustainable Development Strategy of Myanmar.① However, LMC countries should have their own financial resources in order to support existing or future TOC cooperation projects. Therefore, the article recommends that the LMC countries should establish a special fund for technical assistance and the members can borrow the grants from the fund for continuing their project or program if there is no support from international community. However, the fund need to be replenished by member countries.

As a conclusion, China, Myanmar, Cambodia, Laos, Thailand and Vietnam established the Lancang-Mekong Cooperation (LMC) Framework in 2016 to promote the collaboration in political, economic and social pillars, to enhance the wellbeing of people in the sub-region, and to maintain peace and security in the area.

The article concludes that all LMC countries need to take effective and speedy measurse to deter the transnational organized crimes; strengthen liaison and coordination with international, regional and intergovernmental organizations for law enforcement; perform effectively the functions of rescuing, receiving, safeguarding, rehabilitation and reintegration of trafficked persons; enhance law and regulation protects against illegal selling, possessing, and transferring wildlife and wildlife species, ancient cultural properties; prevent damage to forest and natural environmental caused by pollution and man-made disasters; set up long-term strategic plans and short-term works plans to fulfil the obligation of international legal instruments; cooperate with international and regional organizations to exchange information; and promote border-control cooperation in order to prevent TOC are implemented effectively in practice and are supported by the further research.

① Myanmar President Office, 2020, President U Win Myint participates in 3rd Mekong-Lancang Cooperation Leaders' Video Conference Meeting; Myanmar takes over MLC Co-chairmanship for next 2 years, https://www.president-office.gov.mm/en/?q=briefing-room/speeches-and-remarks/2020/08/25/id-10083, last visited on Apr. 4, 2020.

Bahasa Indonesia as Compulsory Language of International Commercial Contract in Indonesia

Dwi Hananta*

Abstract: To protect the national interests, Indonesia formulated the law that obliges the use of Bahasa Indonesia in international commercial contracts involving Indonesian entities. However, the stipulation is not followed by the provisions concerning the infringement's effect. The court decisions on those cases vary with or even contradict each other. Inconsistency as such affected the businesses and investments in Indonesia. The reformulation of the law that can balance national interests and the international need to reduce trade barriers is urgently required. Some authors have reviewed the court's decisions on this matter from the perspective of national law, but this research will provide another view from private international law principles.

Using the qualitative research method, this research found that this subject is a matter of overriding mandatory rules. In terms of the mandatory rule that does not expressly prescribe the infringement's effect, the court may order the contracting parties to exercise remedis under the contract as in the circumstances reasonable. In this case, the appropriate and proportional remedy to the infringement is by ordering specific instruments to the parties to translate the existing contracts into Bahasa Indonesia. The proposed requirements for the reformulation of the law are: expressly describe the provision as an overriding mandatory rule, provide the provision of the effect of infringement, and provide the form of remedies to having the translation in Bahasa Indonesia.

Keywords: Compulsory Language, Contract, Overriding Mandatory Rule

Introduction

Increasing numbers of Regional Trade Agreements during the last ten

* Ph. D Candidate of SwupL/Judge of Indonesia District Court.

years have shown that international trade relations are getting more intense regionally and globally.

International commercial contracts, which are the basis of international trade relations, are the key to the implementation of trade relations. As stated in the principle of *pacta sunt servanda*, the agreements must be kept, or the agreements are legally binding and must be performed, the agreements become laws to the signatory parties.

International laws and domestic laws are applied to such commercial contracts. Lorenzo stated that, the law applicable to contracts can fulfill three different functions: first, a "supplementary function", filling the contractual gap with default rules. Second, an "interpretative function", determining the meaning of ambiguous or obscure contract terms. Third, a "restrictive function", voiding contractual clauses contrary to mandatory rules.①

In the Indonesian law context, there is a crucial legal issue of concern to lawyers and business practitioners. On September 30, 2019, the President of the Republic of Indonesia issued Presidential Regulation No. 63 of 2019 concerning the Use of the Indonesian Language as the implementing regulation of Law No. 24 of 2009 concerning the National Flag, Language, Emblem, and Anthem (hereinafter referred to as the Regulation on Language and the Law on Language). The regulation requires the Indonesian Language (*Bahasa Indonesia*) should be applied in all Memoranda of Understanding (MoU) and/or agreements that involve government institutions of the Republic of Indonesia, government agencies of the Republic of Indonesia, Indonesian private entities, and individuals as Indonesian citizens. If the agreement involves foreign parties, the Indonesian language version can be accompanied by a version in the foreign parties' language and/or in English.

Even though the language used on the regulation and the Law are imperative in nature or compulsory (marked by the word "must"), they do not provide any sanctions for violations of using the Indonesian language in inter-

① Six to Sanchez Lorenzo, Choice of Law and Overriding Mandatory Rules in International Contracts After Rome I, Yearbook of Private International Law, Sellier *European Law Publishers & Swiss Institute of Comparative Law*, 2010, Vol.12, p.67.

national contracts to be applied in Indonesia. Therefore, using *Bahasa Indonesia* in contracts involving foreign parties is debatable: on one hand it is mandatory as it is stated in the regulation and the Law; on the other hand it is voluntary as there is no sanction for the violation of using *Bahasa Indonesia* in contracts involving foreign parties.

Judgments of the Indonesian courts vary on the issue of language applied in international contracts. It is because the Indonesian legal system does not recognize the principle of *stare decisis*, meaning that lower courts are not bound to follow decisions of higher courts. However, in some cases, the court may use or cite previous interpretations of an article, law, or regulation. One of the court decisions attracting public discussion is the Supreme Court's decision on the case of Nine AM Ltd. v. PT Bangun Karya Pratama Lestari①. The Supreme Court reinforced the Jakarta High Court's and District Court of Jakarta Barat's decisions, which stated that "A loan agreement that is made and signed in English without containing an Indonesian equivalent/translation is prohibited because it was made for prohibited reasons, so it does not meet the essential requirements of the validity of an agreement as referred to in Article 1320 of Indonesian Civil Code. Therefore the agreement is null and void."

On the other hand, Amlapura District Court in Bali Province of Indonesia raised a judgment on Alexander William Ford v. Man Lee Ford Cheung's case.② The court concluded that the receivable and liability agreement provided in English is a breach of the Law on Language, but that breach is not against the essential requirements of the validity of an agreement. As long as the motive of an agreement is not a fake motive, not prohibited by the prevailing laws and/or is not based on motives that are contrary to decency or public order, then it is legal and binding on the parties making it.

Inconsistency of courts' judgments on the issue of language applied to

---

① Supreme Court of the Republic of Indonesia, Decision on the Case of Nine AM Ltd. v. PT Bangun Karya Pratama Lestari, No. 601 K/Pdt/2015, last visited on Aug. 31, 2015.

② District Court of Amlapura, Decision on the Case of Alexander William Ford v. Man Lee Ford Cheung, No. 254/Pdt.G/2019/PN Amp, last visited on Apr. 1, 2020.

international contracts in Indonesia affected business actors and investors' decision to invest in Indonesia. Courts face a dilemma of either enforcing law and regulation or playing their role in improving Indonesia's economy by reducing barriers to trade through their decisions.

One of the lawmakers' considerations to pass the Law of the Indonesian Language is that Language is a means to unify, identify, and realize the existence of the Nation symbolizing sovereignty and honor of the State. The Law also promotes *Bahasa Indonesia* to become an international language.

Law on language which obliges the use of Indonesian Language in international contracts in practice seems to undermine the government's effort to ease the difficulty of doing business in Indonesia. One of the indicators measured on the ease of doing business is contract enforcement. If the court's judgments are inconsistent in interpreting the Indonesian language's obligation in international commercial contracts, business actors and investors will perceive Indonesia as unfriendly to them.

Since the national law and regulations do not provide provisions on the consequences of the failure to fulfill the obligation to use *Bahasa Indonesia* in the international commercial contracts involving Indonesian legal entities, they should elaborate the consequences that do not harm the contracts violate the Law.

This study will discuss the questions as follows:

1. What should be the consequences of the absence of *Bahasa Indonesia*'s use as the compulsory language in international commercial contracts?

2. How is the Law supposed to regulate language used in international contracts soas to balance national interests and the international need to reduce trade barriers?

This research uses a normative research method with a qualitative research approach to study the related Indonesian law and court decisions deepened with the analysis of international conventions and comparative study of other national law and court decisions, which are the primary sources. It also uses the doctrine, articles, and reports as secondary sources. The result of this research will be delivered with a descriptive research method.

This paper is organized as follows: the introduction is used to set forth the background information on which the later analysis in this paper will depend, in conjunction with the problem statement, research questions, and research methodology, which will guide this paper. Section Ⅰ examines the major cases and the related Indonesian national applicable law to analyze how the law stands. Section Ⅱ analyzes the topic from the perspective of private international law principles embracing the Law on Language as overriding mandatory rules. Section Ⅲ contains a comparative study of the Turkish Law. Section Ⅳ discusses the nature of the overriding mandatory rules, and Section Ⅴ is dedicated to the issue of the effect of infringement of overriding mandatory rules.

The whole research is briefly restated and concluded in the last section concluding the research questions' answer.

1. The Applicable Law and Analysis of the Cases

1.1 Case of Nine AM Ltd. v. PT Bangun Karya Pratama Lestari (BKPL)①

Under the loan agreement written in English only, Nine AM Ltd. provided a loan for BKPL. The provision of choice of law designated Indonesian law to govern the agreement. A deed of fiduciary security executed in Bahasa Indonesia was concluded to secure the loan. Starting from December 2011, BKPL discontinued repayment, resulting in BKPL defaulting on the loan.

After issuing a demand letter and receiving no response, Nine AM Ltd. petitioned the court seeking payment and interest of the overdue principal, to which BKPL responded with a tortious act claim, challenging the loan agreement under Languange Law because it was made without translation/not accompanied by the contract version in *Bahasa Indonesia*.

District Court of Jakarta Barat granted the request of BKPL. Hence the Loan Agreement was declared null and void. As a consequence, the Court ordered BKPL as the borrower to repay the remaining loan principal without any interest owed or lost profit that the lender may have suffered during the

① The Case Brief, Cited from Akset, Court Nullifies English Language Contract, https://aksetlaw.com/news-event/newsflash/court-nullifies-english-language-contract, last visited on Jun. 22, 2015.

loan terms.[①]

The decision issued with considerations that the absence of using *Bahasa Indonesia* in the loan agreement is an infringement of the Law on Language. Therefore under Articles 1335 and 1337 of the Indonesian Civil Code, it constitutes a prohibited cause or a violation of the law, so it does not fulfill the conditions required in Article 1320 of the Indonesian Civil Code.

The Appeal Court of Jakarta affirmed the District Court of Jakarta Barat's decision,[②] and subsequently it became legally binding after the Supreme Court reaffirmed the decisions.

For the record, the Supreme Court's decisions are not taken unanimously. Justice Sudrajat Dimyati gives a dissenting opinion that "what is meant by lawful cause, which is an objective requirement of a contract, in essence, is the content or material of the agreement itself which may not contradict with the law, morals, and public order. So the lawful cause is not about the formality or form of an agreement, but the material/content."

The decisions in Nine AM Ltd. v. BKPL exercise the provisions in the Law on Language and consider the breach of the Law on Language is against the conditions that must comply with a contract to be validly stated under Article 1320 of the Indonesian Civil Code.

Article 1320 of the Indonesian Civil Code contains four conditions: (1) consent between those who bind themselves (the contracting parties), (2) capacity of the respective parties to conclude the obligation, (3) a certain (specific) subject matter, and (4) a legal cause. The first two are conditions pertaining to the subject of the contract, and the rest are conditions pertaining to the object of the contract.

The annulment of the loan agreement between Nine AM Ltd and BKPL by the courts was based on the non-fulfillment of the fourth condition of the

---

① District of Jakarta Barat, Decision on the Case of PT Bangun Karya Pratama Lestari v. Nine AM Ltd., No. 451/Pdt.G/2012/PN Jkt Brt, last visited on Jun. 20, 2013.

② Appeal Court of Jakarta, Decision on the Case of Nine AM Ltd v. PT Bangun Karya Pratama Lestari, No. 48/PDT/2014/PT DKI, last visited on May 7, 2014.

Article 1320 of the Indonesian Civil Code, "a legal cause".

A "legal cause" means that what has to be performed by either party is not contrary to the law, public order, or public morality. A contract whereby one of the parties undertakes to commit a crime is null and void because it has an illegal cause. The statement conforms with Article 1335 of the Indonesian Civil Code, which states that whenever the subject matter of the agreement is not certain or based on a false cause, or whenever the cause is not legal, the contract is void by law. Up to this point, the decision seems adequate, but then we see a further understanding of "a legal cause".

According to Justice Subekti, as cited by Agus Yudha Hernoko, a cause is the substance of the agreement itself, so the causes are the interchangeable performances and compensations of the parties.① In line with that, Justice Wirjono argued that a cause in the law of contracts is the substance and the objective of the contracts, which led to an agreement.② Ahmadi Miru and Sakka Pati's also held that "the fourth condition regarding the legal cause, is also a condition on the substance of the agreement."③

Through those statements, we can simply see that those scholars and justices agreed that "a legal cause" is regarding the substance of the agreement. Obviously, the language of the agreement is not the substance of the agreement, so it is not "a legal cause" meant by the law.

The other relevant condition to this case is "the mutual consent between those who bind themselves". As Subekti said, in concluding a contract there have to be at least two persons (parties) who take opposite positions and have the intention to come to a mutual agreement (consent). Hence, consent

---

① Subekti in Agus Yudha Hernoko, *Hukum Perjanjian, Asas Proporsionalitas dalam Kontrak Komersial* (*Law of the Contracts, Proportionality Principles in the Commercial Contracts*), Jakarta: Kencana, 2010, p.194.

② Wirjono Projodikoro, *Azas-azas Hukum Perjanjian* (*Principles of the Contracts Law*), Bandung: Mandar Maju, 2011, p.37.

③ Ahmadi Mirru and Sakka Pati, *Hukum Perikatan, Penjelasan Makna Pasal* 1233 *sampai* 1456 *BW* (*Law on the Agreement, explanation of Article* 1233 *to* 1456 *Indonesian Civil Code*), Jakarta: Rajawali Pers, 2011, p.69.

means a meeting in minds.[①]

In Nine AM Ltd. v. BKPL, both parties did not take "mutual consent" as an issue. So do the court's decisions. It means that clearly, both parties bind themselves into the loan agreement with out mutual consent. As both parties have voluntarily given their consent to the contract, it is questionable if one of them files a case of annulment to the contract they have signed.

The question that needs to be examined by the lawyers is "whether both parties signed the contract in an equal position?" If it is not, then the claim is unjustified. Nevertheless, if the contract was signed in an unequal position, the court might consider the breach of Law on Language as an overriding mandatory provision and strike the balance between party autonomy and the protection of weaker parties.

1.2 Case of Alexander William Ford v. Man Lee Ford Cheung

In 2008, an English citizen, Ford, was married in Macau to Cheung, a Chinese citizen. Since 2009, they lived in Bali and became PT Alba Indah's shareholders, an Indonesian legal entity that ran tourism businesses. Jointly they owned 100% (a hundred percent) of the company's shares.

Their marriage did not go well. During the divorcing process, the couple agreed to divide their marital assets, including the company's shares. As stated in the "Receivable and Liability Agreement", in April 2019 Ford transferred 51% of his shares of the company (USD 1, 5000, 000) to Cheung with periodic or stage payments, whereas the sale of the shares has also been stated in the minutes of the general meeting of shareholders of the company. The agreement was written in English without translation in *Bahasa Indonesia*.

In June 2019, Ford and Cheung's marriage end in divorce. Later, Ford considered that Cheung had not fulfilled several clauses of their agreement, so he was filing a case against Cheung. Ford asked the court to declare the agreement null and void because it did not comply with the Law on Language provisions.

---

① Subekti in Hartono, et. al., op. cit. p.15

The District Court of Amlapura has decided that the breach of Law on Language is not against the essential requirements of the validity of an agreement; furthermore, it stated that "the Law on Language does not regulate sanctions for the breach of Article 31 of Law on Language, then the conditions for filing an annulment of the contract also oblige the entitled party to prove that the obliged party can or has harmed him with such a contract." Based on those considerations, the court stated that "the Receivable and Liability Agreement" is valid and binding for the parties.

The consideration of the District Court of Amlapura is in accordance with the analysis of the decisions above, but it still leaves a legal issue. Even the Court acknowledges the use of *Bahasa Indonesia* in an agreement involving Indonesian entities is "compulsory and duly complied with by the contracting party", the court overruled the compulsory provision and did not consider the consequences of the infringement of the Law.

1.3 Case of PT Citra Abadi Kota Persada v. MDS Investment Holding Ltd. and PT ACR Global Investments

In 2014 PT Citra Abadi Kota Persada (PT CAKP), an Indonesian company, and MDS Investment Holding Ltd. (MDS Ltd.), a British Virgin Islands Company, signed a share purchase agreement of PT Perdana Gapuraprima Tbk., (GPRA, an Indonesian public company).

The agreement concluded that MDS Ltd., as the investor, will buy the shares of GPRA from PT CAKP and upon the completion of transaction 2, the investor will own no less than 51.59% stake in GPRA on a fully diluted basis. The agreement is written in English and it is governed by and construed in accordance with Indonesian Law.

The agreement was not made in the form of a notarial deed, but it has been legalized by the notary to certify that the agreement and the signatures are authentic or a true copy.

Instead of accomplishing transaction 2 in six to twelve months after transaction 1, MDS Ltd. asked for some new conditions, i.e. a position for its representatives in the invested company's management board. MDS Ltd. also askd for relaxation to execute transaction 2. PT CAKP filed a claim against MDS

Ltd. for the failure to fulfill the agreement.

District Court of Jakarta Timur issued a decision that granted the claim.[①] The Court declared the share purchase agreement valid and valuable, and ordered MDS Ltd. as the defendant to pay an amount of compensation to PT CAKP.

The Appeal Court of Jakarta reviewed the District Court's decision.[②] By citing the Supreme Court Circular Letter No. 7 of 2012 on the Implementation of the Resolution of Supreme Court 2012 Chamber Plenary Meeting as Guidelines of the Exercise of the Courts Duties,[③] The Appellate Court decided that the lawsuit based on the agreement written in English is formally unacceptable, for it needs to be translated in *Bahasa Indonesia* first.

The referenced Circular shipulates "Certificate and other foreign documents submitted as evidence at trial shall comply whih the requirements of legalization both in the country of origin and in Indonesia. It also must be translated by a sworn official translator in the Republic of Indonesia".

Different from the previous decisions of the other cases as mentioned above, the Appellate Court's decision on the case of PT CAKP v. MDS Ltd. and PT ACR Global Investments did not decide whether the agreements made in foreign languages were valid or not. The Court stated that the agreement should be translated by the sworn official translater before filing the case to the court. The meaning is, even though the agreement was not written/translated into *Bahasa Indonesia* at the time of the parties signing it, the agreement may (unilaterally) be translated into *Bahasa Indonesia* before a party files the case to the court. As long as the agreement was translated

---

① District Court of Jakarta Timur, Decision on the Case of PT Citra Abadi Kota Persada v. MDS Investment Holding Ltd. and PT ACR Global Investment. No. 275/Pdt.G/2018/PN Jkt Tim, Aug. 21, 2019.

② Appeal Court of Jakarta, Decision on the Case of PT Citra Abadi Kota Persada v. MDS Investment Holding Ltd. and PT ACR Global Investments, No. 135/PDT/2020/PT DKI, Apr. 17, 2020.

③ Supreme Court of the Republic of Indonesia, Circular Letter on the Implementation of the Resolution of Supreme Court 2012 Chamber Plenary Meeting as Guidelines of the Exercise of the Courts Duties, No. 2 of 2012, Sep. 12, 2012.

by a sworn official translater, the agreement may be acceptable.

The Court argued that a free translation of the agreement provided by the plaintiff might cause differences of understanding, so the Court considered the lawsuit as obscure.

Studied further, the Circular Letter cited by the Appellate Court is actually related to the obligation of legalization of documents which has lately been regulated in the Minister of Foreign Affairs of the Republic of Indonesia Regulation Number 13 of 2019 concerning the Procedures for Document Legalization at the Ministry of Foreign Affairs,① which applies to a) documents issued in Indonesia that will be used abroad, b) documents issued outside Indonesian territory or issued by the representatives of foreign countries in Indonesia that will be used in Indonesia, and c) documents issued by the representatives of foreign countries in Indonesia that will be used abroad.

The Circular Letter serves as a guid when the courts examine disputes over contracts made abroad, not the contracts made in Indonesia in a foreign language.

Dispute on the annulment of the agreement for the reason of the absence of using *Bahasa Indonesia* does not only occur in the cases with foreign elements. This kind of case could also happen to the agreement signed by both parties of Indonesian nationality or Indonesian legal entities, using English as contracting language, like the case of PT Dunia Retail Indonesia v. PT Mulia Intipelangi. ②

The Supreme Court reinforced the decisions of the Appellate Court of Jakarta and the District Court of Jakarta Barat that rejected the lawsuit demanding the annulment of the agreement provided without *Bahasa Indonesia* translation and that precisely granted the reconvention of the defendant, and de-

---

① Minister of Foreign Affairs of the Republic of Indonesia, Regulation Concerning the Procedures for Documents Legalization at the Ministry of Foreign Affairs, No. 13, promulgated Aug. 8, 2019.

② Supreme Court of the Republic of Indonesia, Decision on the Case of PT Dunia Retail Indonesia v. PT Mulia Intipelangi, No. 1124 K/PDT/2020, May 5, 2020, reinforcing the decision of the Appeal Court of Jakarta No. 320/PDT/2019/PT DKI, Aug. 1, 2019 and decision of the District Court of Jakarta Barat No. 670/Pdt.G/PN Jkt Brt, Jul. 18, 2018.

clared that the agreement was valid and binding to the parties.

Other than that, in the voluntary jurisdiction, there was also a court order issued by the District Court of Tangerang on the request of the requesting party PT Berkah Karya Bersama.[①] It determined that a translation by a sworn official translater of an investment agreement with its supplemental agreement was valid and had the equal legal force to the translated document.

The request is submitted to meet the Law on Language conditions, which enacted view years after the signature of the agreement. The Court considered that even the request was requested by one party (*ex parte*), the translation had been accepted by the other signing party so that the Court assigned the translation of the agreement as valid and enforceable.

1.4 The Applicable Law of the Cases

The decisions, as analyzed above, laid their considerations only on the national applicable law, with different interpretations. The decisions on Nine AM Ltd. v. BKPL considered the agreement as infringement of Law on Language for it was made with a prohibited cause. The decision on the case of Ford v. Cheung viewed the prohibited cause was only for the essential requirements of the validity of an agreement, not for the agreement's form. The Appeal Court and the Supreme Court's decision on the case of PT CAKP v. MDS Ltd. and PTACR Global Investments rejected the case's formality and ordered the parties to translate the agreement first before filing the case.

Apart from the statutory regulations concerning the decisions above, a law also regulates the agreement written in a foreign language. It is the Law on Notary[②]. A notary is a competent public official to draw up an authentic deed as the strongest and the fullest written evidence. They are expected to

---

① District Court of Tangerang, Court Order upon Request of Effendi Syahputra as the Director of PT Berkah Karya Bersama, No. 70/Pdt.P/2016/PN Tng, Feb. 11, 2016. The agreement was written in English at the time of the signature (2002), and in 2015, after the enactment of the Law on Language (2009), the agreement was translated by a sworn official translater.

② The Republic of Indonesia, Law concerning the Amendment of Law No. 30 of 2004 concerning Notary, No. 2, promulgated Jan. 15, 2014.

secure legal certainty.

The Law on Notary emphasized using *Bahasa Indonesia* as the official language in the making of authentic deeds. As stated in Article 43 of the Law on Notary, a notarial deed must be done in the Indonesian language. The deed can also be done in a foreign language if the parties agree, but in that case, the deed must also be translated into *Bahasa Indonesia*. However, these statutes also do not provide provisions on the consequences of the failure to fulfill the obligation to use *Bahasa Indonesia* in the authentic deeds.

The agreements as the object of the claims above were not made in the form of an authentic deed so that the judgments of those agreements did not take the Law on Notary into their considerations.

However, the aforementioned decisions do not include sufficient consideration regarding the key factor of the cases: the existence of a foreign element or connecting factor.

Foreign elements or connecting factors are the factors or circumstances that raise private international law issues,① The key is deciding which law applies to certain cases. Those factors that give rise to the private international issues are 1) nationality, 2) domicile or residence, and 3) place of domicile of the legal entity.

In Nine AM Ltd. v. BPLK, the foreign element is the place of domicile of the plaintiff, which is in Texas, United States of America. In the case of Ford v. Cheung, the foreign element is the parties' nationality. The plaintiff is an English citizen, and the defendant is a Chinese citizen. The two made an agreement related to an Indonesian legal entity. In the case of PT CAKP v. MDS Ltd. and PT ACR Global Investments, the defendant is a British Virgin Islands company, a foreign legal entity.

Since those three cases contain foreign elements, the instrument of private international law should prevail in those cases.

---

① Ari Purwadi, *Dasar-dasar Hukum Perdata Internasional*, Surabaya: Pusat Pengkajian Hukum dan Pembangunan (PPHP) Fakultas Hukum Universitas Wijaya Kusuma, 2016, p.64.

2. The Use of Bahasa Indonesia in International Contracts as Overriding Mandatory Rule

As stated by Huala Adolf, there are at least four principles relevant to the international commercial contract law: 1) national mandatory laws, 2) freedom of contract or party autonomy, 3) *pacta sunt servanda*, and 4) good faith.[①]

In Adolf's opinion, mandatory laws are the most important principle. The validity of every transaction made by the parties is determined by national law. The national law should be defined, obeyed as mandatory or compulsory law. The parties have no right to override it. In this term, Adolf using the words "supremacy of national law".

The private international law is the law concerning transnational private law mainly sourced from national law. According to Hardjo wahono, private international law is a part of the national law of a state. So it is understandable if there are mandatory laws in private international law cases, national law should prevail.

Indeed, the provisions of Indonesian Law on Language and Law on Notary stipulating *Bahasa Indonesia*'s use as the compulsory language of the international commercial contracts involving Indonesian entities are the mandatory laws. However, they connot automatically be considered as overriding mandatory rules.

This common understanding can be seen in international conventions. For example, from Article 9 of The Regulation (EC) No. 593/2008 of the European Parliament and of the Council of June 17, 2008, on the law applicable to contractual obligations (Rome I), we can conclude that not all mandatory rules are overriding mandatory ones, but only those "the respect for which is regarded as crucial by a country for safeguarding its public interests, such as its political, social or economic organization".

---

① Huala Adolf, *Hukum Transaksi Bisnis Transnational* (*Transnational Business Transaction Law*), Bandung: Keni Media, 2020, p.40.

According to Hardjo wahono, in practice, it is not easy to determine whether a law can be categorized as an overriding mandatory rule or not. This issue is usually answered through legal interpretation and construction measures of law at the domestic level, by considering the substance of the fundamental law as the background of the applied law.

> The characterization of a rule as an overriding mandatory rule is difficult. It rests with the authority called upon to decide (national court or arbitral tribunal, in some cases), which assesses, almost discretionary, on a case-by-case basis. Even in the less common cases, when their enactment characterizes certain provisions as overriding mandatory rules, the court/arbitral tribunal will assess whether they meet all the conditions to be considered overriding mandatory rules.①

Only a relatively small number of autonomous private international law codifications in the states provide specific rules, let alone a definition for overriding mandatory provisions. Some private international codes contain rules on overriding mandatory provisions without defining this concept. Without providing a full definition, the legislation usually hints at certain features of overriding mandatory norms. There is no specific provision on the application of overriding mandatory norms at all in other countries.② With the absence of any special act on private international law, Indonesia is included in the third category.

Article 9 (1) of the Rome I defines overriding mandatory provisions as provisions the respect for which is regarded as crucial by a country for safeguarding its public interests, such as its political, social, or economic organ-

---

① Carmen Tamara Ungureanu, Overriding Mandatory Rules in International Commercial Contracts Dispute Resolution: A Romanian Perspective, *Cuardernos de Derecho Transnacional*, Oct. 2020, Vol. 12, pp.784-794.

② Tamas Szabados, Overriding Mandatory Provisions in the Autonomous Private International Law of the EU Members States-General Report, *ELTE Law Journal*, 2020, No.1, Hungary: Eötvös University Press, 2020, pp.9-35.

ization, to such an extent that they apply to any situation falling within their scope, irrespective of the law otherwise applicable to the contract under the Rome I Regulation.

Adolf stated that the reasoning that gives the background of the application of the overriding mandatory rules is the presumptions generally containing or reflecting the fundamental policy of the states that enforced it and that if such rules are overridden by private international laws' principles or by the agreement of the parties, automatically those rules will lose their meaning as rules that contain fundamental policy.

As the main object of this research, *Bahasa Indonesia* is stated in Article 36 of the Constitution of the Republic of Indonesia 1945, "language of the State".

According on the Central Bureau of Statistics of Indonesia (Statistics Indonesia), in the 2010 population census, there are in total 1,331 ethnic groups under 633 large ethnic categories in Indonesia.[①] Those ethnic groups speak different languages of at least 718 kinds.[②] For this reason, the national language is needed as a means to unify, identify, and realize the existence of the Nation symbolizing sovereignty and honor of the State.

The other consideration of the stipulation of the Law on Language is that language, along with the national flag, emblem, and anthem, is the manifestation of the culture rooted in the history of a struggling nation, unity in the cultural diversity, and equality in realizing the ideals of the nation and the Unitary State of the Republic of Indonesia.

The four symbols reflect the state sovereignty in the social order in interstate relations and reflect the independence and existence of the free, unified, sovereign, just, and prosperous state of Indonesia. Those symbols rec-

---

① Statistics Indonesia, Mengulik Data Suku di Indonesia (Explore the Ethnic Group Data in Indonesia), Badan Pusat Statistik, https://www.bps.go.id/news/2015/11/18/127/mengulik-data-suku-di-indonesia.html, last visited on Mar. 2, 2021.

② Erwin Hutapea, Indonesia Punya 718 Bahasa Ibu, Jangan Sampai Punah! (Indonesia has 718 Mother Languages, Don't Extend It!), https://edukasi.kompas.com/read/2020/02/22/21315601/indonesia-punya-718-bahasa-ibu-jangan-sampai-punah?page=all, last visited on Feb. 22, 2020.

ognize Indonesia as a nation and state and are respected and proud symbols the state.

The provisions of the obligation to use *Bahasa Indonesia* in international contracts must be seen as a unity of the other provisions. Article 31 Par. 2 of the Law on Language stated that in the Memoranda of Understanding (MoU) and/or agreements which involve Indonesian entities and also foreign parties, the Indonesian language version could be accompanied by a version in the language of the foreign parties and/or in English. In this comprehensive view, the efforts to achieve both objectives: to reflect the state sovereignty and the social order in interstate relations, are feasible.

For these reasons, the provisions of the use of *Bahasa Indonesia* as the compulsory language of Indonesian international contracts must be considered as an overriding mandatory rule.

3. A Comparison to Turkish Compulsory Language

The Republic of Turkey is the other one of few countries that applies the law on commercial contracts' compulsory language. Law No. 805 of 1926 concerning the Compulsory Use of Turkish Language in Economic Enterprises (hereinafter referred to as Law on the Turkish Language), regulates the procedure of Turkish enterprises' records keeping. According to Article 1 of the Law on the Turkish Language, all Turkish companies and enterprises are obliged to conduct their business transactions, conclude their agreements, and keep their correspondences, records, and books in the Turkish language within Turkey. The term "companies and enterprises" also includes natural person merchants.

The Law's main focus on the Turkish Language is the place where the agreement is signed. This law does not apply to the agreement concluded outside Turkey by a Turkish company even though the results and effects of the agreements arise within Turkey's jurisdiction.

This provision is different from the Indonesian Law on Language, whose main focus is the agreements'subject. As long as one or both parties of the agreements are Indonesian entities, the agreements must be written in

Bahasa Indonesia.

According to Article 2 of the Law on the Turkish Language, foreign companies must use the Turkish Language for the documents and books to be presented to the Turkish governmental authorities within Turkey. Moreover, foreign companies are required to use the Turkish language for the transactions and communications made with Turkish citizens and Turkish companies.[①]

The obligation for foreign companies to use the Turkish language is only limited to the circumstances mentioned above. In this framework, even within Turkey, there is not any obligation to use the Turkish language, nor when a foreign company concludes a transaction with another foreign company or while the operation is related to its internal business.

According to Article 3 of the Law on the Turkish Language, foreign companies may also use a language other than the Turkish language. According to the relevant article, the text in the Turkish language is required to be added next to the text in a foreign language. However, it is the Turkish version of the text that should be signed and attested; even though the text in a foreign language is signed, the text in the Turkish language shall prevail over it.

Both Law on the Turkish Language and Indonesian Law on Language allow foreign companies to have a translated version in another language. The difference is that the Turkish law stipulates that the Turkish Language shall prevail in the case of the use of the bilingual agreement. In contrast, the Indonesian law stipulates that the prevailing language is determined by the parties as stated in the agreement.

Different from the Indonesian Law on Language, Law on the Turkish Language expressly set forth sanctions applicable in case of violation of its provisions, stated that documents and records that are prepared contrary to the provisions of the Law should be invalid. Such agreements shall be considered null and void and shall not confer any rights or obligations on their parties.

---

① Erdem & Erdem, The Act on Compulsory Use of Turkish Language in Economic Enterprises, http://www.erdem-erdem.av.tr/publications/law-post/the-act-on-compulsory-use-of-turkish-language-in-economic-enterprises/, last visited on Mar. 5, 2021.

Furthermore, Law on the Turkish Language stipulates that failure to comply with the Law may lead to an administrative fine (Article 4 and Article 7 of Law on the Turkish Language).

Although this Law is quite old, its provisions are still in vigor and thus enforceable. No specific law has been subsequently enacted to hinder its application.[①] Gucuk and Talaz noted few decisions in which Law on the Turkish Language has been applied by the Turkish Courts, among others are: [②]

-702062160-1979: The Court refused to enforce a due date clause which was in English and contained in a bank security letter in Turkish given to a government office;

-702062159-2006: In a dispute between a Turkish bank customer and a Turkish branch of a foreign bank, the court of appeals found that the lower court should have considered Law No. 805;

-702062158-2014: In a dispute between a foreign pharmaceutical company and a Turkish distributor, the court dismissed the case because it found the arbitration clause was invalid in the contract as it was drafted in English;

However, Turkey's Court sees the arbitral clause or arbitration agreement in a distinct view, even though both are included in the same contract. The Court's decision No. 2020/19 E and 2020/184 K dated February 2, 2020, stated that if one of the parties is not Turkish, then it is not mandatory to use Turkish in the arbitration agreement. Therefore, a non-Turkish arbitration agreement is valid if one of the parties is foreign, and thus the arbi-

---

① Akdogan Uslas, Compulsory Use of the Turkish Language in Agreements Executed in Turkey, https://www.hg.org/legal-articles/compulsory-use-of-the-turkish-language-in-agreements-executed-in-turkey-18372, last visited on Mar. 8, 2021.

② Courtney Kirkman Gucuk, Can Talaz, Turkey's Court of Cassation Refuses to Enforce an Arbitration Clause in English Based on a Turkish Language Requirement, http://arbitrationblog.kluwerarbitration.com/2018/09/29/turkeys-court-of-cassationrefuses -to-enforce-an-arbitration-clause-in-english-based-on-a-turkish-languagerequirement/Kluwer Arbitration Blog, last visited on Sep. 29, 2018.

tration objection raised by the defendant is to be accepted by the court.[①]The Court adopted a pro-arbitration approach.

Baysal and Cevik held that when taking a look back at the decisions in which the Law on the Turkish Language has been applied, it seems that Turkish courts are making an effort to circumvent the application of the mandatory provisions of this law as possible as they can. Although the provisions of the Law are mandatory, Turkish courts abstain from their ex officio application. It is only when a party raises the Turkish language requirement do the Turkish courts examine the question of whether or not the contract violates Law.[②]

Moreover, Baysal and Cevik concluded that even if a party were to raise an objection based on the Turkish language requirement, Turkish courts would not directly jump to the conclusion that the contract itself is void. In those cases, Turkish courts would examine whether raising the Turkish language requirement, in turn, constitutes an abuse of rights. In many instances, Turkish courts concluded that a party, who had previously relied on any part of the contract, couldnot later argue that the contract is void for violating the provisions of the Law.

4. The Nature of Overriding Mandatory Rules

As said by Lorenzo, one of the functions of the applicable law to a contract is the "restrictive function", which restricts the party autonomy or freedom of a contract and is recognized by most of the modern legal systems.

---

① Fatih Isik, Istanbul Regional Court of Appeal Decisions Regarding Law No. 805 on Mandatory Use of Turkish Language in Arbitration Agreements, https://www.mondaq.com/turkey/trials-appeals-compensation/943936/istanbul-regional-court-of-appeal-decisions-regarding-law-no-805-on-mandatory-use-of-turkish-language-in-arbitration-agreements, last visited on Jul. 9, 2020.

② Pelin Baysal and Bilge Kağan Cevik, Can One Arbitrate With a Turkish Party Based on a Contract in a Language Other Than Turkish?, https://gun.av.tr/insights/articles/can-one-arbitrate-with-a-turkish-party-based-on-a-contract-in-a-language-other-than-turkish? utm_source=Mondaq&utm_medium=syndication&utm_campaign=LinkedIn-integration, last visited on Aug. 19, 2019.

Ungureanu classified the limitation of party autonomy as follows: "In domestic contracts, the parties are bound to observe 'public policy' and 'good morals'. In international contracts, party autonomy is limited by 'public policy' and 'overriding mandatory rules'."

Public policy may be a limitation for both domestic and international contracts, but overriding mandatory rules only apply as a limitation for international contracts.

By citing some scholars' opinion, Ungureanu concluded that overriding mandatory rules are a specific form of public policy. The main difference between them is not the content but the way they operate. Overriding mandatory rules are provisions that apply directly to specific situations, without involving negative/critical assessments regarding the chosen law; their effect is "repellant"; the chosen law is refused without having its content analyzed. Public policy is a negative way, implying the non-application of the chosen law, in whole or in par. If it contravenes the public policy of the, this time, the refusal is based on the content of the chosen law.

Mota defined an overriding mandatory rule as "a substantive and imperative rule that has the prerogative to override the rule of conflict or competence-attribution clause in accordance with the (especially important) goals that it pursues, given they may be explicitly classified (by the legislator), or interpreted as such".①

Following are the outline of that definition:

(ⅰ)"Substantive law" refers to the body of rules that determine the rights and obligations, duties and causes of action of the subject of law that can be enforced by law, which is compounded with the "procedural law", the set of rules by which the substantive law is created, applied and enforced.

(ⅱ) "Imperative" means its nature compulsory or mandatory provisions, which should be obeyed and generally followed by a threat of sanctions or consequences of breach.

① Miguel Afonso do Carmo Mota, *Overriding Mandatory Provisions in a European Context*, Lisbon: Catolica Global School of Law, 2018, p.6.

(ⅲ)"has the prerogative to override the rule of conflict or competence-attribution clause" is the primary nature of the overriding mandatory rules. A choice cannot circumvent the application of the law of another country. In other words, these provisions are internationally binding. They are also to be distinguished from the "provisions that cannot be derogated from by agreement". Van Bochove mentioned Article 3 (3) and (4) as well as Article 6 (2) and 8 (1) of the Rome I Regulation: not only are overriding mandatory rules enforceable irrespective of a choice of law by the parties, but they also supersede the law applicable based on the objective choice of law rules of the Regulation.①

(ⅳ) "in accordance to the (fundamental) goals that it pursues": because of its nature as a fundamental policy, the stipulation of overriding mandatory provisions is considerd to safeguard its public interests, mainly its political, economic, and social order.

(ⅴ)"given they may be explicitly classified (by the legislator), or interpreted as such": Some private international law codes, such as Belgian Private International Law Act Article 20, Bulgarian Private International Law Act Article 46, English Private International Law (Miscellaneous Provisions) Act Section 14 (4), Hungarian Private International Law Act Article 13, Lithuanian Civil Code Article 1.11 (2), and Polish Private International Law Act Article 8, contain rules on overriding mandatory provisions without defining this concept. The other states such as Austria, Denmark, Estonia, Germany, Latvia, Slovenia have no specific provision on the application of overriding mandatory norms. Without being explicitly classified by the legislator, whether a provision is an overriding mandatory rule needs to be interpreted.

UNIDROIT, an independent intergovernmental organization, whose purpose is to modernize, harmonize, and coordinate private and in particular commercial law between States and groups of States and to formulate

① Laura Maria van Bochove, Overriding Mandatory Rules as a Vehicle for Weaker Party Protection in European Private International Law, *Erasmus Law Review*, Nov. 2014, No. 3., pp.147-156.

uniform law instruments, principles, and rules to achieve those objectives,① has presented its fourth edition of the UNIDROIT Principles of International Commercial Contracts in 2016 (hereinafter referred to as PICC).②

The Official Commentary of the PICC states that the mandatory rules are "predominantly laid by specific legislation, and their mandatory nature, may either be expressly stated or inferred by way of interpretation."③ A provision that is not expressly stated as an overriding mandatory rule can be interpreted by using the doctrines such as Mota's definition.

PICC gives a dominant position to the mandatory rules over the concluded contracts. The Principles acknowledges the overriding mandatory rules in a broad notion, which are enacted autonomously by States, derived from international conventions or general public international law, or adopted by supranational organizations.

5. Effects of the Infringement of Overriding Mandatory Rules

PICC is one of the sources of private international law that can be used as a reference due to the absence of national law stipulating the effects of the infringement of overriding mandatory rules.

As a member of UNIDROIT, the Indonesian court may take the pandect of the PICC's provisions into consideration in judging international commercial contract disputes, even though Indonesia has not expresslied ratified the Principles yet.

As general rules for international commercial contracts, PICC return

---

① Institute International Pour L'Unification Du Droit Prive (UNIDROIT) has its seat in the Villa Aldobrandini in Rome. Set up in 1926 as an auxiliary organ of the League of Nations, the institute was, following the demise of the League, re-established in 1940 on the basis of a multilateral agreement. UNIDROIT, History and Overview, https://www.unidroit.org/about-unidroit/overview, last visited on Feb. 11, 2021.

② PICC 2016 was concluded at UNIDROIT's 95th session in May 2016. The Governing Council adopted the amendments and additions to the 2010 UNIDROIT Principles of International Commercial Contracts.

③ Official Commentary of Article 1.4 PICC, Par. 2.

the effect of the infringement of overriding mandatory rules to the binding norms from which such rules originate. The Art. 3.3.1 Par. 1 PICC states that "Where a contract infringes a mandatory rule, whether of national, international or supranational origin, applicable under Art. 1.4 of these Principles, the effects of that infringement upon the contract are the effects, if any, expressly prescribed by that mandatory rules."

If there is no provision of the effects expressly prescribed in the originate rules, PICC provides guidance as stated in Par. 2 of Art. 3.3.1: "Where the mandatory rule does not expressly prescribe the effects of an infringement upon a contract, the parties have the right to exercise such remedies under the contract as in the circumstances are reasonable."

Moreover, PICC also mentions how to determine what is reasonable regard. As stated in Par. 3 of Art. 3.3.1. PICC, it is to be had in particular to:

(a) the purpose of the rule which has been infringed;

(b) the category of persons for whose protection the rule exists;

(c) any sanction that may be imposed under the rule infringed;

(d) the seriousness of the infringement;

(e) whether one or both parties knew or ought to have known of the infringement;

(f) whether the performance of the contract necessitates the infringement; and

(g) the parties' reasonable expectations.

Regarding those provisions, whenever a court judges a case based on the overriding mandatory rule where the effect of such infringement is not expressly prescribed, the court should consider: 1) what is reasonable in the circumstances and 2) which kind of remedies fits the infringement.

The official commentary of PICC 2016 provides explanations and examples of each criterion to determine the contractual remedies available in the circumstances. Some of the criteria relevant to *Bahasa Indonesia*'s provision as compulsory language are analyzed as follows.

Among the most critical factors to be taken into consideration is the purpose of the mandatory rule and whether the attaining of its purpose would or would not be affected by granting at least one of the parties a remedy under the contract.

According to Article 3 of the Indonesian Law on Language, specifically related to international contracts, the purposes of the stipulation of the Law are to keep the honor which shows the sovereignty of the nation and the Unitary State of the Republic of Indonesia and create order, certainty, and standardization of the use of the language.

The reasoning for this purpose is subjective—from the point of view of the interests of the state. However, that is the nature of overriding mandatory rules, regulated and dictated by the national law.

Granting remedies under the contract may also depend on whether one or even both of the parties knew or ought to have known of the mandatory rule or its infringement.

In the case of the infringement of the use of Bahasa Indonesia as a compulsory language in international commercial contracts, both parties signed the contracts and obviously, they are aware of the use of language in their contract. Thus under the maxim "everyone is presumed to know the law", the parties may not escape liability for violating that law merely by "using unaware of its content" as an excuse.

The Provision of remedies in PICC is formulated in a broad and flexible understanding. As it is said in its explanation, Notwithstanding the infringement of the mandatory rule, one or both of the parties may, depending on the circumstances of the case, be granted the ordinary remedies available under a valid contract (including the right of performance), or other remedies such as the right to treat the contract as being no effect, the adaptation of the contract or its termination on terms to be fixed.

By considering the criteria for determining what is reasonable in the circumstances, it is unfair if the court grants annulment to the contracts upon the lawsuit of the party of the contracts, since both parties know that the agreement is provided in English without translation in *Bahasa Indonesia*, by the time they sign the contracts. It should also be noted that the purpose of the Law on *Bahasa Indonesia* is not to protect the parties of the contracts, even if the party is of an Indonesian entity, but more to protect national interests in general.

We see those lawsuits of infringement of Indonesian Law on Language submitted by the party and aggrieved by the other party related to the implementation of the contents of the contracts, not related to the loss due to the absence of using Bahasa Indonesia in the contracts.

The remedies decided by the courts should be appropriate and proportional to the infringement. In the cases of infringement of Indonesian Law on Language, several essential considerations need to be taken into account:

1. Disputes on international commercial contracts are related to the parties' interests, the business climate and the need to reduce the trade barriers. So in the case of infringement of the Law on Language, it is necessary to find solutions that balance the national interests and the international need to reduce the trade barriers.

2. Civil procedural law in the Indonesian courts is carried out in *Bahasa Indonesia*, so are the court decisions. According to Article 4 of Presidential Regulation No. 63 of 2019, court decisions are classified as state documents, so they are obliged to be provided in *Bahasa Indonesia*. The submission of a contract in a foreign language as evidence in Indonesian courts needs to be translated or at least should be accompanied by a contract in *Bahasa Indonesia*.

According to those relevant criteria and the essential considerations, the appropriate and proportional remedy to the infringement of Law on Language in *Bahasa Indonesia*'s use in an international commercial contract involving Indonesian entities is ordering specific performance to the parties to fulfill the provisions of the Law on Language.

Therefore, the court may issue an interlocutory or provisional decision giving the order to translate the contract into *Bahasa Indonesia* by a sworn official translator chosen by the parties or appointed by the court. Hence, the dispute examination process is carried out based on the contract's translation. Or else, if the annulment of a contract written in English is the only demand by the plaintiff, the court may issue a decision giving an order of a remedy to both parties to translate the contract.

By the court order of the remedy, the contracting parties forced to accomplish their content of the contract, rather than just making non-use of *Bahasa Indonesia* in the contract as an excuse to avoid the contract they have been concluded.

Conclusion

The obligation of using Bahasa Indonesia in the international contracts is not followed by an explicit provision concerning the effect of the infringement of that obligation.

The court's decisions to those cases are varied, even contradicting each other. That causes the uncertainty that may affect the business climate. Given that there are foreign elements contained within such case, the instrument of private international laws should be applied.

According to the private international law principles, this research concluds that the obligation of using *Bahasa Indonesia* in international contracts in Indonesia is an overriding mandatory rule, so in examining such cases, it must be treated by its nature.

Indonesian courts may take the pandect of the PICC's provisions into consideration. Article 3.3.1 of the PICC offers guidance when the mandatory rule does not expressly prescribe the effect of an infringement of those contracts. The parties have the right to exercise such remedies under the contract as in the circumstances are reasonable.

Applied to those cases, the reasonable regards are the purpose of the rule that has been infringed and whether one or both parties knew or ought to have known the infringement.

Based on those relevant criteria and the essential considerations, the appropriate and proportional remedy to the infringement of Law on Language in the use of Bahasa Indonesia in an international commercial contract involving Indonesian entities is ordering specific performance to the parties to fulfill the provisions of the Law on Language.

The fulfillment of the Law on Language provisions may be ordered by interlocutory/provisional decisions or by substantive decisions (depending on the plaintiff's substantive dispute).

In order to balance the national interests and international need to reduce trade barriers, it is an urge to ensure certainty. Besides, the law's stipula-

tion concerning the use of language in international commercial contracts is supposed to be in lenient provisions, rather than strict provisions.

First, to ensure certainty, the law is supposed to expressly describe the obligation of using *Bahasa Indonesia* in international commercial contracts in Indonesia as an overriding mandatory rule.

Second, the law is also required to provide the provision of the effect of the infringement of overriding mandatory rules.

Third, the remedy to the effect of the infringement of the Law on Language shall be having the translation of the contract in *Bahasa Indonesia*, as it is by the order of the interlocutory/provisional decision or of the decision issued by the court, depending on the dispute substance.

For the business actors as the signatory parties, it is important to notice the obligation to use Bahasa Indonesia in their international commercial contracts to ensure their contracts enforceable. Anyway, they can still determine the prevailing language of their contracts.

Comprehensive and Progressive Agreement for Trans-Pacific Partnership and the Significance on Future Regional Free Trade Agreement

Haile Anadrgie*

Abstract: The fundamental aim of this article is to examine Comprehensive and Progressive Agreement for Trans-Pacific Partnership (CPTPP) in terms of its contents and the implication on future trade negotiation of free trade agreements. It also investigates the impact of CPTPP on the members and regional geopolitics. The article argues that CPTPP incorporats many of the negotiated elements as part of the Trans-Pacific Partnership (TPP), yet with some significant differences like suspending some items from the TPP. The relative importance of CPTPP is worthwhile, especially in the current global context, because of threats to WTO rules' effective operation, including its dispute resolution mechanism. In this respect, CPTPP is a game-setter in that it locks in institutional and rules-based reform, sets new standards for future free trade agreements (FTAs) and provides incentives to consolidate and reorder Asia-Pacific supply chains.

Keywords: CPTPP, Challenge, Opportunity, Impact, Regional Agreement

1. Introduction

On 28 May 2006, Trans-Pacific Strategic Economic Partnership Agreement, a free trade agreement, come effectively from four countries: Singapore,

* Former V/Dean of Debre Markos University School of Law, Ethiopia and PhD candidate of International Law School, SWUPL.

Chile, New Zealand and Brunei.[①] In 2007, the member states decided to expand the negotiation scope of this agreement to financial services, investment, and exchange with the United States. In September 2008, the United States Trade Representative (USTR) notified the United States to participate in negotiations to expand and the united states was officially involved in some discussions of opening up the financial services market. As time went on, the number of Countries interested in the talks increased to twelve. Those twelve countries managed to sign an agreement called Trans-Pacific Partnership (TPP) on 4 February 2016.

All of a sudden, the United States withdrew immediately after Donald Trump took office. The remaining eleven members restarted negotiations. The CPTPP was signed in Santiago, Chile, on 8 March 2018. The agreement specifies that its provisions enter into effect 60 days after ratification by at least 50% of the signatories (six of the eleven participating countries). For those Parties who have not yet ratified the CPTPP, it enters into force 60 days after the date on which that signatory has notified the Depositary (New Zealand) in writing of the completion of its applicable legal procedures.[②] Until 1 January 2019, Australia, Canada, Mexico, New Zealand, and Singapore implemented the second round of tariff cuts. Japan's second tariff cut took place on 1 April 2019.

CPTPP member countries contribute a significant portion to the world economy. The eleven countries' combined economies represented 13.5 per cent of the global gross domestic product (GDP), approximately US $10 trillion, making the CPTPP area the third largest free trade area in the world by GDP after the North American Free Trade Agreement and European Single Market.

The parties to CPTPP represent approximately half a billion people, which is immense, as slashed tariffs encourage significant shifts in global

---

① Phan Quan Viet, Opportunities and Challenge When Vietnam Joins TPP, *International Research Journal*, 2015, Vol.15, p.1.

② The CPTPP Enters into Force: What Does It Mean for Global Trade? https://www.whitecase.com/careers, last visited on Mar. 31, 2020.

supply chains.[①]The CPTPP's high-standard provisions on the digital economy, investment, financial services, labour and the environment establish new "rules of the road" that will have broad country-specific and collective impact.[②] As noted by Christopher and et al., the CPTPP, like its predecessor, the TPP, is touted as a 'next-generation' trade agreement, building on the core structure of WTO Agreements and existing bilateral FTAs. Nevertheless, CPTPP went further than WTO and FTA rules in several key areas, such as digital trade and electronic commerce, intellectual property, labour environment and state-owned enterprises (SOEs). The provisions implicate that CPTPP has a tangible impact on trade in goods and services among the Parties and have repercussions as they are used as a model for other agreements.

Therefore, this article explores critical points on the main contents of CPTPP in part II, including those that changed from the TPP. In part III, the paper explores the overall implication of CPTPP on some selected countries and the upcoming free trade agreements in the international trade regime. Part IV depicts the prospects of CTPP in setting standards in future free trade agreements. Finally, part V provides concluding remarks.

2. CPTPP: Is It a Verbatim Copy of TPP?

The CPTPP is nearly identical to the TPP but suspends 22 elements of its predecessor. The rest provisions are incorporated in TPP signed in 2016 by the original 12 parties (including the United States). Most of the suspended provisions had been inserted into the original TPP text at US negotiators' demand to safeguard various domestic stakeholders' interests.

---

① Alan Oxley, Comprehensive and Progressive Agreement for Trans-Pacific Partnership, https://www.rmit.edu.au/rmit/.../apec/apec-currents-the-comprehensive-and-progres, last visited on 15 Jan. 2020.

② Cristopher F. et al., The CPTPP Enters into Force: What does it Mean for Global Trade, https://www.whitecase.com/.../alert/cptpp-enters-force-what-does-it-mean-global-trade, last visited on 4 Apr. 2020.

The suspended conditions cover market exclusivity rules for biological drugs, strict copyright enforcement priorities, and investor-state dispute settlement. The final text of the CPTPP Agreement has been reduced from 622 pages to 584 pages with the removal of the suspended provisions, which, according to Article 2 of the CPTPP, will remain suspended until the 11 signatories decide; otherwise by consensus.

The rationale for setting these provisions aside for later consideration and debate, as opposed to completely removing them from the legal text, was a negotiating tactic led by Japan and Australia to leave the door open for the eventual return to the United States' agreement. In the absence of the United States signalling interest to rejoin and rekindle the incentive of preferential access to US markets, it is unlikely that the 11 countries can or would indeed want to reach a consensus on 'not suspending' any of the contentious provisions.

The CPTPP preserves all of the original and substantive TPP commitments in market access for goods, services, investment, state-owned enterprises, government procurement and business mobility. In other words, all of the existing annexes from the TPP Agreement remain unchanged, and all tariff reduction and elimination schedules, services and investment liberalizations, as well as market access for government, procured works will take place as scheduled in the original commitments, with a majority taking effect from day one of entry into force of the agreement.

Therefore, CPTPP is not substantially different from its predecessor, TPP. It reflects the aspirations of participating countries to implement the TPP outcomes, demonstrating their firm commitments to market opening, protectionism combating, as well as enhancing and advancing regional economic integration.[①] It is deeper and broader, with commitments that best match the needs of large and small businesses. The CPTPP, among other things, includes the most detailed standards for the intellectual property of any trade agreement and protections against intellectual property theft

① Benson Simon, "*$ 13.7 trillion TPP pact to deliver a boost in GDP*", *The Australian*, last visited on 25 Apr. 2019.

against corporations operating abroad, investment, labour, environment, and other contemporary issues.[1] The preamble of the CPTPP indicates that corporate social responsibility, cultural identity and diversity, environmental protection and conservation, gender equality, indigenous rights, labour rights, inclusive trade, sustainable development and traditional knowledge. The preamble also emphasizes the importance of preserving public interest, which is at the agreement's centre.[2] Those provisions of CPTPP, which are deemed essential and novel in the author's view, are depicted in the following sections.

2.1 CPTPP Introduces Digital Trade/E-commerce Governance

The CPTPP can be considered novel to recognize electronic commerce's potential to generate economic growth and development opportunities. E-commerce is a relatively new phenomenon, and the previous trade agreements did not have a detailed regulatory and institutional framework. In the CPTPP, the E-Commerce Chapter seeks to facilitate business-related data transfers and trade in digital products.

Firstly, the CPTPP introduces a prohibition on data localization measures and aims to promote the adoption of domestic frameworks capable of building confidence among e-commerce users and avoiding the imposition of unnecessary barriers to the use and development of e-commerce.

Secondly, the CPTPP provides a commitment to allow the cross-border transfer of information by electronic means when such activity is for business conduct. This part of the agreement contains provisions covering electronic authentication and signatures, online consumer protection, the protection of personal information of the users of e-commerce, unauthorized commercial electronic messages, and the value of cooperation on cyber-security matters.

Thirdly, the CPTPP envisages a system of a prohibition on imposing

---

① Goodman Matthew P. "From TPP to CPTPP", *Center for Strategic and International Studies*, last visited on 12 Jun. 2020.

② CPTPP, https://www.mfat.govt.nz/assets/CPTPP/Comprehensive-and-Progressive-Agreement-for-Trans-Pacific-Partnership-CPTPP-English.pdf, last visited on Apr.4, 2020.

customs duties on electronic transmissions. The chapter also prohibits parties requiring access to the source code of software owned by a person of another Party as a condition for the import, sale or use of the software.

All in all, CPTPP aims to minimize unnecessary barriers to e-commerce: encouraging the adoption of paperless trading, prohibiting customs duties on electronic transmissions between the Parties, requiring non-discriminatory treatment of digital products, minimizing unnecessary barriers relating to the cross-border transfer of information by electronic means, and prohibiting the location of computing facilities and access to source code.

2.2 CPTPP Heightens Standard of Investment Protection

Of course, the Investment Chapter of CPTPP is not entirely new compared to the pre-existing trade agreements, as there were attempts like TRIMS. However, the Investment Chapter of CPTPP establishes high-standard provisions for investors and covers the entire lifecycle of an investment—from establishment or acquisition to management, operation, expansion and disposition. The chapter's requirements include the core obligations of national treatment, most-favoured-nation (MFN) treatment[①], expropriation and compensation, performance requirements and transfers[②]. While the agreement includes Investor-State Dispute Settlement (ISDS) provisions, the scope for investors to make ISDS claims is narrowed (e.g. private companies cannot make ISDS claims relating to investment contracts they have entered into with governments). Supply chain, goods, rules of origin, certification-The Agreement supports the development of CPTPP-wide supply chains by generally allowing for "accumulation" within the CPTPP region. This confirms that the ability to further process or add one signatory country to products in another signatory country (which will then be treated as originated in the latter country) has become a standard feature in modern trade agreements. The agreement also includes trade facilitation provisions on self-certification of origin, advanced rulings and customs clearance timelines.

---

① CPTPP, Article 9.4

② CPTPP, Article 9.5

2.3 CPTPP Adopts Negative Listing in Service Trade

The Cross-Border Trade in Services Chapter seeks to facilitate cross-border trade in services, including in sectors such as accountancy, construction, engineering and architecture services. How to market access commitments for services and investment in CPTPP is through a 'negative list' framework. This format provides exporters and investors with a simple way to determine whether the services and investment provisions apply to their business area in another CPTPP market. Under a 'negative list' approach, Parties commit to provide market access except in areas where restrictions are listed in individual Parties' services and investment schedules. These restrictions are known as 'non-conforming measures' or 'reservations'. Each country's 'negative list' has two parts. Annexe I sets out existing measures (laws, regulations, decisions, practices and procedures) that CPTPP Parties retain the right to maintain in their present form. Such actions may restrict the access of Foreign Service suppliers or investors or discriminate in favour of domestic service suppliers or investors. These existing measures are subject to a 'ratchet' clause. This means that CPTPP Parties automatically commit to extend the benefits of any future autonomous liberalization of these measures to all other CPTPP countries. Measures in Annex I capture the current level of access provided in a market and cannot be made more restrictive in the future. Annex II lists reservations for sectors and activities where CPTPP Parties reserve the right to maintain existing discriminatory measures and to adopt new or more discriminatory actions in the future. The ratchet clause does not apply to any measure covered by Annex II. In other words, if a CPTPP Party does not list any restrictions for a particular industry sector, it means that the Party is committed not to apply any measures that would be inconsistent with certain Chapter obligations.①

2.4 CPTPP Introduces Long-Ignored Labor Issues

Setting labour standard in trade deal was not common in the previous

① Goodman, Matthew P. (2018), No.13.

trade agreements, for it is a very sensitive issue. In this respect, the Labor Chapter of CPTPP constitutes the most tangible outcome on trade and labour in any FTA negotiated between states to date, in terms of its provisions' scope and nature. CPTPP provides binding commitments that require a Party to uphold through its domestic laws. The rights incorporated in the CPTPP are a set of standards outlined in the International Labor Organization (ILO) Declaration: freedom of association and collective bargaining, elimination of forced labour, abolition of child labour, and eliminating employment discrimination. ① The CPTPP also records the Parties' recognition that labour standards should not be used for protectionist trade purposes and that it is inappropriate to encourage trade or investment by weakening or reducing labour laws. Accordingly, CPTPP Parties agree not to derogate from their laws (or offer to do so) in a manner affecting trade or investment between them.

Besides, each CPTPP Party commits to discourage, through initiatives it considers appropriate, importing goods produced by forced or compulsory-labour from other sources and encouraging enterprises in its jurisdiction to adopt voluntary corporate social responsibility initiatives on labour issues. They help level the playing field for companies and employees by setting minimum labour obligations for all CPTPP Parties. This ensures that laws that are not effectively enforced do not underpin CPTPP parties' competitive advantage in trade or do not reflect internationally recognized labour rights.

All obligations in the chapter are subject to the CPTPP dispute settlement mechanism; however, the Labor Chapter has specific procedures for labour consultation that must be used before the dispute settlement provisions of CPTPP are employed. Besides, the Disputes Settlement Chapter requires Parties to make every attempt to resolve disputes through cooperation and consultations before resorting to the procedures provided in the chapter. The inclusion of binding dispute settlement applicable to the labour commitments, with the potential of trade sanctions or monetary compensation for

① Greater Market Access, Lower Tariffs for Singapore Companies when CPTPP Enters into Force, *Channel News Asia*, last visited on Jul. 24, 2020.

breaches, reduces policy space and creates some risks for the government in potentially dealing with unfounded actions.

2.5 CPTPP Elevates Environmental Standards

In terms of environmental standards, the CPTPP is called a "21st century" FTA because it has established advanced trading rules that are not necessarily included in other FTAs (about 300 worldwide) or the WTO agreements in many areas.① The Environment Chapter in the original TPP, which consists of 23 articles and many provisions, remains almost intact in the CPTPP. The Environment Chapter aims to promote mutually supportive trade and environment policies, promote high levels of environmental protection and effective enforcement of environmental laws, and enhance the CPTPP Parties' capacities to address trade-related ecological issues. The Environment Chapter includes both binding and non-binding commitments relating to environmental protection. ② Three multilateral environmental agreements (MEAs)—Montreal Protocol on Substances that Deplete the Ozone Layer, London Protocol to the International Convention for the Prevention of Pollution from Ships, and the Convention on International Trade in Endangered Species—are incorporated.

Four objectives guide CPTPP members' policy in negotiating environment chapters in trade agreements: to promote sustainable development; to ensure trade and environment provisions are mutually supportive; to ensure the government has the flexibility to regulate the environment following national circumstances and to ensure that environmental provisions are not used as a disguised form of protectionism. The CPTPP Environment Chapter supports and promotes these objectives and represents the most comprehensive environmental outcome in any new CPTPP members' FTAs. These provisions can give impetus and support to related initiatives in the WTO and

① Mitsui & Co. Global Strategic Studies Institute Monthly Report, September 2018, CPTPP as a Landmark "21ST Century" Agreement.

② The CPTPP Enters into Force: What Does it Mean for Global Trade? https://www.whitecase.com/careers, last visited on Mar. 31, 2019.

elsewhere to incorporate the issue of environment in trade dealing.

All obligations in the chapter are subject to the CPTPP dispute settlement mechanism; however, the Environment Chapter has specific procedures requiring consultation that must be used before the dispute settlement provisions of CPTPP are employed. Besides, the Disputes Settlement Chapter requires Parties to make every attempt to resolve disputes through cooperation and consultations before resorting to the procedures provided in the chapter.

2.6 CPTPP Incorporates Detail Sanitary and Phytosanitary Measures

Imports, particularly primary products, can face measures designed to protect human, animal or plant life or health against pests, diseases and food-borne risks (referred to collectively as SPS measures: sanitary: human and animal health; and phytosanitary: plant health)①. For example, imported fruit may require treatments and inspections to ensure the absence of pests, and food may be necessary to have pesticide levels below certain maximum residue limits. All CPTPP Parties are members of the WTO SPS Agreement, which allows countries to determine their protection level for health and safety and requires that any restrictions on trade should be non-discriminatory, transparent and scientifically justified. Here, it made clear that CPTPP is a WTO plus agreement established basing the later rule. CPTPP provisions are built on the WTO Agreement on the Application of Sanitary and Phytosanitary Measures and provide a solid framework for

---

① The SPS is given an extended definition under the WTO framework in the form of an Annex. Annex A(1)(a) defines an SPS measure as any measure taken to protect animal or plant life or health from the establishment or spread of pests, diseases, disease-carrying organisms, or disease-causing organisms. Annex A(1)(b) defines an SPS measure as any measure taken to protect human, or animal life or health within the territory of the Member from risks arising from additives, contaminants, toxins or disease-causing organisms in foods, beverages or feedstuffs. Annex A(1)(c) defines an SPS measure as any measure taken to protect human life or health from risks arising from diseases carried by animals, and Annex A(1)(d) defines an SPS measure as any measure taken to prevent or limit other damage within the territory of the Member from the entry, establishment or spread of pests.

CPTPP Parties to implement their WTO-related SPS commitments (concerning both new and existing SPS measures). CPTPP encourages better and more consistent SPS regulatory practice, intending to benefit exporters and importers across the region potentially.

2.7 CPTPP Guarantees Intellectual Property Protection

The Intellectual Property (IP) Chapter sets out several obligations for CPTPP countries. These obligations cover copyright, patents, plant variety rights, trademarks, geographical indications, industrial designs, domain names, and intellectual property rights enforcement. The chapter also contains provisions on traditional knowledge, traditional cultural expressions and genetic resources. Many of the intellectual property obligations in CPTPP go further than the multilateral treaties CPTPP member states have agreed like the World Trade Organization Agreement on Trade-Related Aspects of Intellectual Property Rights (TRIPS Agreement) or their previous FTAs.[①]

The CPTPP requires Parties to adopt or maintain due process requirements regarding any regime they provide to protect geographical indications (GIs).[②] Besides, the CPTPP requires Parties to provide more uniformity in civil and criminal procedures to enforce intellectual property rights. Greater uniformity of enforcement procedures throughout CPTPP countries can reduce the regulatory and business compliance cost for member states' businesses when enforcing their intellectual property rights in other CPTPP Parties. The IP part also contains several provisions on traditional knowledge. In the Agreement, Parties recognize the relevance of traditional knowledge to intellectual property systems, commit to work together on traditional knowledge issues and preserve their ability to take measures to respect, preserve and promote traditional knowledge and traditional cultural expressions. The Parties also agree to pursue quality patent examination. These include an opportunity to inform patent offices of each Party, using databases or digital libraries containing information on traditional knowledge, and coop-

---

① CPTTP, New Zealand Ministry of Foreign Affairs and Trade Report, 2018, p.59.

② CPTTP, New Zealand Ministry of Foreign Affairs and Trade Report, 2018, p.60.

erating in the training of patent examiners on how to deal with applications related to traditional knowledge.

2.8 CPTPP Emphasizes on Transparency and Anti-corruption

Another new trend in CPTPP is the incorporation of transparency and anti-corruption chapter. The CPTPP includes some novel transparency provisions intended to assist businesses operating in other CPTPP markets and combat bribery and corruption. It imposes procedural requirements to ensure that Parties promptly, impartially, and reasonably administer measures covered by the agreement. The CPTPP is also the first international agreement in which FTA has agreed to include specific transparency-related provisions on pharmaceutical and medical device reimbursement (or subsidy) programmers. The provisions in annexes to the chapter are intended to promote transparency and due process to list pharmaceuticals and medical devices for reimbursement. In this regard, one can argue that CPTPP is a standard-setter for future agreements to come.

3. Implication of CPTPP on the Future Regional Free Trade Agreement

The CPTPP is called a "21st century" FTA, for it has established advanced trading rules in many ways. The implication may be categorized into three kinds. Firstly, the CPTPP has developed novel practices that have substantial significance for the coming free trade agreement and the WTO reforms. Secondly, the CPTPP has immense benefit to its members regarding social, economic and political dynamism. Thirdly, the CPTPP's impact on main actors Asia Pacific region, such as China, is also beyond doubt. Hence, in this section, the author tries to address the significant implication of CPTPP in some selected members, the Asia Pacific region and the legal framework of international trade law as a whole.

3.1 Selected Country-Specific Implications

Each CPTPP signatory has existing bilateral and multilateral agreements

with some, but not all, of the other Parties. As the CPTPP opens new markets and, in some cases, imposes new rules on the domestic treatment of data, intellectual property, labour rights, and more, each Party has a unique set of economic and political circumstances to consider. The impact of CPTPP is highly dependent on the countries' profile in terms of development, existing membership to FTA and domestic policies.

3.1.1 Australia

Australia is already well connected among the CPTPP Parties, having bilateral FTAs with Chile, Japan, Malaysia, New Zealand, and Singapore, a multilateral deal with the Association of Southeast Asian Nations (ASEAN) including Brunei Darussalam and Vietnam, an agreement with Peru signed in February 2018 but not yet in force. However, further trade liberalization among existing FTA partners and the prospect of increased market access to Canada and Mexico are significant.

The Australian Department of Foreign Affairs and Trade (DFAT) has specifically highlighted potential benefits for (i) exporters of goods, including new reductions on Japanese beef tariffs, unique access for dairy products into Japan, Canada and Mexico, and elimination of all tariffs on industrial products; (ii) exporters of services, including the legal guarantee and enforceability of CPTPP Parties' reforms in the professional services sector, preferential temporary entry arrangements for Australian workers, and new opportunities for government procurement contracts in a range of sectors; and (iii) Australian investors, including the introduction of higher screening thresholds for investments in Mexico and Canada. The CPTPP will impact critical areas of trade and commerce across the Australian economy. The Australian government has stated that it "will help support Australian businesses to grow and see annual benefits of up to [AUD] $15.6 billion to [the] national economy by 2030." State parties are required to reduce barriers to trade and foreign investment. Significant changes include eliminating tariffs on AUD 12.7 billion of Australia's dutiable exports to countries party to the CPTPP. Private foreign investment is projected to increase as the Foreign Investment Review Board (FIRB) threshold for private foreign investment is lowered for signatories to the CPTPP.

Despite the anticipated benefits, particularly for exporters in Australia's critical agricultural sector, some economists have estimated the ultimate real national income boost will be just 0.5 per cent by 2030—the lowest of all Parties. In other words, because of Australia's established trade ties with most CPTPP members, Australia's benefit is the least compared with other members.

3.1.2 Canada

Compared to other CPTPP members, Canada's existing network of FTAs is relatively limited, focused on its hemisphere. Of the CPTPP members, Canada has only completed bilateral FTAs with Chile and Peru and is connected to Mexico via NAFTA. While Canada is negotiating deals with Japan and Singapore and is undergoing exploratory discussions with ASEAN, including Brunei Darussalam, Malaysia and Vietnam, most of the trade relationships established by CPTPP are new. Thus, the CPTPP represents a significant opportunity for Canada to diversify its trade links and build more robust export markets in Asia.① Much has been made of the "first-mover advantage" gained by the original class of six ratifying members, who have the first opportunity to establish markets under the CPTPP. For Canada, this advantage is incredibly potent, as it now enjoys newfound trade benefits in markets like Japan. To be more specific, Canada's food and agriculture industry, in particular, is poised to benefit, gaining preferential access where it currently faces high tariffs, such as in Japan, Vietnam and Malaysia. Overall, Government of canada expected benefits in the financial services, fish and seafood, forestry, and metals and minerals sectors. Overall, Canada's GDP gains are estimated to reach US $4.2 billion, higher than under the TPP, because it is no longer competing with the United States under the same agreement.

3.1.3 Japan

Following the United States' withdrawal from the TPP, Japan drove the process forward to salvage the deal. It would not have done so were the

---

① CPTPP Broader Implication, https://www.whitecase.com/careers, last visited on Mar. 31, 2019.

political and economic benefits not significant. Politically, Japan's role in realizing the CPTPP positions it as a regional leader, particularly vis-à-vis China. The CPTPP sets a floor for the anticipated US-Japan FTA negotiations and gives Japan leverage amid other ongoing negotiations. Economically, Japan is making a strategic compromise. While some key sectors will take a hit—agricultural, forestry and fisheries output is expected to lose US $1.3 billion—overall, the economy is estimated to receive a US $71 billion boost once the CPTPP is fully implemented.

3.1.4 Mexico

Mexico's interest in becoming part of the CPTPP process arose from a strategic view to strengthen trade and investment ties with the Asia Pacific region and raise the bar for its entire network of FTAs, including NAFTA. Moreover, in light of existing uncertainty surrounding the future of its trade relationships with Canada and the United States under the new and yet-to-be-approved USMCA, Mexico is seeking to rebalance its geopolitical interests towards the Asia Pacific region.

The CPTPP allows Mexico to have FTAs with six additional Asia Pacific nations, including Australia, Brunei Darussalam, Malaysia, New Zealand, Singapore and Vietnam. The openness of the CPTPP process to allow membership to new potential candidates could also allow Mexico to exploit new trade and investment relationships with other Asian countries and Latin American neighbours.

Given the enormous and innovative scope of the CPTPP as a "new generation FTA," Mexico will benefit not only from non-tariff barriers with its CPTPP partners but also from comprehensive treaty coverage and strict protections in several areas, such as digital trade, regulatory coherence, intellectual property rights (IPR), SOEs, services, labour and environment, transparency and corruption. Perhaps one of the most substantial advantages of the CPTPP for an emergent economy such as Mexico will be to gain access to technology-intensive manufacturing opportunities in telecommunications, digital trade and aerospace.

Upon the entry into force of the CPTPP, over 700 Mexican agricultural and industrial products will benefit from new market access opportunities

under the agreement, including Mexican auto parts, light vehicles, electrical equipment, medical devices, electronic goods, and a long list of fruits, vegetables and other perishable goods, such as meat, poultry, avocados, and orange juice.

3.2 CPTPP's Regional Economic and Geopolitical Implication

Proponents of TPP were explicit about emphasizing its role as an instrument of foreign policy. This "securitization" of the agreement can be seen in the United States, which has long used FTAs to reinforce its alliances. Indeed, it lies behind many of the earlier agreements in the Asia Pacific region. Speaking at the ASEAN Business and Investment Summit on 21 November 2015, President Obama declared, "TPP is more than just a trade pact; it also has significant strategic and geopolitical benefits." The president went on to say that TPP is a long-term investment in our shared security and universal human rights. He emphasized the agreement's role in building trust among members and deepening US ties to its allies in the region, concluding that the "TPP sends a powerful message across the Asia Pacific." The statement further said that America's foreign policy rebalance to the Asia Pacific will continue on every front. The United States will keep its commitments to allies and partners, and that we are here to stay and that you can count on us.① Even more, in his 2016 State of the Union address to Congress, President Obama urged support for TPP: "With TPP, China does not set the rules in that region—we do."

Therefore, it was vivid that TPP was framed within a strategy to build U.S.-Japan relations and counter China's influence in East Asia at both economic and strategic level. Provisions on transparency and competition policies about state-owned enterprises would also force changes in sensitive policies in other future regional agreements. Indeed, from the Chinese perspective, the TPP had been perceived as hostile to its interests. For

① Press Statement, 14 Statement, https://www.whitehouse.gov/the-press-office/2015/11/20/remarks-president-obama-asean-business-and-investment-summit, last visited on May. 18, 2020.

instance, an editorial in *China Daily* stated that "TPP has been heavily criticized for its spirit of confrontation and containment, as China, the world's second-largest economy and a traditional powerhouse in the eastern Pacific, is excluded from the Pacific trade pact."

Looking to the regional effect of CPTPP, without the participation of the US and with some provisions suspended, its impact is found to be minimal. However, the CPTPP has geopolitical implications involving Japan as a significant regional key player counterbalancing the growing competition in the Asia region. Nonetheless, the recently concluded Regional Comprehensive Economic Partnership (RCEP), where China, as a member, will counter balance the influence of CPTPP in the future. The RCEP is a trade agreement comprising 24 per cent of global GDP and 46 per cent of the worldwide population, making it the world's largest trade bloc. In comparison, the CPTPP without US participation makes up 13.5 per cent of global GDP and 14 per cent of the worldwide population. According to an economic forecast, full implementation of the CPTPP will enhance exports between member states by 6 per cent by 2030. ①

4. Future Prospect of the CPTPP

Firstly, CPTPP will positively influence the future multilateral agreement on trade. CPTPP is at the forefront of trade and investment integration in the Asia Pacific region. It is envisaged that in the longer term, membership of CPTPP would expand to include other economies. However, without the participation of China and the United States, the two biggest economies across the Pacific Ocean, it is a worthy question whether CPTPP will be as comprehensive and progressive as it declares. If one of the world biggest economy joins CPTPP, the agreement will act as a critical stepping stone towards the objective of free and open trade within the region and beyond, and

① China Briefing, What the CPTPP and RCEP Mean for China and Asia-Pacific Trade, https://www.china-briefing.com/news/cptpp-rcep-impact-china-asia-pacific-trade, last visited on Apr. 19,2019.

can serve as a critical player for a Free Trade Area of the Asia Pacific (FTA-AP). As such, CPTPP is likely to exercise considerable influence on economic integration in the Asia Pacific region well into the future.

Secondly, CPTPP can involve many economically powerful states in the future and thereby be a very powerful Free Trade Agreement (FTA). Countries including Colombia, Indonesia, the Philippines, South Korea, Thailand, and the United Kingdom, have indicated varying degrees of interest in joining the agreement. Colombia became the first country to give New Zealand, the CPTPP Depositary, formal notificationof its stake in joining the deal in June 2018.[①] Besides, the government of the United Kingdom has applied for membership in the CPTPP to stimulate exports after Brexit and has held informal discussions with several members.

Thirdly, the potential for the USA to come back to the negotiation table is not closed. On 25 January 2018, former US President Donald Trump, in an interview, announced his interest in possibly rejoining the TPP if it were a "substantially better deal" for the United States.[②] On 12 April 2018, he told the former White House National Economic Council Director Larry Kudlow and the former US Trade Representative Robert Lighthizer to join the new deal. Therefore, there is a probability that the US may reconsider its withdrawal and rejoin the CPTPP. All these indicate that CPTPP has a great potential to be a giant free trade agreement involving a substantial portion of the world economy and to become a standard-setter, even for multilateral trade negotiation and the upcoming WTO reforms.

5. Conclusion

CPTPP is nearly identical to the TPP except for a handful of provisions that the remaining member countries agreed to suspend. CPTPP contains

---

① The CPTPP Enters into Force: What Does it Mean for Global Trade? https://www.whitecase.com/careers, last visited on Mar. 31,2019.

② Pacific Trade Pact Takes off With Tariffs Cut in Six Nations, http://www.reuters.com, last visited on Dec, 30, 2020.

comprehensive, progressive and advanced rules representing many so-called 21st-century trade issues. These issues include digital commerce, liberalization of trade in services and investment, customs and marketing facilitation, technical barriers to trade, labour standards, environment, anti-corruption and more. Experts agree that some of the high standards preserved in the CPTPP reflect the direction of the future development of global trade as it suits modernized values and ideas.

CPTPP has diverse economic and political effects on members and beyond. CPTPP signatories are countries with very different import/export profiles and in various economic development stages. The agreement has multiple effects in terms of adjacent domestic rule, export promotion and overall development. Their support for the CPTPP shows an appreciation among significant economies of the need for systematic liberalization of services and investment if economic growth is sustained. The establishment of the CPTPP shows the determination and confidence of the Asia Pacific region's economies in supporting trade liberalization, economic integration and multilateral cooperation with equality and mutual benefit while not being too dependent or dominated by specific markets like the USA. CPTPP constantly affects the domestic and international economy of members and nonmembers in terms of geological grouping and trade negotiation strategy.

Protection of Foreign Investment under the Regional Comprehensive Economic Partnership

Juvelin Rezara*

Abstract: After almost a decade of negotiations, the ASEAN countries and its five partners ultimately agreed to sign the Regional Comprehensive Economic Partnership (RCEP) in November 2020. The agreement contains multidimensional economic cooperation, but the present research focuses only on protecting the foreign investment, which is a pillar for improving the investment environment among member countries. The study aims to examine the specificity of the RCEP legal mechanism for protecting foreign investment. As this agreement is regulated differently from the previous multilateral and regional agreements, the research relies on a qualitative approach comprising pragmatic analyses and comparative methods. Henceforth, the study concerns foreign investors' protection in the agreement by determining the interpretation of the agreement's aims on foreign investors' protection, comparing the agreement with the existing regeional trade agreements (RTA) in the Asia-Pacific region, and pointing out the implication of investment protection for the economic level of member countries. Although some country members did not entirely enforce the agreement, RCEP's prospective implication on investment protection in member countries will fertilize the quality and increase foreign investment among developed, developing, and least developed countries (LDCs) involved.

Keywords: Protection, Foreign Investment, Regional, Free Trade Agreement

Introduction

In the RCEP agreement, foreign investment is defined as an asset that

---

* Juvelin Rezara, a doctorate candidate, studies international economic law in the school of International at Southwest University of Political Science and Law (SWUPL).

foreign investors own or control directly or indirectly. It includes shares, stocks, and other forms of equity participation in juridical person, bonds, debentures, loans, intellectual property rights, and movable or immovable property. The investment agreement aims to create an enabling investment environment among member countries, which means that it notably establishes cooperation among fifteen (15) members to improve and promote the investment climate. The Chapter on Investment regularizes the provisions relating to investment protections, liberalization, promotion, and facilitation. These provisions are set to upgrade and enhance the existing ASEAN-plus-one FTAs on Investment. The agreement also highlights the regulations and commitment of parties to impose a most-favored-nation and national treatment concerning the purposes of Article 10.4 and commitments on the prohibition of performance requirements beyond their multilateral obligations under the WTO Trade-Related Investment Measures Agreement. A schedule of reservations and non-conforming measures, which provides for the parties' investment commitments using the negative list approach with standstill and ratchet mechanism, is also included in the investment part in the RCEP, with investment facilitation provisions that address investor aftercare such as assistance in resolution of complaints and grievances that may arise. The investment dispute settlement mechanism is also stressed in the chapter for maintaining good flows of investment within member countries. The State parties and their investors have a commitment and right to protecting probable losses and disputes.

In this regard, problems come to mind: firstly, to what extent is the foreign investment protection under the RCEP against unfair treatment and threats Secondly, is the RCEP investment protection realistic for establishing a reliable regional organization among the State parties? And thirdly, except for China, Japan, South Korea, what are the obstacles for the countries not to enforce the agreement fully? And what suggestions should be applied to those countries?

Consequently, the study considers the shortage of regional investment governance in protecting foreign investment within country partners, which is calculated to affect the harmonization of differing regional investment pro-

tection standards and public policy innovation. To explain more about the research objective, the first part of the research focuses on the standard of foreign investment protection, which comprises minimum standard of treatment, protection of investment for security, protection of foreign investment property rights, and the protection of foreign investment under the regulation on dispute settlement. The second part explores differences between the RCEP and other RTA investment protection. The third part of the study talks about challenges on enforcing the RCEP rules thoroughly within member countries and suggestions. And the last part of the study concerns the possible profit of country members in protecting foreign investment according to the commitment under the agreement.

Methods

This research is a doctrinal study based on analysis of data relating to RCEP on foreign investment protection, interpretation of rules, and comparatively commenting on the rules and the other RTA rules such as WTO rules on the protection of foreign investment and CPTP's. Pursuant to the aims and expected result of the research, the study qualitatively examines the investment protection in the RCEP overall and points out the significance of RCEP foreign investment protection rules. In extension, the first part of the research studies analysis on rules protecting foreign investment and foreign investors' rights, whereby the provisions of RCEP on the protection of investment are commented on and compared with the other parallel regional FTA. By all means, the research did not stick only to analysis, but extended to the comparative approach, a familiar and efficient trend of contemporary research academics, because the enforcement of the RCEP rules in every member country requires a multidimensional approach to identify the gaps that may pose obstacles flawless of the enforcement of investment rules in

the country which is economically fragile.① On the other hand, most of the members in the said agreement did not ratify it yet; therefore, the research seeks to show up the way for the countries that do not have relative capacities to ratify the deal directly. But it demands deep analysis on how to adjust domestic rules and extend the ability of those States in hosting foreign investment efficiently in terms of protection against act hindering rights, and against threats and damages in domestic investment.

Discussion

1. Standard of Foreign Investment Protection under the RCEP

In the field of the regional agreement, foreign investment protection is a crucial part that determines the commitment of member countries to protect the rights and assets of foreign investors. Expressly, under the view of international investment, foreign investment needs a well-founded mechanism that provides a standard of investment treatment comprising rights to fair and equitable treatment and security of the investment environment. The investment agreement chapter in the RCEP recognizes these principles in protecting foreign investment among member countries.

1.1 Minimum Standard of Treatment

In general, foreign investment protection focuses on the minimum standard of treatment, which comprises fair and equitable treatment.② This principle is superseded by the customary international law, which defines the standard of treatment that has to treat the alien; the therapy is based on multidimensional areas, the investment an area whereby this treatment shall apply for foreign investors and their investment in the host country. In the

① The LDCs members are the most worried because it is still volatile whether the investment agreement of RCEP may benefit them through business operating by foreign investors or may undermine the traditional investors.

② Peter K. Yu, The RCEP and Trans-Pacific Intellectual Property Norms. *Vanderbilt Journal of Transnational Law*, May 2017, Vol. 50, No. 3, pp.673-740.

breath of foreign investment policy, the said principle is used to set investment legal protection to attract foreign investors.

All the previous international or regional investment agreements set out the principle of minimum standard of treatment; therefore, the RCEP agreement adopts the principle as commitments of the member countries.① Under the RCEP, the focus is based on legal perceptions that every member country shall not be a subject of matter Covered Investments made by investors of the other party which constitute a violation of the minimum standard of foreign investment through denial of justice in any judicial or administrative proceedings; or fundamental breach of due process; or targeted discrimination on manifestly unjustified grounds, such as gender, race or religious belief; or manifestly abusive treatment, such as coercion, duress, and har assment.② The specificity of RCEP investment policy is that it accentuates the principle of customary international, inter alia, the minimum standard of treatment of the aliens for protecting the rights, and that it even avoids the threats to investors of state members. The concept of fair and equitable treatment does not require treatment beyond what is accorded under customary international law. Regarding this principle for protecting foreign investment, the state party shall allow all transfers relating to a covered investment to be made freely and without delay into and out of its territory, and may prevent or delay a transfer through the equitable, non-discriminatory, and good faith application of its laws and regulations relating to bankruptcy, insolvency or the protection of the rights of creditors including employees; issuing, trading or dealing in securities, futures, options; recovery of the proceeds of crime; financial reporting; ensuring compliance with awards; taxation; and social security, public retirement.

1.2 National Treatment and Most-Favored-Nation

The national treatment and Most-Favored-Nation (MFN) are the legal

① Desierto, Diane A., ASEAN Investment Treaties, RCEP, and CPTPP: Regional Strategies, Norms, Institutions, and Politics. *Washington International Law Journal*, April 2018, Vol. 27, No. 2, pp.349-406.

② See RCEP Chapter 10, Article 10.5

concepts applied for granting protection of foreign investors under the customary international law. Regarding the national treatment, State members shall accord to foreign investors and covered investments the treatment no less favorable than that in, the establishment of the investment, acquisition, expansion, management, conduct, operation, and sale or other disposition investments in its territory. In addition, State members shall adopt and maintain measures that prescribe special formalities in connection with foreign investments, including all requirements that the assets be legally constituted under its laws or regulations, provided that such formalities do not materially impair the protections afforded by that Party to investors of another Party and covered investments. And for the MFN, the member countries shall protect, to the extent possible, any confidential information provided from any disclosure that would prejudice the legitimate commercial interests or the competitive position of the investor or the covered investment. In short, this framework of investment agreement provides foreign investors with dynamic methods of enforcing treaty-based standards, and, more importantly, the treaties contain similar substantive standards of protection.

1.3 Protection against Expropriation, Compensation, and Security

No country member shall expropriate or nationalize a covered investment or through any measures equivalent to expropriation or nationlization. The agreement specifies two forms of prohibited expropriations: (1)a direct expropriation where a covered investment is nationalized or directly expropriated through formal transfer of title or outright seizure, and (2) an action or a series of late actions by a Party that has an effect equivalent to direct expropriation but without formal transfer of title or outright seizure. However, some grounds are accepted as an exception of expropriation when the expropriation or nationalization is for a public purpose, in a non-discriminatory way, on payment of compensation, and particularly in accord with the laws.

In analyzing most cases where the LDCs are most attacked by expropriation,[①] it generates doubt about the standard of LDCs in RCEP.

Set aside by the agreement also that to compensate the foreign investment is a commitment of state members considered in line with the international standards. It is a State's responsibility to assure rights of aliens against unproportioned expropriation.[②] The compensation shall be paid without delay, be equivalent to the fair market value of the expropriated investment at the time when the expropriation was publicly announced. Still, some countries have special treatment regarding this. The compensation shall be effectively realizable effectively and freely transferable. In addition, the compensation shall be prompt, adequate, and full.[③] However, in the case of delay, the compensation shall include an appropriate interest following the expropriating party's laws, regulations, and policies which are supposed to apply on a non-discriminatory basis. Compared to nother investment policies, RCEP draft investment has a separate annex to clarify the rules on expropriation (including tests for indirect expropriation).

In the event of losses, members shall accord to investors of another Party, and their covered investments, with regard to measures it adopts or maintains relating to losses suffered by investments in its territory owing to armed conflict, civil strife, or state of emergency, treatment no less favorable than that it accords. For security exceptions, a party may furnish access to any information the disclosure of which it determines to be contrary to its essential security interests.

1.4 Protection of Foreign Investment Property Rights

Intellectual property (IP) is an independent chapter but is confined as a part of foreign investment protection in the RCEP agreement; it aims to

---

① Akinsanaya Adeoye, International Protection of Direct Foreign Investment in the Third World, *International and Comparative Law Quarterly*, January 1987, Vol. 36, No. 1, pp.58-75.

② Borchard Edwin, Minimum Standard of the Treatment of Aliens, *Michigan Law Review*, February 1940, Vol. 38, No. 4, pp.445-461.

③ Brice M. Clagett, Protection of Foreign Investment under the Revised Restatement, *Virginia Journal of International Law*, Fall 1984, Vol. 25, No. 1, pp.73-98.

reduce IP-related barriers to trade and investment by promoting economic integration and cooperation in utilizing, protecting, and enforcing intellectual property rights (IPR). It intends to provide a balanced, inclusive approach to protecting and enforcing intellectual property rights in the region. Aside from featuring provisions relating to harmonizing the protections for the standard suite of intellectual property rights, it provides for the protection of intellectual property rights beyond the level of the WTO agreement on trade-related and technological protection measures and enforcement in the digital environment, as well as appropriate procedures and penalties against unauthorized copying of a cinematographic work on a commercial scale. Accordingly, supporting the intellectual property rights holders is also covered by the agreement to streamline and align procedures for establishing certain intellectual property rights, such as those relating to electronic filing of applications and making relevant information available online. It is required under the agreement to develop to every state regime the exhaustion of intellectual propriety rights and national treatment for according a treatment no less favorable. And it affirms the rights to fully use the flexibilities as duly recognized in the Doha declaration on the TRIPS Agreement and Public Health, including provisions related to genetic resources and traditional knowledge. The State members have an obligation to protect the intellectual propriety rights of foreign investors; however, every country may have different policise according to its legal system. In addition, all the States have to agree on the international conventions known as having competence for good-regulation of intellectual property rights: the Paris Convention for the Protection of Industrial Property done in Paris on March 20 1883, as revised at Stockholm on July 14, 1967, and amended on September 28, 1979; the Berne Convention for the Protection of Literary and Artistic Works done at Berne on September 9, 1886, as revised at Paris on July 24, 1971, and amended on September 28, 1979; the Patent Cooperation Treaty done at Washington on June 19, 1970, as amended on September 28, 1979, and modified on February 3, 1984 and October 3, 2001; the Protocol Relating to the Madrid Agreement Concerning the International Registration of Marks adopted at Madrid on June 27, 1989, as amended on October 3, 2006, and

November 12, 2007; the WIPO Copyright Treaty adopted in Geneva on December 20, 1996; the WIPO Performances and Phonograms Treaty adopted in Geneva on December 20, 1996; the Marrakesh Treaty to Facilitate Access to Published Works for Persons Who Are Blind, Visually Impaired, or Otherwise Print Disabled adopted in Marrakesh on June 27, 2013. The legal protection of IPR of foreign investment is indispensable for maintaining flows of foreign investment environment; the more the IPR of foreign investors is protected, the more they have the incentives to invest and expand their business.①

1.5 Dispute Settlement Mechanism

The development of treaty-based promotion standards and foreign investment protection through investor-state arbitration mechanisms allows enforcement of action against the host state.② The RCEP dispute settlement mechanism provides an effective, efficient and transparent process for consultations and dispute resolution. In detail, salient features of the RCEP dispute settlement process include:

(1) choice of forum: provisions allow the Complaining Party to select the forum within which to address a dispute that concerns substantially equivalent rights and obligations in the RCEP Agreement and another international trade or investment agreement to which the Parties to the dispute are party, to the exclusion of other possible fora;

(2) consultations: provisions require a Responding Party to first enter into consultations with a Complaining Party, if requested;

(3) good offices, conciliation, or mediation: provisions allow Parties that are party to the dispute to voluntarily undertake alternative methods to settle their disputes;

(4) establishment of a panel: provisions allow a Complaining Party to request the establishment of a panel to resolve a dispute in circumstances

① Menkes Jerzy, Protection of Foreign Investment Property under International Law, *Polish Quarterly of International Affairs*, 2000, Vol. 9, No. 4, pp.63-84.

② Karr Spenser, A Battle for Choice: Selecting Investor-State Arbitrators under the RCEP, *Temple Law Review*, Fall 2017, Vol. 90, No. 1, pp.127-128.

where the Responding Party does not reply to a request for consultations or does not enter into consultations within the stipulated time line, or where consultations have failed to resolve the dispute within the specified time line;

(5) and rights for interested third parties: provisions enable interested third parties to participate in disputes and their views to be taken into account during the panel process. This Chapter also includes detailed provisions on the functions of panels, panel procedures, implementation of the panel's final report, compliance review proceedings, compensation, and suspension of concessions or other obligations. Another necessary provision in this Chapter is an article on Special and Differential Treatment involving the Least Developed Country Parties whereby the Complaining Party is obligated to exercise due restraint in raising matters under this Chapter where a Least Developed Country Party is involved. Furthermore, although RCEP encompasses WTO agreements mostly in dispute settlement mechanisms and many multilateral agreements, it does not contain an ICSID dispute settlement mechanism.

2. Difference between RCEP and Other RTA in Protecting Foreign Investment

Recently, RTA has become a prevailing practice of the third world to establish FTA which includes investment agreement. In Asia-Pacific region, RCEP and CPTPP are the most significant multilateral investment agreements, and some members of the RCEP are a signatory of the CPTPP.①

2.1 Protection of Foreign Investment under RCEP and CPTPP

As said above, the RCEP aims to create a liberal, facilitative and competitive investment environment in the Asia-Pacific region. The negotiations for investment under the RCEP cover four pillars: the promotion, protection, facilitation, and liberalization of investment. The provision of RCEP on investment agreement is not entirely different from the substantive and procedural frameworks under the CPTPP. The CPTPP provides clear rules that

① These countries are Singapore, Japan, Malaysia, Australia, New Zealand, Vietnam and Brunei.

require fair and non-discriminatory treatment of the inward investment of each other's investors while at the same time preserving the ability of the parties to achieve legitimate public policy objectives.[①] Remarkably, the CPTPP defines investment as every asset that an investor owns or controls, directly or indirectly, through a commitment of capital or an expectation to gain or profit. In particular, the agreement requires a contracting country to treat investors from other contracting countries fairly and equitably regarding the establishment, acquisition, expansion, management, operation, or sale of the investments. In the event that the investment properties are subject to expropriation or nationalization, the CPTPP requires the authority to compensate an amount equivalent to the fair market value immediately before the expropriation takes place. Moreover, compensation must be prompt and adequate to cover the loss incurred.

The CPTPP provides the essential elements of investment protections found in other trade agreements as well as BITs which consist of protecting investment among member countries against discrimination, including national treatment and most-favored-nation standards(MFN); prohibiting expropriation except for cases determined for public goods in the host State such as for public purpose, with due process, in a no-discriminatory manner and with payment of compensation; protecting investment against denial of justice; requirement of fair and equitable treatment; and prohibiting trade-distorting measures like local content requirements; provision on repatriation of capital and appointment of senior managers without regard to nationality. The particularity of the said agreement is investors can force these obligations through ICSID. Generally, the text of the RCEP investment chapter is not significantly different from the CPTPP, given that these standard provisions

① Government of Canada, How to Read the Comprehensive and Progressive Agreement for Trans-Pacific Partnership (CPTPP), 2019, http://www.international.gc.ca/trade-commerce/trade-agreements-accordscommerciaux/agr-acc/cptpp-ptpgp/chapter summaries-sommaireschapitres.aspx? lang=eng, last visited on Now. 15, 2019.

underlie most investment treaty provisions.[①]

In terms of dispute settlement mechanism, the RCEP procedure is quite different from CPTPP and other RTA. Its provisions on investment set out procedures for the peaceful understanding between disputing parties inter alia conciliation and negotiation that relies on the investors' home state to bring the claim on behalf of the investors. Concerning all inter-state disputes in the RCEP, DSM is provided for in Chapter 19 of the agreement to protect investor rights. If a party to the RCEP breaches any of its obligations under the RCEP, the investor shall request its home state to escalate its claims. The investor's home state shall bring a claim against the host state under the RCEP.[②] This procedure requires prior negotiation and consultation; these shall be taken before stepping to arbitration. The procedure is squarely more resilient compared to the CPTPP one. However, it does not recognize the ICSID provisions significantly. The inclusion of an ISDS mechanism became controversial during negotiations of the RCEP, and this was, therefore, carved out to avoid further delays in its conclusion.[③] Accordingly, the remedies attainable are limited to a finding by a panel in the form of a report that the host state has failed in its obligations under the RCEP[④] if such a report is issued then: where a measure at issue is not in conformity with the host state's obligations under the RCEP, the host state must bring the non-conforming measure into conformity; or, where the host state has failed to carry out its obligations under the RCEP, the host state must carry out those measures. Where the host state fails to comply with this order, the home state may then bring a compliance review, which will lead to either

---

① Collins C. Ajibo, et al., RCEP, CPTPP and the Changing Dynamics in International Trade Standard-Setting, *Manchester Journal of International Economic Law*, December 2019, Vol. 16, No. 3, pp.425-440.

② RCEP, Article 19.3(1)

③ Lars Markert and Anne-Marie Doernenburg, "Regional Comprehensive Economic Partnership (RCEP)—What You Need to Know: Investment Protection Perspective (Part II)", https://www. lexology. com/library/detail. aspx? g = b934a88d-3344-46aa-8736-961b74643877, last visited on Jan. 27, 2021.

④ RCEP Article 19.15.

payment of compensation by the host state to the home state, or, if the disputing parties do not agree with compensation, the home state may suspend concessions given to the host state under the RCEP.

In contrast, Chapter 9 of the CPTPP deals specifically with dispute resolution between foreign investors and contracting states; it provides modernized procedures that allow investors to access directly to arbitration without considering prior recourse to domestic proceedings or peaceful remedies.① In the agreement, the host state grants consent to arbitration via the CPTPP itself, with an open invitation to investors to initiate arbitration. There is no need for prior recourse to domestic remedies before the initiation of arbitral proceedings. The claimant under the CPPT has options to access ICSID rules of procedures for arbitration proceedings if both disputing parties are parties to the convention; may also choose UNICTRAL rules for claiming their rights or any other laws agreed by the disputing parties. ② Arbitration tribunals constituted via the ICSID mechanism in the CPTPP may only award separately or in combination the monetary damages and interest thereon; and restitution of property with the provisions that provide that the State may pay monetary damages and any applicable interest instead of restitution. There is no punitive damages under the agreement.③

Regarding foreign investment protection under the RCEP and CPTPP, both mega-agreements are pretty similar in protecting the investors through customary international law based on the principle of minimum standard of treatment, national treatment, and most-favored-nation cited above. But considering all the provisions relating to investment protection, the CPTPP

---

① Tony Dymond, Cameron Sim and Bejamin Teo, Debevoise and Plimpton LLP "Investment Treaty Arbitration in the Asia-Pacific: The Impact of the CPTPP and the RCEP", https://globalarbitrationreview.com/review/the-asia-pacific-arbitration-review/2022/article/investment-treaty-arbitration-in-the-asia-pacific-the-impact-of-the-cptpp-and-the-rcep, last visited on Fer 27, 2021.

② TPP, as incorporated in the CPTPP (TPP/CPTPP), Article 9.19.4.

③ CPTPP, Article 9.29(6).

is more liberalised than the RCEP.[①] The CPPT does not force the settlement of disputes through domestic proceedings or negotiations; it gives a comprehensive range of options for investors to join international arbitration like ICSID, UNICTRAL, and other regional arbitration where parties are members. The RCEP, as is known, does not rely on the ICSID disputes settlement mechanism nor UNICTRAL; the resolution is encouraged through negotiation or consultation between disputing parties under the domestic proceedings.

2.2 Protection of Foreign Investment under RCEP and WTO

Accordingly, some chapters of the RCEP agreement recognize provisions under WTO to be applied in issues about trade climate among members. As stipulated in Chapter 2 of the said agreement, national treatment of internal taxation and regulations is applied to foreign investment within country members. All RCEP countries are members of the WTO agreement, which means they have obligations to maintain all treatment conformable to the standard of protection of foreign investment and investors. Regarding the interests involved, in general, both the industrial and the newly industrialized countries are essentially interested in a multilateral investment agreement to provide with greater transparency, predictability, stability and better economic efficiency for investments. This interest is supported by confederations of industries with far-reaching expectations, with their primary interest in efficiently protecting assets. Under the WTO, foreign investment protection is based on transparency, non-discrimination, free transfer, and settlement of disputes.

The term "transparency" is construed as publishing acts and relevant information in the host country and procedural or administrative transparency. The analysis in the World Bank Report in 2003 evokes the substantial leverage of protecting and promoting foreign investment by predictability and stability, and transparency on the distribution of the international flows of investment. However, the developing countries had reservations about such

① Kawharu, Amokura, The Admission of Foreign Investment under the TPP and RCEP, *Journal of World Investment & Trade*, 2015, Vol. 16, No. 5-6, pp.1058-1088.

procedural transparency as they feared that such a broader understanding of transparency could restrict their ability to pursue an independent national policy.

Concerning non-discrimination, based on a GATS-type positive list approach, the wording of the Doha Mandate already indicates the line of thought. According to such a bottom-up approach for protection against discrimination, each WTO member could negotiate the particular sectors it will open for foreign investors even in the pre-establishment phase. Even OECD countries might have requests for exemptions. It is not the more desirable top-down approach. However, it would mean a second increase in value than the European Bilateral Investment Treaties, which do not offer such a commitment in the pre-establishment phase. But again, here, the developing countries were skeptical.

Concerning Exceptions and balance-of-payments safeguards, the principle of free transfer should be guaranteed. Exemptions may amend it through well-defined as balance-of-payments safeguards Clauses. They might follow the relevant regulations in international treaties.

In comparison to the RCEP provisions on investment, the WTO trade-related investment looks similarly narrower; the protection of foreign investment is not specific, and the DSM does not provide options for foreign investors to settle the dispute in the ICSID or UNICTRAL, yet requires the member to resolve the dispute through court (panel and appellate body), arbitration, consultation, negotiation or conciliation.

3. Suggestion for Facing Challenges on Enforcement of the RCEP in Terms of Investment Protection

RCEP is a new agreement; most signatory countries struggle to ratify and enforce the provisions thoroughly. The enforcement is the root of international or regional agreements; member countries have to ensure the enforcement of the provisions in the agreement. The previous regional agreements have shown decay of the agreement due to weak enforcement, such as the case of CPTPP, which generates the withdrawal of the USA.[①] In this regard, RCEP members have to consider the strategies carefully for enforcing the agreement to avoid disaccord between member countries later. Therefore, to deal equitably with enforcement, every country must adjust domestic rules and policy to be compatible with investment protection under the agreement and fulfill commitment under the agreement on protection of foreign investment.

3.1 Adjusting National Policy for Foreign Investment Pursuant to the RCEP

In the Asia-Pacific region, foreign investment has been hugely significant for economic development. In the latter half of the twentieth century, in a bid to attract foreign investment, countries in Asia modernised their laws and policies governing foreign investment, which were intended to encourage cross-border investment by extending various protections to foreign investments, such as promises of non-discrimination and fair and equitable treatment, as well as by granting foreign investors the right to bring their claims directly against host states through ICSID mechanisms.[②]

Expressly, most countries in Asia-Pacific will likely face pressure in the RCEP investment agreements because the provisions may leverage domestic investment development. The riskiest countries have investment commitments in other agreements, like the CPTPP and even related investments under the WTO.[③] Arguably these agreements surpass the capacity of the fragile developing countries and LDCs involved. The lack of public engagement with potential FTA commitments generates negative investment impacts because the negotiations are held behind closed doors. In terms of possible regulatory constraints under the RCEP and CPTPP, the core issue for developing and LDCs concerns the extent to which it will lose the ability to determine the

---

① Jeffrey J. Schott, "US Trade Policy Options in the Pacific Basin: Bigger Is Better", Peterson Institute for International Economics, 2017, https://piie.com/system/files/documents/schott20170216ppt.pdf, last visited on Oct. 30.

② Kenneth J. Vandevelde, A Brief History of International Investment Agreements, *UC Davis Journal of International Law & Policy*, 2005, Vol. 157, No. 12, p. 171.

③ Kawharu, Amokura, The Admission of Foreign Investment under the TPP and RCEP, *Journal of World Investment & Trade*, 2015, Vol. 16, No. 5-6, pp.1058-1088.

conditions for screening the entry of foreign investment.

So far, the attractiveness of foreign investment has become a pillar of economic growth; most countries over the world want to attract capital, technology, expertise, goods, and services that are needed and guard against the possible disadvantages of foreign investment such as competitive threats to the domestic industry. National policies regarding the admission of foreign investment may reflect these concerns by encouraging quality investments with measures such as tax incentives while restricting or screening investment in sensitive sectors. Most of the RTAs and even the RCEP do not deal with admission, while they encourage the state parties to admit investment into their territories subject to their national laws. The right of national treatment applies only once an investment has been made and preserving the host state's regulatory autonomy to pursue national policy goals regarding the conditions of entry for foreign investment. The position approximates the developmental state perspective, which sees a role for the State to support national comparative advantages through measures such as restrictions on foreign ownership. The investor may establish investments in the circumstances where domestic investment is allowed. Many countries are now reassessing the balance that should be reflected in their treaties between the interests of host states and foreign investors; most of their attention has been focused on the regulatory issues associated with the protections, such as fair and equitable treatment. Commonly, the combination of deficiencies in the negotiating process and the impact of the agreed rules on regulatory discretion puts the legitimacy of the regulations into serious question, especially when vital national policies are at stake.

A better policy from a rule of law perspective may be for a host state to create an excellent investment environment for those investments provisions under the RCEP while excluding those investments that it does not wish to treat fully in accordance with other principles. Considering national treatment rights in discussions on the regulatory implications of investor protections is that they constrain regulatory freedom. All countries should maintain a screening regime for foreign investment, and, in this respect, it shares an interest with many other TPP and RCEP countries that also screen foreign investment. It needs strong political support for closer regional economic ties.

4. The possible Impact of the RCEP in Member Countries in Protecting Foreign Investment

Despite the challenges that member countries may face when enforcing the agreement, pursuant to RCEP investment rules stated above, the RCEP as a mega-investment may provide many advantages on investment protection within countries involved. The sectors that would benefit from the agreement are developing a legal framework for protecting foreign investment, especially the promotion of SMEs in the international market. The developing countries and LDCs would gain experience from the developed countries.

4.1 Development of Legal Framework on the Protection of Foreign Investment among Member Countries

The pillar of investment development in developed countries is establishing strong protection of investor rights against different forms of discrepancy in the operation.[①] To provide guarantee for foreign investment increase more the effectivity mechanism for attracting investors in the country, by all means, that establishment of reliable legal policies for favor investors without discrimination determined as prolific method helped much the economy of the developed country flourished since ever.[②] Every member of the RCEP would benefit from the investment. The RCEP agreement stipulates all provisions according to the specific economic levels of all countries, such as developed, developing, and least developed countries. Commitment are not in total similar to well-balanced interest and more sustainable. Partly, it is often a problem to define the interest of countries with different econom levels, especially that LDCs with no advanced technologies, enterprises, and

---

① Fred L. Morrison, The Protection of Foreign Investment in the United States of America, *American Journal of Comparative Law*, 2010, Vol. 58, pp.437-454.

② Matsui, Yoshiro, Japan's International Legal Policy for the Protection of Foreign Investment, *Japanese Annual of International Law*, 1989, Vol. 32, pp.1-17

weak domestic economic strategies to fulfill their benefit. Investment protection may facilitate reform in developing countries and promote investment in each country party.[①] In referring to a holistic approach, the objective of the enhancement of protection of foreign investment is to encourage investment climate within the members to assess the global goods. Each country member shall promote its domestic investment by encouraging investment among the parties, organizing joint investment promotion activities, organizing and supporting various briefings and seminars on investment opportunities, and conducting information exchanges. Under the agreement, the parties can freely promote their investment to attract foreign investment among party countries.

Further, improving the flows of investment into members is the main point of the Chapter because the investment has recently been deemed very important on how to develop the State's economy rapidly. On the other hand side, each party of the agreement has to facilitate the investment climate. It is every party's commitment to facilitate the investment by improving laws and regulations to conform to the intent of the RCEP agreement, creating the necessary environment for all forms of investment, simplifying its procedures for investment, and establishing investment centers. In addition, the treatment of foreign investment is determined according to the circumstances of every country. Like Art 10.61. (h): "to adopt a given rate or amount of royalty under a license contract with any license contract in existence at the time the requirement is imposed or enforced, or an investor and a person in its territory, provided that the requirement is imposed or enforced in a manner that constitutes direct interference with that license contract by an exercise of non-judicial government authority of a party". This provision shall not apply to Cambodia, Lao PDR and Myanmar. Meanwhile, the enforcement of RCEP depends on every country's circumstances; some of the countries in RCEP have a reserve right on some provisions that are not compatible with the country's economic development.

---

① See Chapter 10 Article 10.16 of RCEP agreement, which determines all Commitment of State on how to activate the flow of investment.

4.2 The Growth of SMEs under the Protection of RCEP

The SMEs under RCEP are protected as they contribute significantly to economic growth, employment, and innovation. Therefore, the member states of RCEP seek to promote information sharing and cooperation in increasing the ability of small and medium enterprises to utilize and benefit from the opportunities, particularly the developing countries whose economic development depends on SMEs. The agreement offers freedom to enterprises by its size and reforms the protectionist domestic legal system among country members—most developed countries ahead against nationalism and protectionism of investment.① Some developing countries in RCEP face their challenges of protectionism; for example, in the case of Indonesia, after the enactment of omnibus law where foreign investment policy almost tends to protect only the interest of domestic SMEs, the corporate enterprises are restricted in many areas.② Chapter 14 of the agreement sets out regulations on SMEs, which is integrally construed as a mechanism of protecting the interest of SME's investment along with its operation. The partnership among MNEs and SMEs is encouraged. All the countries shall strengthen their cooperation by the implementation of efficient rules and regulations on investment, improving cooperation to enhance SME's access to markets and participation in global value chains, promoting and facilitating partnerships among businesses, encouraging the use of innovation and advanced technology as well as promoting awareness, understanding, and effective use of the intellectual property system among small and medium enterprises. RCEP promotes good regulatory practices, builds capacity to formulate regulations, policies, and programs that contribute to small and medium enterprise development, and share the best practices to enhance capability and competitiveness. The agreement may promote fair competition among do-

---

① Richard B. Lillich, The Foreign Claims Settlement Commission and the Protection of Foreign Investment, *Iowa Law Review*, Summer 1963, Vol. 48, No. 4, pp.779-793.

② Law number 20 the year 2008 concerning Small, Micro, and Medium-scale Enterprises. http://eng. kppu. go. id/wp-content/uploads/LAW-OF-THE-REPUBLIC-OF-INDONESIA-20-OF-2008.pdf, last visited on Fer. 28, 2021.

mestic and foreign SMEs or between SMEs and corporate enterprises among country parties.[①] In addition, some economists affirmed that RCEP is supposed to relatively benefit every country member since its investment policy provides the opportunity for LDCs and developing countries to access the market of developed country members.

Conclusion

The RCEP agreement has set out a larga number of regulations in the protection of foreign investment for member countries. The minimum standard of treatment is considered a prominent provision of the agreement that determines thorough foreign investment protection among State members, encompassing fair, equitable, and non-discriminatory treatment. The RCEP treatment of foreign investment is also referred to as national treatment and most-favored-nation treatment, which requires country members to treat investment favorably. In addition, the dispute settlement mechanism under the RCEP will protect the foreign investment on the reclamation of their rights. The agreement is considered to improve investment protection in every country involved; however, some challenges slow ratification and enforcement of the deal in signatory countries. And there is as well a possible challenge that is prominent for the country members to conduct stricter enforcement of the policies according to every country's economic level: the treatment of country members may be incompatible with the flexibility of the agreement. Every country member shall be treated according to its economic level so that they can benefit. There is even more disparity between the substantive investment protection standards in the RCEP investment chapter and the more concise and restrained language is needed. Still, in comparison to other agreements paralleled with RCEP in ASEAN countries, the investment chapter of the RCEP draft provides determinative tests

① Siquiros, Jose Luis, Bilateral Treaties on the Reciprocal Protection of Foreign Investment, *California Western International Law Journal*, Spring, 1994, Vol. 24, No. 2, pp.255-276.

intended to guide the task of interpreting treaty standards. Further, the impact of this current COVID-19 is amongst the most significant challenges that RCEP faces; this pandemic has paralyzed pre-existing economic growth in every country in RCEP, especially the LDCs, which bear enormous losses. So the country members have to adopt convergent strategies to fully apply the agreement in business climate among members.

Indonesia's Legal Response to the Regional Comprehensive Economic Partnership Enforcement

Marcellino Gonzales*

Abstract: The Regional Comprehensive Economic Partnership (RCEP) was born amid the current uncertain world economy. The RCEP is considered to be the most significant trade agreement in the world outside of the World Trade Organization (WTO) when viewed from world coverage of the total Gross Domestic Product (GDP), foreign direct investment (FDI), population, and trade. However, this Agreement also raises new challenges, especially for each country that has joined the RCEP Agreement, in preparing legal provisions for welcoming this RCEP. The recklessness in preparing legal foundations in trade and investment sectors can raise new problems for RCEP members. This paper will only specifically discuss whether there are any impacts on the RCEP implementation. And specifically, how does Indonesia's legal instrument readiness protect their national interests facing the challenges from RCEP? The method was descriptive analysis, which is a research method used to gain an overview of the situation and circumstances by presenting the data obtained as they are and also seeing the real situation. Then, various analyses are carried out to compile some conclusions. While, studies conduct through normative juridical approach; it is a research method to gain an overview of the situation and circumstances of the RCEP, by way of exposure data obtained as it is, then through the various analyses compiled some conclusions.

From the discussion, it can be concluded that firstly, RCEP brings a positive impact in developing supply chains that have been disrupted due to the COVID-19 pandemic and the China-US decoupling. Secondly, RCEP is significant momentum in making a giant leap towards legal transformation in the economic sector, particularly for Indonesia; thus far, in facing this RCEP challenge, Indonesia already has a new legal instrument which was recently enacted on October 5th 2020. This law is known as the Job Creation Law or the In-

* Ph. D candidate of SWUPL, judge of Indonesia District Court.

donesia Omnibus Law. It has provided a significant shove for changes to the formation of laws in the Indonesian economic sector.

Keywords: RCEP, Indonesia Job Creation Law, Indonesia Omnibus Law

1. Introduction

According to international trade theory, free trade agreements (FTAs) are accepted because the benefits that the countries involved in this trade obtain derive from a comparative advantage.① A nation will specialize in producing a product if it has a comparative advantage. With this kind of specialization, the world can generally develop total world output with the same amount of resources. At the same time, economic efficiency will continue to increase. Theoretically, an FTA can guarantee that the countries involved in this Agreement will benefit from the formation of trade creation and trade diversion.

The latest trend of FTAs shows that many countries globally have been involved in various trade agreements and investment agreements, both bilateral and regional agreements. They realized that trade and encouraging foreign capital were ways to develop their national economy and fulfill their needs.

However, turmoil that has occurred in the world recently, such as the tension between the two largest economic giants in the world, America and China, which affects the world economic map and is related with the weakness of WTO in solving problems between the two major countries, and most recently the impact on the world economy caused by the COVID-19 pandemic, which caused the economic conditions of the countries in the world to be even more stricken and affected to a lower level, and this made them think of various ways to get out of their economic downturn.

---

① Amalia Adininggar Widyasanti, *Perdagangan Bebas Regional Dan Daya Saing Ekspor: Kasus Indonesia* (*Regional Free Trade and Export Competitiveness: The Case of Indonesia*), Buletin Ekonomi Moneter dan Perbankan, 2010, p.6.

Strategic steps that can be taken are to increase trade cooperation between countries and encourage foreign capital to enter to increase export potential and import substitution, so as to increase foreign capital earnings and be able to save it, with the hope that cooperation can rise from the impact of the global economic downturn caused by various current issues, in particular the COVID-19 pandemic. Increasing the economic income of countries by finding a way or solution to simplify the trade process from upstream to downstream and attract foreign investment is the main reason why such cooperation is needed. The hope is to help accelerate the economic growth of the affected countries so that they altogether will soon recover.

In the midst of the current uncertain world economy, the Regional Comprehensive Economic Partnership (RCEP) was born, which is a comprehensive Asian economic partnership that was initiated by Indonesia when it assumed the leadership of ASEAN in 2011. This cooperation aims to consolidate five FTAs which ASEAN already has with its six trading partners. The negotiations were declared on November 11th, 2020 with the agreement of 15 countries, consisting of 10 ASEAN countries and 5 ASEAN partners, namely, China, Japan, South Korea, Australia and New Zealand, and the agreement was signed by the 15 countries on November 15th, 2020.

The RCEP is considered to be the largest trade agreement in the world outside of the WTO when viewed from world coverage of the total Gross Domestic Product (GDP) (30.2 percent), foreign direct investment (FDI) (29.8 percent), population (29.6 percent), and trade (27.4 percent), which is slightly below the EU-27 whose world coverage of trade was recorded at 29.8 percent. [①] The Peterson Institute for International Economics have forecasted that RCEP will add almost US$ 200 billion to the global economy and an average of 0.2 percent per year to the GDP of its members, therefore creating employment and improving the standards of living of the people in member

① CNN Indonesia, Mengenal RCEP dan Untungnya Buat Indonesia (Get to know RCEP and the Benefit for Indonesia), https://www.cnnindonesia.com/ekonomi/20201116073151-92-570136/mengenal-rcep-dan-untungnya-buat-indonesia, last visited on Dec. 14, 2020.

countries.[①]

The Indonesian Minister of Trade, *Agus Suparmanto*, revealed various reasons why Indonesia needs a RCEP trade agreement in a virtual press conference. The reasons are:

1. Indonesia needs RCEP to deal with uncertain international trade dynamics; this is closely related to the weakening of trust in the WTO and the multilateral system, which has shifted many countries to regional, especially bilateral agreements.

2. Indonesia anticipates the impact of the trade war between the United States and China. According to him, countries that have direct trade relations with the US and China are beginning to shift dependence on the two countries to competition in other regions. This also cannot be separated from the anticipation of the US protection policy on its trade balance. In fact, this is a new trend that other countries are emulating and will have an impact on the advancement of international trade.

3. RCEP is a measure to mitigate the impact of the COVID-19 pandemic, which suppressed world trade previously less conducive, and the world economy needs a recovery stage that cannot be done alone and quickly.

Indeed, these 15 countries have their plan of interests, like China, whose participation in the RCEP is an extraordinary step. RCEP holds great significance for China. Once implemented it will become the largest trade bloc in Asia and is expected to amount to US$12.4 trillion in trade, and this opportunity will be open also for China to involve and increase businesses expansion.[②] Actually, China already has bilateral trade deals with many RCEP members and still hopes for a trilateral pact with Japan and South Korea. The conclusion of the RCEP agreement is expected to strengthen economic relations between all three countries and ASEAN nations, and could lead to

① Ministry of Finance and Economy, Brunei Darussalam, "The RCEP Agreement", http://www.asean 2021.bn/Theme/news/news-21.02.21.aspx, last visited on Mar. 15, 2021.

② Dorcas Wong, RCEP FTA Signed: What Can Foreign Investors in China Expect?, China Briefing, https://www.china-briefing.com/news/rcep-fta-signed-what-can-foreign-investors-in-china-expect/, last visited on Dec. 15, 2020.

further bilateral arrangements among all members, particularly China.[①] Likewise, by joining RCEP, Australia hopes they can get their main benefits, which are:[②]

- a new single set of rules and procedures for accessing preferential tariffs in any of the 15 RCEP markets
- a new scope for trade in services throughout the region, including telecommunications, professional and financial services
- improved mechanisms for tackling non-tariff barriers, including in areas such as customs procedures, quarantine and technical standards
- greater investment certainty for businesses
- rules on e-commerce to make it easier for businesses to trade online
- a common set of rules on intellectual property
- agreed rules of origin that will increase the competitiveness of Australian inputs into regional production chains

However, this Agreement also raises new challenges for each country that has joined the RCEP Agreement in preparing legal provisions for welcoming this RCEP. The recklessness in preparing legal foundations in trade and investment sectors can raise new problems for RCEP members. Many doubts arise from various circles regarding the influx of imported goods that will be eroding domestic products. That is what India worried about, so it resigned from this RCEP. In addition, there are concerns that RCEP will only benefit certain parties and hinder the economic growth of countries that are not prepared yet.

These facts are interesting to discuss deeper. Reflecting on these, next, the author will try to analyze and describe more about the readiness of one of the RCEP members, Indonesia. The form of enthusiasm here is specifically

---

① Johnston, Eric, What Does RCEP Mean for Japan and Its Asian Neighbors? https://www.japantimes.co.jp/news/2020/11/15/national/politics-diplomacy/rcep-japan-asia-trade/, last visited on Dec. 15, 2020.

② Prime Minister of Australia, Regional Trade Deal to Boost Export Opportunities for Aussie Farmers and Businesses, https://www.pm.gov.au/media/regional-trade-deal-boost-export-opportunities-aussie-farmers-and-businesses, last visited on Dec. 15, 2020.

regarding legal instruments which are considered to be a formal way of securing all worrying forms. Based on that, the scope of discussion in this paper will only specifically discuss:

1. Are there any impacts on the RCEP implementation?

2. How does Indonesia's legal instrument readiness protect their national interests facing the challenges from RCEP?

2. Methodology

A method is a tool to help and answer to find the truth symbolically, methodologically, and consistently, then held the analysis and construction of the data collected and processed following the purpose of research. The method was descriptive analysis, which is a research method used to gain an overview of the situation and circumstances, by presenting the data obtained as they are and also seeing the real situation. Then, various analyses are carried out to compile some conclusions; while, studies conduct through normative juridical approach. It is a research method to gain an overview of the situation and circumstances of the RCEP, by way of exposure data obtained as it is, then through the various analyses compiled some conclusions. Meanwhile, the study was conducted with normative juridical approach, literature and scientific papers related to the object of research and sociological juridical approach. In other words, the study was also conducted based the condition as well as the facts related with the regulations especially the regulations related to the trading and investment area in Indonesia.

In analyzing RCEP and the transformation of Indonesian law in the economic sector, the use of internal legal logic research is very important, specifically directing the focus of this research primarily to compiling a description, the criteria for evaluating a correct argument about the law, in this case, the laws and regulations on the administration of the investment system. In this connection analysis, deductive logic should be used. Deductive reasoning is used to conclude general matters into individual cases. This analyzing method should be used because the understanding about RCEP itself is quite new and there has not been much scientific law discussion regarding

itself and its relation to the steps of transforming economic law in Indonesia through the new conception of Indonesian Job Creation Law.

3. The RCEP and the Implication for Indonesia

3.1 The Idea of RCEP

The Regional Comprehensive Economic Partnership (RCEP) is a significant trade pact proposed by ASEAN to increase trade between its member countries plus free trade agreement (FTA) partners. It is said to be the most significant trade cooperation in the world because it involves 15 countries (10 ASEAN member countries plus Australia, New Zealand, South Korea, Japan, and China), which cover 30% of the world economy, 30% of the world's population, and no less than 2.2 billion potential customers. Top officials from the 15 nations inked the RCEP, after nearly a decade of making, on the final day of the 37th ASEAN Summit hosted virtually by Vietnam in 2020. The completion of negotiations is a strong message affirming China, Eastern Asia, and ASEAN's role in supporting the multilateral trade system. In addition, the Agreement will contribute to developing supply chains that have been disrupted due to the Covid-19 pandemic and the China-US decoupling and support the regional and world economic recovery.

Clearly, the purpose of RCEP itself is to establish a modern, comprehensive, high-quality, and mutually beneficial economic partnership that will facilitate the expansion of regional trade and investment, and contribute to global economic growth and development. Accordingly, it will bring about the market and employment opportunities to businesses and people in the region. The RCEP Agreement will work alongside and support an open, inclusive, and rules-based multilateral trading system. The four key features of the RCEP agreement are elaborated as follows: ①

(1) **Modern.** The RCEP Agreement is an agreement not made just for

① Summary of the RCEP Agreement, https://asean.org/storage/2020/11/Summary-of-the-RCEP-Agreement.pdf, last visited on Dec. 13, 2020.

today but is also an agreement for tomorrow. It updates the coverage of the existing ASEAN Plus One FTAs (ASEAN's FTAs with the five dialogue partners) and takes into consideration changing and emerging trade realities, including the age of electronic commerce, the potential of micro, small and medium enterprises, the deepening regional value chain, and the complexity of market competition. The RCEP Agreement will complement the World Trade Organization (WTO), building on the WTO Agreement in areas where the Parties have agreed to update or going beyond its provisions.

(2)**Comprehensive.** The RCEP Agreement is comprehensive, in terms of both coverage and depth of commitments. On its coverage, the RCEP Agreement comprises 20 Chapters and includes many areas that were not previously covered in the ASEAN Plus One FTAs. The RCEP Agreement has specific provisions covering trade in goods, including rules of origin; customs procedures and trade facilitation; sanitary and phytosanitary measures; standards, technical regulations and conformity assessment procedures; and trade remedies. It also covers trade in services including specific provisions on financial services, telecommunication services, professional services, as well as the temporary movement of natural persons. In addition, there are chapters on investment, intellectual property, electronic commerce, competition, small and medium enterprises (SMEs), economic and technical cooperation, government procurement, and legal and institutional areas including dispute settlement. In terms of market access, the RCEP Agreement achieves liberalization in trade in goods and services and has extended coverage to investment.

(3)**High-Quality.** The RCEP Agreement contains provisions that go beyond the existing ASEAN Plus One FTAs, while recognizing the individual and diverse levels of development and economic needs of the RCEP Parties. The RCEP Agreement addresses the issues required to support the Parties' engagement in global and regional supply chain and complements market access commitments with trade and investment enabling rules that are business-facilitating while at the same time preserving legitimate public policy objectives. The RCEP Agreement strives to boost competition in a way that drives productivity, which is sustainable, responsible, and constructive. In addition, the RCEP Agreement has the added value of bringing

together a single rulebook to help facilitate the development and expansion of regional supply chains among Parties.

(4) **Mutually beneficial.** The RCEP Agreement brings together countries with diverse levels of development. Thus, the RCEP Parties have recognized that its success will be determined by its ability to mutually bring benefits. The RCEP Agreement is designed to achieve this objective in a number of ways, including through appropriate forms of flexibility and provisions for special and differential treatment especially for Cambodia, Lao PDR, Myanmar, and Vietnam, as appropriate, and additional flexibility for the least developed Parties. In addition, the RCEP Agreement includes technical cooperation and capacity building that will be made available to support the implementation of commitments made under the RCEP Agreement and for the Parties to maximise the benefits accruing there. The RCEP Agreement also includes provisions that will ensure that economies with different levels of development, businesses of differing sizes and the broader stakeholders can all benefit from the Agreement.

A description of the RCEP above shows that this Agreement is expected to provide benefits for its member countries. However, apart from the expected benefits, it is inevitable that this Agreement can also have some impacts, both positive and negative. Many experts provide their opinion or analysis on this RCEP. Forexample, during a webinar held on November 10th, economic experts, business owners, civil organizations and parliamentarians expressed their concerns about it.

Rashmi Banga said FTAs like RCEP may further restrict policy and fiscal space of developing countries. In her analysis based on smart methodology, assuming tariffs are removed on all products between RCEP countries, she finds that for most ASEAN countries, imports post-RCEP imports RCEP will rise more than their exports, leading to worsening of their balance of trade concerning RCEP members. Developing countries are more vulnerable and expected to be hit harder and take more time to recover.① She also expressed her fear of RCEP, especially the impact on ASEAN countries:

> ASEAN countries can only benefit from RCEP if they can use the potential on Regional Value Chains which should link with the Global Value Chains. But mostly in regional cooperation, such as RCEP, most ASEAN Countries will lose the preferential access...

Kate Lappin, also had a statement about her worry for RCEP and the impacts:

> FTAs such as RCEP would also increase the pressure on governments to privatize, as public services need to be traded and compete on the market. It will have negative impacts on equality, including corrosive impacts on gender equality... free trade rules shift the weight of who has power in the economy away from workers and in the hands of MNCs and narrow economic interests. In fact, by constraining the policy space of future governments, deals like this are constraining the potential for future poor-worker governments to alter the economic rules.

From the businessman side, *Ian Syarif*, owner of *PT. Sipata Moda Indonesia*, a local textile company, said that free trade agreements like RCEP would bypass diversified trade opportunities and benefit the organized country like China with the sole focus on industrial efficiency. RCEP will also increase possible transshipment activities where goods will be shipped to other RCEP participating countries with zero tariffs and eventually re-exported to Indonesia, bypassing the trade remedies that the Government has im-

① This Statement was Conveyed in the Webinar Forum in Chiangmai, Thailand, November 11th, 2020 with theme "RCEP Will Impact The Future of Developing Countries", https://igj.or.id/wp-content/uploads/2020/11/Press_Release_RCEP_Will_Impact_The_Future_of_Developing_Countries.pdf, last visited on Dec. 15, 2020.

posed.①

All of these practitioners' opinions will generally underline the readiness of ASEAN countries in facing the other five RCEP partners, particularly China, which is one of the most influential and dominant countries in economic terms. So, it will be excellent if the 15 countries can place pretty and equally according to their portion, in the sense of the main principle to help each other and encourage each member's economic growth.

3.2 Domestic Law Improvement as a Solution to the Negative Impacts of RCEP on Indonesia

The description of RCEP and its implications for the member countries can be pointed up more clearly in the explanation above. Considering the importance of this Agreement, Indonesia also realizes that responding to the impact that will arise from this RCEP agreement requires some strategic steps, so that it does not cause new problems for Indonesia itself. The adverse effects of a decision are a consequence that must be accepted. Notably, in this case, the existing anxieties must be reduced to a measurable and controllable level. In this case, the best instrument is to form strategic and targeted laws. Even though these laws are deemed unable to fulfill the sense of justice of all the stakeholders, it is hoped that they can create order and can be the answer to any problems that may arise in the future in protecting Indonesia's own interests.

In an advanced legal system, with the creation and development of laws that are professionally and logically designed, there is no doubt that legal products can influence, even change the joints of people's lives.② The faster the law responds to the reform voice / legal change in society, the greater

---

① Press Release of the IGJ Forum in Chiangmai, Thailand, 2020, https://igj.or.id/wp-content/uploads/2020/11/Press_Release_RCEP_Will_Impact_The_Future_of_Developing_Countries.pdf, last visited on Dec. 14, 2020.

② Munir Fuady, *Sosiologi Hukum Kontemporer "Interaksi Hukum, Kekuasaan, dan Masyarakat"* (*Sociology of Contemporary Law "The Interaction of Law, Power and Society"*), Jakarta: Kencana, 2011, p. 61.

the law role is in changing that society. On the other hand, the slower the law responds to voices of reform in society, the smaller the function and role of law is in changing that society because society itself has changed.

In line with this thought, the Indonesian Government is currently trying not to be slow in responding to the voice of reform in society, but rather trying to accelerate the response to the voice of reform / legal change in society, with the expectation that the role played by law in that society will also be greater. This is particularly so in reading the changes that have occurred in the world, where the Indonesian Government is very aware that if it cannot see or read world changes, it will be difficult for Indonesia to develop, and at the end of the day it will continue to throw away more opportunities for cooperation that benefit Indonesia. Meanwhile, to advance development, the participation in international cooperation is an absolute must for every nation. This is where the role of law in a country should be.

From that explanation, we can see that there are two aspects of the tendency of legal changes in society: One hand, laws that tend to be changed and laws that tend to be conservative. For example, family law or laws regarding individual property are everywhere conservative and rarely changed. On the other hand, law of business, state administration, etc., tend to change according to the wishes and developments in society. Specifically, regarding the RCEP Agreement, it can be concluded that it is part of business law that can change frequently because it is closely related to economic policy, so obviously the Indonesian Government must prepare itself and accelerate the response to the voice of reform / legal change.

RCEP, which was initiated in 2011, and then finally completed by signing in 2020, has a long process of almost 9 years in the discussion. In that period of time, there were also many changes and developments that occurred in the world, affected the world economy, and directly or indirectly had an impact on Indonesia. For example, in 2019, 33 Chinese companies decided to invest overseas. However, none of the 33 companies visited Indonesia. 23 chose Vietnam, the other 10 went to Malaysia, Thailand and Cambodia. Besides, in 2017, 73 Japanese companies chose to relocate. But again, Vietnam is one of the main goals. A total of 43 companies chose to invest in

Vietnam. Meanwhile, 11 companies went to Thailand and the Philippines. Only 10 companies invested in Indonesia. *Jokowi*, said the Government needed to be careful in overcoming this problem. According to him, one of the reasons Vietnam is the main destination for foreign investors is a more concise regulation.①

Learning from this, the Indonesian Government finally accelerated the formation of a Job Creation Law which was finally completed on October 5th, 2020, exactly one month before RCEP was signed on November 15th, 2020. Approval of the Job Creation Law by the Indonesian Parliament was responded to with large demonstrations in a number of regions in Indonesia. Not infrequently, demonstrations led to chaos. The base of his pontificate was mainly related to the changes in the articles of labors. The Job Creation Law originates from a bill proposed by Jokowi in April 2020. This law is also often referred to as the Omnibus Law on Job Creation. Prior to the creation of the Job Creation Law, the omnibus law was relatively unfamiliar to Indonesians. The Omnibus Law itself became known to the public for the first time in the country when it was mentioned in Jokowi's inauguration speech of his second term in October 2019. ②

Why is the Job Creation Law named the omnibus law? In terminology, "omnibus", which comes from Latin, means for everything. In a legal context, the omnibus law is a law that can cover all or one law that regulates many things.According to Busroh, Omnibus law is a law whose substance is to revise and/or repeal many laws. This concept developed in common law countries with Anglo Saxon legal systems such as the United States, Belgium, England and Canada. The omnibus law concept offers solutions to problems caused by over-regulation and overlapping regulations. If the problem is solved in the

---

① Ihsanuddin, Presiden Jokowi Kecewa Calon Investor Banyak Lari ke Negara Tetangga (President Jokowi is Disappointed that Many Potential Investors Run to Neighboring Countries), https://nasional. kompas. com/read/2019/09/04/16425441/, last visited on Des. 2020.

② Muhammad Idris, Mengapa UU Cipta Kerja Disebut Omnibus Law? (Why Is the Job Creation Law Called the Omnibus Law?) https://money.kompas.com/read/2020/10/17/073311026, last visited on Dec. 20, 2020.

normal way, it will take a long time and cost a lot. Not to mention that the process of designing and forming laws and regulations often creates deadlocks or is not in accordance with interests.[①] Omnibus law allows the parliament to amend several laws at one time.

One of the countries in the world that adopted the omnibus law concept was Serbia in 2002 to regulate the autonomous status of Vojvodina Province. The law formed under this concept covers the jurisdiction of the Vojvodina Provincial government regarding culture, education, language, media, health, sanitation, health insurance, pensions, social protection, tourism, mining, agriculture and sports. Apart from Serbia, the concept of omnibus law has also been adopted by other countries and regions such as Argentina, Australia, Austria, Belgium, Canada, Chile, Czech Republic, Denmark, Estonia, Finland, France, Germany, Greece, Hungary, Iceland, Ireland, Israel, Italy, Japan, Latvia, Liechtenstein, Lithuania, Luxembourg, Malta, the Netherlands, New Zealand, Norway, Poland, Portugal, Romania, Russia, Slovak Republic, Slovenia, Spain, Sweden, Switzerland, Taiwan, and United Kingdom. In Southeast Asia, Vietnam and the Philippines are two countries that have already practiced the omnibus law. Vietnam has been successful in attracting a lot of investment after the Government provided various facilities for investors in various sectors, such as incentives, tax exemptions and permits. These conveniences were provided after the issuance of the omnibus law.

The Job Creation Law was passed in the end, because of many opportunities that had been wasted, which was caused by so many overlapping regulations especially in the economic sector in Indonesia. The question will be: why is the Job Creation Law considered to be a solution for Indonesia to complete some homework in the economic sector? This is because the Job Creation Law covers at least 11 clusters that are considered problematic and hinde-

---

① Firman Freaddy Busroh, Konseptualisasi Omnibus Law dalam Menyelesaikan Permasalahan Regulasi Pertanahan (Conceptualization of the Omnibus Law in Solving Land Regulation Problems), *Arena Hukum*, 2017, Vol. 10, No. 2, p.241.

ring Indonesia up to now, i.e.:[①]

- the simplification of land permits;
- investment criteria;
- employment;
- the ease and the protection of SMEs;
- the ease to start a business;
- the support to do research and innovation;
- governmental administration;
- sanction-imposing;
- land-controlling;
- the ease of governmental projects;
- special economic zone.

Additionally, these 6 sectors regarding taxation are covered:

- investment funding;
- territorial system;
- individual taxpayer;
- taxpayer compliance;
- business climate fairness;
- facilities.

Thus this law has streamlined regulations in terms of numbers and also simplified rules to make them more targeted. With the existence of 11 clusters and 6 sectors that have been illustrated, the Indonesian Government has subsequently issued the implemented regulations related to the Job Creation Law, which is expected to have an immediate impact on efforts to recover the national economy as well as become momentum for the awakening of the Indonesian nation.

And it is hoped that this Job Creation law will become an entry point for reforming all practices that hinder investment into Indonesia and also the readiness of Indonesia to protect the its people's interests and especially the domestic business, in reducing the negative impacts of joining the RCEP A-

① Tata Soesatya, Break the News: Omnibus Law Has Passed! https://engliven.com/2020/10/13/omnibus-law-passed/, last visited on Dec. 20, 2020.

greement. With the enactment of this law, it is also hoped that it can encourage foreign investors to invest in Indonesia so that they can create more job opportunitie than are actually needed by the Indonesian people, especially with the impact of the COVID-19 pandemic that hit hard Indonesia's domestic business and thereby decreasing job opportunities.

Thus, the Job Creation Law, known as the Indonesian Omnibus Law, is a big step for Indonesia to make changes and improvements to domestic law. This is done to prepare for all the possibilities that arise from implementing any cooperation mechanism that involves Indonesia in the world in general, and RCEP in particular, or in other words, this law is expected to be Indonesia's initial asset in fortifying its national interests.

The Job Creation Law is a major transformative step for Indonesia, after a long period of process in making systematic and integrated rules, even though this is changing the mindset of law formation that puts forward dynamic and strategic steps in the same direction with the development of life in society. Besides, the existence of the Job Creation Law provides an impetus for cultural change in forming a law which initially required a long time and much consideration in creating a condition. Still, with the formation of this law, it can also be seen how much the effort was to cut bureaucracy in the process so that people adapt to it more swiftly, and their interests are more easily accommodated and protected.

This significant step will provide "culture shock" for experts and researchers, particularly in Indonesia. It proves that the law does not always have to fall behind in reading the development of society. Still, changes in society must be mapped out in the legal provisions that will be made. It requires the continuity of the government policies in shaping and directing the development of a nation. With a clear path of state leadership, the results enjoyed by the community can be reflected in the form of laws which are based on a transparent and sustainable foundation in an appropriate period.

The descriptions above illustrate that RCEP is huge momentum in making a big leap towards legal transformation in the economic sector for all the countries that are members of it, especially for the developing countries which hope to obtain more economic benefits from this Agreement. Particu-

larly for Indonesia, RCEP has provided a significant shove for changes to the law formation as a whole in the economic sector.

Although it is not ideal and will continue to be improved, this step provides more real hope for business actors, and potential investors who intend to make and put their investment in Indonesia. After nearly several decades, there had been no legal umbrella that could facilitate and provide legal certainty in securing economic activities for business actors both domestic and abroad to Indonesia. Every year, the untidy and overlapping regulations from the center to the regions became homework for the Indonesian Government before the Job Creation Law appeared and made it very inconvenient for economic actors working in Indonesia. And RCEP has given its own momentum to the legal transformation in the financial sector in Indonesia so that it can optimally compete with other member countries to get the maximum benefits from trade opportunities arising from this Agreement while still prioritizing the principle of prudence and protecting domestic interests.

At the end of the discussion on RCEP and legal transformation in the economic sector in Indonesia as the implication of the Agreement itself, it proves that the world economy is part of active life which should not be separated from business law that can change frequently. This realized, in the future the laws governing the economic sector can grow and develop to balance the dynamics of society, which is the main engine driving the nation's economy. Obviously, with the lively economy, the Indonesian Government must prepare itself and always accelerate the response to the voice of reform / legal change in the economic sector, since the economy is one of the most important milestones for the nation's progress.

4. Conclusion

From the discussion above, it can be concluded that:

1. RCEP can bring both positive and negative impacts. The positive effect will benefit all the members if they work together to build a strong relationship. The positive impact will be that the Agreement will help develop supply chains that have been disrupted due to the COVID-19 pandemic and

the China-US decoupling, and support the regional and world economic recovery. The purpose of RCEP itself is to establish a modern, comprehensive, high-quality, and mutually beneficial economic partnership that will facilitate the expansion of regional trade and investment, and contribute to global economic growth and development. Accordingly, it will bring about the market and employment opportunities to businesses and people in the region. On the other hand, negative impacts can also occur if members are not careful in carrying out strategic steps, namely:

- For most ASEAN countries, imports post-RCEP will rise more than their exports, leading to the worsening of their balance of trade concerning RCEP members. Developing countries are more vulnerable and expected to be hit harder and take more time to recover.
- Signing RCEP will bind the hands of governments in taking measures for the public interests in crises to come, be it health or environmental. Further, the free trade rules shift the weight of who has power in the economy from workers to MNCs and narrow economic interests. In fact, by constraining the policy space of future governments, deals like this are denying the potential of future poor-worker governments to alter the financial rules.
- RCEP will bypass diversified trade opportunities and benefit the organized country like China, which focuses on industrial efficiency. RCEP will also increase possible transshipment activities where goods will be shipped to some RCEP participating countries with zero tariffs and eventually re-exported to the other member countries bypassing the trade remedies that the latter have imposed.
- The idea that an international agreement will be signed without prior scrutiny and an assessment of its impact is unacceptable.

2. Thus far, in facing this RCEP challenge, Indonesia already has a new legal instrument that was recently enacted on October 5th, 2020. This law is known as the Job Creation Law or the Indonesia Omnibus Law, with 45 Government Regulations and 4 Presidential Regulations as the implementation regulations. This law is considered to be a reference for Indonesia to face unfavorable impacts when RCEP is implemented in Indonesia. The Job Creation Law covers at

least 11 clusters that are considered problematic and hindering Indonesia up to now, and additionally, 6 sectors regarding taxation are covered also. Thus this law has streamlined regulations in terms of numbers and also simplified regulations to make them more targeted. Therefore, the Job Creation Law, known as the Indonesian Omnibus Law, is a big step for Indonesia to make changes and improvements to domestic law. This is done to prepare for all the possibilities that arise from implementing any cooperation mechanism that involves Indonesia in the world in general, and RCEP in particular, or in other words, this law is expected to be Indonesia's initial asset in fortifying its national interests. RCEP is significant momentum in making a giant leap towards legal transformation in the economic sector, particularly for Indonesia; RCEP has provided a substantial shove for changes to the formation of the laws in the financial industry. Although it is not ideal and will continue to be improved, this step provides more real hope for business actors and potential investors who intend to make and put their investment in Indonesia. After nearly several decades, there had been no legal umbrella that could facilitate and provide legal certainty in securing economic activities for business actors both domestic and abroad to Indonesia.

5. Suggestion

Some suggestions from the discussion above will be as follows:

1. Facing the RCEP, all member countries must play an active role and strive to prioritize the spirit of togetherness that the ASEAN group has always had to this day, even though there is competition that produces turmoil. Still, everything can always be resolved with a spirit of togetherness. Strategic steps that can be taken are to enhance trade cooperation between countries and encourage foreign capital to enter to increase the export potential and import substitution, increase foreign capital earnings, and save it. Improving the economic income of countries by finding a way or solution to simplify the trade process from upstream to downstream and attract foreign investment is the main objective of this cooperation. The main goal is to help accelerate the economic growth of the affected countries so that they all will

soon recover. This goal will be achieved by hand-in-hand cooperation with the same spirit and vision for the future.

2. Looking at the importance of RCEP and its possible impacts in the future, the Indonesian Government should be optimistic and is currently trying not to be slow in responding to the voice of reform in society. Even though Indonesia already has the Job Creation Law or Indonesia Omnibus Law, it still has a lot of goals to achieve after joining RCEP. Other steps are needed, like monitoring the implementation of the Job Creation Law and regulations derived from the center to the regions. Those efforts will make Indonesia more ready to achieve the goals after joining the RCEP.

3. Indonesia must better its performance in improving its laws in various fields by basing it on the continuity of the government policies in shaping and directing the development of the nation. With a clear path of state leadership, the outcomes enjoyed by the people can be reflected in the laws, which are based on a transparent and sustainable legal foundation in an appropriate period. It will make Indonesia always ready to face challenges from the international community, including those from RCEP itself.

Myanmar-Singapore Comparative Study of the New Rule of Law

Myat Hsu Win*

Abstract: The Rule of Law means that everyone in a state, including the government, is subject to the law. The Rule of Law is the cornerstone to get international peace and security and political stability; to achieve economic and social progress and development; and to protect people's rights and fundamental freedoms. It is also situated alongside the other pillars of a democratic society. Therefore, every citizen should know the principles of Rule of Law. If our country has Rule of Law, we can get stability, tranquility and prosperity.

The key ingredients of a Rule of Law-based system are reduction in corruption, protection of economic rights and good governance. Corruption is a significant barrier to the Rule of Law and sustainable development. The negative impacts of corruption obstructs economic growth and development, erodes public confidence, legitimacy and transparency, and hinders the making of fair and effective laws, as well as their administration, enforcement and adjudication. So, corruption attacks the foundation of democracy, institution and the Rule of Law.

Nowadays, corruption is becoming more widespread as a "culture" in society. So, every country has policy agendas to prevent, detect and investigate corruption. Although Myanmar is combating corruption, the problem of corruption is escalating. Therefore, the anti-corruption sector is really important to reform in Myanmar the Rule of Law. The main focus of this paper is a comparative study of the Rule of Law between singapore and Myannmar, especially in anti-corruption.

Keywords: Rule of Law, Anti-corruption

---

* Ph. D Candidate of SWUPL, officer of MOLA, Myanmar.

Introduction

The Rule of Law is a legal principle that requires everyone, including the government, to obey the law. Rule of Law is of paramount importance for linking to the other essential elements of democracy for ensuring the stability and prosperity of community. So, it is an intensely important part of our lives. The principle of Rule of Law has been developing gradually with civilization. Rule of Law is not only important to judges, prosecutors, lawyers, government officials, security personnel, administers and parliamentarians but also to businessmen, builders, consumers, journalists, doctors and labor organizations.

Rule of Law affects sustainable economic growth, political stability and economic rights of citizens. Several countries have recognized this and started to uphold and maintain the Rule of Law for sustainable development. The key ingredients of a Rule of Law-based system are reduction in corruption, protection of economic rights and good corporate governance (both private and public). Corruption is one of the significant barriers to the rule of law.

Corruption includes abuse of authority, bribery and willful misconduct; therefore, it is related to the public interest. It has main effects on administration and human rights and also deteriorates the economy, politics and moral ethics. As the global economy is rapidly developing nowadays, corruption has grown transnationally in different form as organized crime. Corruption attacks the foundation of democracy, institutions and the Rule of Law.①

The United Nations (UN) also supports assistance to Member States in implementing the UN Convention Against Corruption (UNCAC) as well as in strengthening capacities to prevent, detect and investigate corruption, and to implement programmes to promote transparency, integrity and accountability

① Development of the Anti-corruption Mechanism in Myanmar, Ngwe Zaw Aung, https://www.unafei.or.jp/publications/pdf/GG11/18_GG11, last visited on Aug. 27, 2021.

in criminal justice and Rule of Law institutions. [①] Furthermore, all ASEAN Member countries have ratified the UNCAC and all ASEAN Heads of State have adopted the Political-Security Community Blueprint as part of ASEAN 2025. This blueprint calls for the promotion of ASEAN cooperation in the implementation of the UNCAC for the prevention and combating of corruption.[②]

Singapore ranked third in the world for its absence of corruption, civil justice, and criminal justice according to the ASEAN countries' index.[③] The rank of corruption in Myanmar was down to 137 in 2020 from 130 in 2019.[④] Although Myanmar have fought corruption, the corruption rank continues to go down. Myanmar is quite different from Singapore with regard to Rule of Law and anti-corruption. Therefore, the main focus of this paper is a comparative study on anti-corruption sector between Singapore and Myanmar in Rule of Law.

1. Rule of Law

1.1 Meanings and Principles of Rule of Law

Rule of law is a principle that enshrines equality for everyone before the law. In 1948, the term "Rule of Law" emerged on the world stage as part of the preamble to the Universal Declaration of Human Rights (UDHR), which affirms that the rule of law should protect the rights and responsibilities of the government and the people.[⑤] Moreover, the UDHR states "the advancement of the rule of law at the national and international levels is es-

---

① Corruption, https://www.un.org/ruleoflaw/thematic-areas/governance/corruption/, last visited on Aug. 20, 2021.

② Helen Yu, Alison Guernsey, What is the Rule of Law? https://iuristebi.files.wordpress.com, last visited on Aug. 18, 2021.

③ https://www.aseanbriefing.com/news/rule-of-law-in-asean-not-all-appealing-2, last visited on Apr. 28, 2021.

④ https://tradingeconomics.com/myanmar/corruption-rank, last visited on Apr. 4, 2021.

⑤ https://www.researchgate.net/publication/326698576_Rule_of_Law_in_Myanmar_and_Current_Situation_2018, last visited on Fer. 25, 2021.

sential for the realization of sustained economic growth, sustainable development, the eradication of poverty and hunger and the protection of all human rights and fundamental freedoms". Furthermore, the United Nations General Assembly asserted that human rights, the rule of law and democracy are interconnected and mutually reinforcing one another. ①

The main principles of Rule of Law are supremacy of law, equality before the law, accountability to the law, fairness in the application of the law, separation of powers, participation in decision-making, legal certainty, avoidance of arbitrariness and procedural and legal transparency under report of the UN Secretary-General Kofi Annan on the Rule of Law and Transitional Justice in Conflict and Post-Conflict Societies, 2004.

Four universal principles of Rule of Law are as follows:

(1) Governments and their civil servants, individuals, and private entities are all accountable for the law.

(2) Laws are equitable, clear, just, publicized, consistent, and protect fundamental human rights

(3) Law-making processes, enforcement and administration of law are transparent, accessible, fair, and efficient.

(4) Justice is provided by impartial, independent individuals who are reflective of the communities they serve.②

The Rule of Law is the cornerstone to get international peace and security and political stability; to achieve economic and social progress and development; and to protect people's rights and fundamental freedoms. It is a foundation of people's access to public services, combating corruption, restraining the abuse of power, and establishing the social contract between people and the state. Rule of law and development are strongly connected, and strengthened rule of law-based society should be considered as an outcome of

---

① https://www.mypilar.org/sites/mypilar.org/files/publication-files/rol_report_emref_09.06.16.pdf, last visited on Mar. 15, 2021.

② https://www.researchgate.net/publication/326698576_Rule_of_Law_in_Myanmar_and_Current_Situation_2018, last visited on Fer. 25, 2021.

the 2030 Agenda for Sustainable Development Goals (SDGs).[①]

Politicians, lawyers, economists and policy-makers often use the term "Rule of Law" to characterize a certain type of legal and political regime. Therefore, the definition of Rule of Law can vary between different nations and legal systems.

1.2 Advantages of Rule of Law

Since 1945, the United Nations has been building international peace and security, human rights and development. After seventy-five years, the complicate political, social and economic transformation of modern society has brought many challenges and opportunities that need a collective response according to the Rule of Law, which is the foundation of friendly and equitable relations between states. The Rule of Law is a principle of governance under which all persons, institutions and entities, public and private, are accountable to laws that are equally enforced and independently adjudicated, and consistent with international human rights norms and standards in the UN system. The General Assembly and Security Council reviewed that the Rule of Law is an essential part of sustaining peace in peace building architecture. Peacekeeping requires the UN system coherence between the political, security, development, human rights, gender equality and rule of law activities of member states.

The Rule of Law means a legal foundation to make our governing institutions, education, housing and health care institutions more effective, accountable and inclusive. Thus, the Rule of Law is essential for the success of any nation state. The UN 2030 Agenda for Sustainable Development Goals (SDGs) have provided a specific goal regarding this: SDG 16 "Peace, Justice, and Strong Institutions" recognises that sustainable development requires the promotion of peaceful and inclusive societies, access to justice and

① What is the Rule of Law, USAID, https://www.un.org/ruleoflaw/what-is-the-rule-of-law/#iLightbox[gallery15269]/0, last visited on Fer. 22, 2021.

effective, accountable, inclusive institutions.①

Strengthening the Rule of Law involves respect for the norms of international law, which are the use of force, and recognition of the primary responsibility of states to protect their populations from genocide, crimes against humanity, ethnic cleansing and war crimes. ② Rule of law is also situated together with the other pillars of a democratic society, including access to justice, gender equality, human rights, free speech, fair and open elections, and accountable and transparent governance. ③

There are many benefits of Rule of Law. The Rule of Law protects it from influence or interference by government, powerful individuals or mob. All citizens get equal protection before the law. The Rule of Law safeguards basic rights such as right to life, personal liberty, freedom of speech and association. Governments are allowed the expression of divergent views such as freedom of the mass media, which includes the radio, television, newspapers and lately the news portals and social media.④ Every citizen must be aware of his or her rights and liberties. If their rights are violated, they can check arbitrariness of those appointed by the government and the rise of dictatorship to prevent arbitrariness and dictatorship.⑤

Where the Rule of Law operates, the ruler and the ruled are equal before the law, no matter their position, rank or status in society. The Rule of Law protects and strengthens democracy, separation of powers and checks and bal-

---

① https://www.bangkokpost.com/opinion/opinion/1421547/the-rule-of-laws-importance-in-aseans-development, last visited on Mar. 12, 2021.

② What is the Rule of Law, USAID, https://www.un.org/ruleoflaw/what-is-the-rule-of-law/#iLightbox[gallery15269]/0, last visited on Fer. 22, 2021.

③ https://www.mypilar.org/sites/mypilar.org/files/publication-files/rol_report_emref_09.06.16.pdf, last visited on Mar. 15, 2021.

④ https://tipsinfluencer.com.ng/the-rule-of-law-meaning-benefits-and-principles-of-rule-of-law, last visited on Mar. 15, 2021.

⑤ https://www.virtualkollage.com/2016/12/the-advantages-of-rule-of-law.html, last visited on Mar. 12, 2021.

ances. All of these contribute to political stability of a nation.[①]

1.3 Anti-corruption for Rule of Law in ASEAN

The Association of Southeast Asian Nations (ASEAN) was set up on 8 August 1967 in Bangkok, Thailand, with the signing of the ASEAN Declaration (Bangkok Declaration) by the founding fathers of ASEAN, namely Indonesia, Malaysia, Philippines, Singapore and Thailand. Brunei Darussalam later joined on 7 January 1984, Viet Nam on 28 July 1995, Lao PDR and Myanmar on 23 July 1997, and Cambodia on 30 April 1999. Today, ASEAN has ten member countries.[②]

Since 1967, ASEAN has embraced the concept of the Rule of Law at the international level. The ASEAN Charter, adopted in November 2007, represents an important paradigm shift in the approach to integration, including promotion of the Rule of Law. One goal relating to the Rule of Law is found in Article 1.7 of the ASEAN Charter, which states that the purposes of ASEAN include"to strengthen democracy, enhance good governance and the Rule of Law, and to promote and protect human rights and fundamental freedoms".[③] The Rule of Law has become a banner through which regional integration projects are being enhanced in ASEAN. Regional integration demands that Rule of Law not only provide stability and predictability in economic relations but also establish a coherent and stable framework for guiding the relations of member states, particularly in resolving issues or disputes among members. [④]

Corruption is a significant barrier to the Rule of Law and sustainable development. The Rule of Law is also stressed as an essential element in ad-

---

① https://tipsinfluencer.com.ng/the-rule-of-law-meaning-benefits-and-principles-of-rule-of-law, last visited on Mar. 15, 2021.

② https://asean.org/asean/about-asean, last visited on Apr. 28, 2021.

③ https://www.dfdl.com/wp-content/uploads/2015/11/Investing_in_ASEAN_2015_DFDL_Rule_of_Law, last visited on Mar. 12, 2021.

④ https://www.researchgate.net/publication/325297458_The_development_of_the_rule_of_law_in_ASEAN_The_state_and_regional_integration, last visited on Mar. 15, 2021.

dressing and preventing corruption. Therefore, all ASEAN member states have ratified the UNCAC and all ASEAN Heads of State have adopted the ASEAN 2025 Political-Security Community Blueprint as part of ASEAN 2025. This Blueprint calls for promoting ASEAN cooperation in implementing the UNCAC to prevent and combat corruption; implementing the Memorandum of Understanding on Cooperation for Preventing and Combatting Corruption; strengthening the implementation of domestic laws and regulations against corruption and of anti-corruption practices in both the public and private sectors within ASEAN; intensifying cooperation in the area of asset recovery; denying safe havens to those found guilty of corruption within the framework of applicable national and international laws to combat corruption; and encouraging the strengthening of the South east Asia Parties Against Corruption network (known as the ASEAN Parties Against Corruption; ASEAN-PAC). ①

Thailand, Indonesia, the Philippines, Malaysia, Cambodia and Myanmar are weak in the Rule of Law in transition to democracies. In those countries, there were many instances where the democratization process was undermined. Weak and corrupt judiciaries, poor access to justice, the ascendancy or strong influence of the military in civil governance, persistence of summary or extrajudicial killings and low capacity of accountability institutions are only among the most visible expressions of the weakness of Rule of Law in these regions.②

Under the ASEAN countries' index, Singapore came third in the word for its absence of corruption, civil justice, and criminal justice.③ Corruption rank of Myanmar was down to 137 in 2020 from 130 in 2019. Transparency International's corruption rank of Myanmar averaged 154.11 from 2003 to

---

① Strengthening Anti-Corruption Efforts of ASEAN and ASEAN Member States, https://asean. usmission. gov/strengthening-anti-corruption-efforts-of-asean-and-asean-member-states/, last visited on Aug. 25, 2021.

② From ASEAN Way to the ASEAN Charter: Toward the Rule of Law? https://www.researchgate.net/publication/325297458, last visited on Mar. 12, 2021.

③ https://www. aseanbriefing. com/news/rule-of-law-in-asean-not-all-appealing-2, last visited on Apr. 28, 2021.

2020.[1] Therefore, there exists a wide discrepancy in the corruption rank between Singapore and Myanmar.

2. Anti-corruption for Rule of Law in Singapore

2.1 Singapore Legal System

Since Singapore is a former British colony, the legal system in Singapore is based on the English common law. On 9 August 1965, Singapore was ejected from Malaysia to become an independent nation.[2] The Indian Penal Code was brought into operation from 1 July 1967 and finally became law in Singapore in 1871. The Indian Criminal Procedure Code brought criminal procedure into line with it. Braddell was responsible for the Civil Law Ordinance (1878), which introduced English law relating to partnership, corporations, banking, principal and agents, carriers by land and sea, insurance and mercantile law, into Singapore.[3] All criminal offences under the Penal Code or other statutes are investigated and tried according to the Criminal Procedure Code. Four main pillars of Singapore law are Constitution, Legislation, Subsidiary legislation and Legal decisions made by judges. [4]

Since the independence, the Department of Law has played a major role in maintaining the rule of law by ensuring that Singapore's legislation reflects a sound, consistent legal policy. Before Government bills may be tabled before Parliament, they must be scrutinized and vetted by the Ministry of Law to ensure that the proposed laws are consistent with Singapore's Constitution and the principle, which underpin the Rule of Law. Moreover, the Ministry of

---

① https://tradingeconomics.com/myanmar/corruption-rank, last visited on Apr. 28, 2021.

② https://www. psd. gov. sg/heartofpublicservice/our-institutions/upholding-the-rule-of-law, last visited on Apr. 5, 2021.

③ A History of The Singapore Legal Service, https://www.sal.org.sg/Resources-Tools/Legal-Heritage/A-History-of-the-Singapore-Legal-Service, last visited on Apr. 12, 2021.

④ https://www. guidemesingapore. com/business-guides/immigration/get-to-know-singapore/introduction-to-singapores-legal-system, last visited on Apr. 12, 2021.

Law is also leading the government's attempts to review and reform the Singapore's laws in order to reflect societal norms and changing circumstances. ①

A constitution is a collection of rules that determine the creation and operation of the government and its institutions. All other laws passed must be consistent with the Constitution. The Singapore Constitution lays down the fundamental principles and basic framework for the three organs of state, namely, the Executive, the Legislature and the Judiciary. The separation of governmental powers among the three branches of government creates a system of checks and balances between them. Article 12 (1) of Singapore Constitution provides that "All persons are equal before the law and entitled to the equal protection of the law."②

According to Hong Kong-based Political and Economic Risk Consultancy (PERC), Singapore is the 2nd least risky country in Asia in the year 2010. Singapore's efficient, transparent and extremely sound legal system has been key to the country's significant growth in recent years. All Singapore citizens are equal before the law irrespective of their race, religion and creed.③

2.2 Rule of Law in Singapore

The rule of law is good governance, a clean and credible justice system and strong legal institutions for the succession of independent Singapore. In 1967, the rule of law was established in the city-state of Singapore. Singapore built together many themes and upheld the Rule of Law as an independent country. The Rule of Law is important not only as an ideal but also as a foundation upon which a nation and its institutions might be built and governed.④

---

① https://www. psd. gov. sg/heartofpublicservice/our-institutions/upholding-the-rule-of-law, last visited on Apr. 5, 2021.

② The Rule of Law and the Singapore Constitution, https://www. supremecourt. gov. sg/news/events/magna/the-rule-of-law-and-the-singapore-constitution, last visited on Apr. 5, 2021.

③ https://www. guidemesingapore. com/business-guides/immigration/get-to-know-singapore/introduction-to-singapores-legal-system, last visited on Apr. 12, 2021.

④ Upholding the Rule of Law, https://www. psd. gov. sg/heartofpublicservice/our-institutions/upholding-the-rule-of-law, last visited on Apr. 5, 2021.

Singapore recognizes the Rule of Law as a universal value. It must be applied to achieve good governance and to promote the general welfare. Today, Singapore remains committed to the Rule of Law as a foundational principle. The Constitution is the supreme law of the land. The laws are interpreted and applied by an independent and respected Judiciary. The President and Parliament are elected through universal right to vote. There is a culture of respect for the law, and an expectation that the law will be impartially enforced, both in Government and in society at large. The Rule of Law must provide good governance to enhance the life of Singaporeans.[①]

Singapore is attractive in that it is a leading business destination for investment and locating major operations, which is affirmed by various international surveys. Those surveys have also given Singapore high ratings for its efficiency, rule of law and lack of corruption. As a result of the development of the Rule of Law, Singapore has generated economic gains and foreign investments.[②]

2.3 Anti-corruption in Singapore

Since Singapore entered self-government in 1959, controlling corruption has been a top priority for the government. It was necessary to ensure the growth of the economy. It is a competitive advantage to attract foreign businesses to invest in Singapore. Corruption control has become a strategic principle of governance. It provides the public with the predictability and confidence to depend upon the government to discharge its duty without bias.[③]

Corruption is a serious problem in many Asia countries, but Singapore is the least corrupt country in Asia according to the annual surveys conducted by the Hong Kong-based Political and Economic Risk Consultancy Ltd. (PERC) and the Berlin-based Transparency International (TI) in recent

---

① K. Shanmugam, The Rule of Law in Singapore -Nus -Faculty of Law, https://law1.nus.edu.sg › sjls › SJLS-Dec-12-357, last visited on Apr. 5, 2021.

② https://www.statecourts.gov.sg/cws/TBD/Documents, last visited on Apr. 12, 2021.

③ Koh Teck Hin, Corruption control in Singapore, https://www.unafei.or.jp/publications/pdf, last visited on Aug. 20, 2021.

years. In 1996, PERC ranked Singapore as the third least corrupt country in the world.①

The basic legal framework of corruption in Singapore is the Prevention of Corruption Act (PCA), which applies to both private sector and public officials. Other laws related to corruption are the Penal Code and the Corruption, Drugs Trafficking and Other Serious Crimes (Confiscation of Benefits) Act (CDSA). CDSA provides for the seizure and forfeiture of proceeds which a person convicted of corruption cannot satisfactorily account for. ② The Corrupt Practices Investigation Bureau (CPIB), which was founded in 1952, is the sole agency responsible for combating corruption in Singapore Singapore's fight against corruption has since been credible, effective, relentless, pursued without fear. A clean government and trustworthy public service have come to be the hallmark of the Singaporean system. ③

The framework of corruption control consists of four pillars in Singapore. They are as follows:

(1) effective anti-corruption acts (or laws);

(2) effective anti-corruption agency;

(3) effective adjudication (or punishment) and;

(4) efficient government administration.④

In order to fight corruption, Parliament and the Heads of Government departments have been formulated strict rules and regulations, which govern the conduct of public officers in Singapore. Strict rules and regulations are: cannot borrow money from any person who has official dealings with him or her; cannot use any official information to further his or her private interest;

---

① John S.T. Quah, Combating corruption in Singapore: What Can be learned? https://datascience.iq.harvard.edu/files/gov2126/files/quah_singapore, last visited on Aug. 20, 2021.

② Koh Teck Hin, Corruption control in Singapore, https://www.unafei.or.jp/publications/pdf, last visited on Aug. 20, 2021.

③ Upholding the Rule of Law, https://www.psd.gov.sg/heartofpublicservice/our-institutions/upholding-the-rule-of-law, last visited on Apr. 5, 2021.

④ Koh Teck Hin, Corruption control in Singapore, https://www.unafei.or.jp/publications/pdf, last visited on Aug. 20, 2021.

cannot engage in trade or business or undertake any part-time employment without approval; cannot receive entertainment or present in any form from members of the public; and a public officer is required to declare his or her assets at his or her first appointment.

Low salaries are an important factor contributing to corruption. The government has an obligation to provide high salaries for combating the corruption. In order to reduce the corruption, the government had to improve the salaries and working conditions in the Singapore Civil Service to stem the brain drain of competent senior civil servants to the private sector by offering competitive salaries and fringe benefits to reduce the gap between the public and private sectors. Accordingly, the salaries of civil servants in Singapore were increased in 1973, 1979, 1982, 1989 and 1994 to reduce the brain drain to the private sector and the gap between salaries in the two sectors.[①]

Singapore government embarked e-Government Action Plans (eGAP) to better serve the nation. This plan aims at delivering excellent public services as well as connecting the citizens to the government. Although the e-government action plan does not totally control corruption, it has an important side benefit. It reduces the visits to government service counters, service turnaround time and cost of delivery. If a government service can now be obtained from the homes via the Internet, what opportunity is there for someone to interfere in between to solicit a bribe for the purpose of greasing the transaction?[②]

3. Anti-corruption for Rule of Law in Myanmar

3.1 Myanmar Legal System

The legal system of Myanmar belongs to the Common Law Legal Fami-

① John S. T. Quah, Combating corruption in Singapore: What Can be learned?, https://datascience.iq.harvard.edu/files/gov2126/files/quah_singapore, last visited on Aug. 20, 2021.

② Koh Teck Hin, Corruption control in Singapore, https://www.unafei.or.jp/publications/pdf, last visited on Aug. 20, 2021.

ly. However, it is not a replica of the Common Law Legal System but a unique combination of Common Law and Civil Law Legal Systems. Myanmar still applies the basic principles of the Common Law Legal Systems, which originate from British Colonial period. The Penal Code, the Code of Criminal Procedure, the Evidence Act and Special Laws are applied in the Courts of the Republic of the Union of Myanmar.

Myanmar regained her independence in 1948. The first Constitution of the Union of Myanmar was adopted in 1947. The second Constitution for the Socialist Republic of the Union of Myanmar was adopted in 1974. A new Constitution of the Republic of the Union of Myanmar was adopted in May 2008 and came into force on 31 January 2011. In order to be in line with the new Constitution, some old laws, which are inconsistent with the social and economic objectives of the State, were amended and repealed.

According to Article 11 of the 2008 Constitution of the Republic of the Union of Myanmar, the three branches of sovereign power are legislative power, executive power and judicial power, which are separated to the extent possible, and exert reciprocal control, check and balance among themselves. Myanmar 2008 Constitution has several "fundamental rights", including various protections against discrimination; rights to education and health care; language and other cultural rights; prohibitions on enslavement, people-trafficking and forced labor; freedom of movement; rights to property and privacy; a right to vote and stand in elections; and freedoms of expression, association and belief. ①

Also, according to Article 19 of the 2008 Constitution and Section 3 of the Union Judiciary Law, the court is independent to render its judgment without any interference of other branches of sovereign power. These laws grant the core elements to taking action against offenders. These norms are embodied in the Constitution and Laws as follows:

(a) No criminal law should be done the retroactive action: any accused person shall be convicted only in accord with the relevant law then in operation. He shall not be penalized to penalty greater than that is

① Constitution of the Union of Myanmar, 2008.

applicable under that law.

(b) Any person convicted or acquitted by a competent court for an offence shall not be retried unless a superior court annuls the judgment and orders the retrial.

(c) The accused shall have the right of defense in accord with the law.

(d) No person shall be held in custody for more than 24 hours without the remand of a competent magistrate.

(e) Punishment should be aimed to reform the moral character of offender.[①]

The 2008 Constitution guarantees the independence and impartiality of the judiciary, and it mandates presumptively public courtroom hearings, a right of defense and a right of appeal.

One of the Myanmar's judicial principle is administering justice independently according to law. In trying and making decisions in criminal cases, judges at all levels have to comply with Penal Code, the Code of Criminal Procedure, and the Evidence Act. All offences under the Penal Code and other laws shall be investigated and tried according to the Code of Criminal Procedure. However, if there is a special rule of the procedure in any law, the procedure shall be subject to that law with regard to investigation or inquiry or trial. Therefore, whoever contravenes the provisions of any existing law in the Union of Myanmar shall be liable to be punished under that law.

3.2 Rule of Law in Myanmar

The government of the Republic of the Union of Myanmar places great importance on the establishment of stability and prosperity of the community where the public understand the concept of the Rule of Law. The Rule of Law is the cornerstone for strengthening democracy and development of the country. One of the basic principles of the Rule of Law is to promote the establishment of a rule-based society in the interest of legal certainty and predictability. Strengthening the Rule of Law is to protect the rights of and provide access to justice for all Myanmar people.

---

① Union Judiciary Law, 2010.

Over the five years of Myanmar's evolving democratic transition, the notion of "Rule of Law" has played a central role in the country's reform agenda. In 2015, the Nationwide Ceasefire Agreement referred to "the Rule of Law". Furthermore, the Union Attorney General Office released their Strategic Plan with the title of "Moving Forward to the Rule of Law".

A new Constitution was adopted in May 2008; parliamentary elections were held in November 2010. Myanmar was at an historic stage in 2010 for its development. The transition to civilian rule under the new 2008 Constitution was the first step in an on-going series of rapid and far-reaching political and economic reforms. Some of these include widespread poverty and corruption, an underdeveloped economy, and weak institutional capacity. ①

In 2015, the World Bank gave Myanmar one of the lowest scores possible in Rule of Law, along with meager rankings in other governance issuse of the public sector.② After two decades of internal repression, civil wars and estrangement from the international community, it has embarked on a process of reform. The country now faces the challenge of advancing Rule of Law, access to justice and other reforms while simultaneously maintaining stability.③ Another fundamental issue of Rule of Law in Myanmar is the lack of legal awareness that adds to the prohibitive environment surrounding formal legal institutions.

Rule of Law reform in Myanmar is just beginning to take root. Myanmar is currently trying to transform every sector. Political leaders, civil society activists, and members of the international community regularly invoke "the Rule of Law" as a necessary part of the country's reform agenda. Another key area of Rule of Law reform in Myanmar is the decentralization of governance, particularly because many community members still view the union

① https://www. aseanbriefing. com/news/rule-of-law-in-asean-not-all-appealing-2, last visited on Mar.15,2021.

② https://www. mypilar. org/sites/mypilar. org/files/publication-files/rol _ report _ emref_09.06.16.pdf, last visited on Mar. 15, 2021.

③ https://www.undp.org/.../Fast_Facts_Rule_of_Law, last visited on Fer. 25, 2021.

government as lacking in transparency and unresponsive to their needs. ①

The 2008 Constitution that conforms to Rule of Law principles serves to protect fundamental rights and provide access to legal recourse, and ensures that executive power is exercised "only on the basis of and within the limits of the law". The Constitution defines the basic structure of the government and makes some commitments to the Rule of Law, including the separation of powers between the three branches of government, which are executive, legislative and administrative, and setting out five writs available to challenge violations of individual rights. The 2008 Constitution guarantees fundamental rights and the possibility to apply for writs that give citizens recourse against unlawful government actions. ②

The Supreme Court is authorized meanwhile to issue five writs, including writs of habeas corpus, writs of mandamus, writs of prohibition, writs of quo warranto and writs of certiorari under the Law Relating to the Application of Writ, 2914 and Section 44 of the 2008 Constitution. The following are meanings of the five writs issued by the Supreme Court.

(a) Writs of Habeas Corpus means a writ issued in writing after causing to bring the detainee to the office of writ and hearing whether or not the detention is in conformity with law by any Court of the Republic of the Union of Myanmar or any competent authority;

(b) Writs of Mandamus means a writ issued in writing to comply with Law by any competent person; or any authority; or any government department for the failure to comply with the power conferred thereon;

(c) Writs of Prohibition means a writ issued in writing not to perform beyond the jurisdiction or against justice in any proceeding of any quasi judicial matter;

(d) Writs of Quo Warranto means a writ issued in writing whether or

① https://www.mypilar.org/sites/mypilar.org/files/publicationfiles/rol_report_emref_09.06.16.pdf, last visited on Mar. 15, 2021.

② https://www.researchgate.net/publication/326698576 Rule of Law in Myanmar and Current Situation 2018, last visited on Fer. 25, 2021.

not it is in conformity with law after hearing whether or not any government department or any empowered authority has carried out in accordance with laws, rules, regulations, by-laws, procedures, orders, notifications, directive issued on person or persons;

(e) Writs of Certiorari means a writ issued in writing to be the decision in conformity with law if it is found that the decision of any court or any quasi judicial matter is not in conformity with law.①

The Government of Myanmar supports strengthening institutions, systems and capacity that ensure people can access administrative and criminal justice that is fair, transparent and accountable based on human rights and rule of law. The Strengthening Accountability and Rule of Law (SARL) project works to strengthen the justice and human rights sector with the Union Attorney General's Office (UAGO), the Office of the Supreme Court of the Union and the Myanmar National Human Rights Commission to support the application of rule of law and administrative justice principles, and to promote awareness and protection of human rights. SARL will also engage the public in understanding and accessing accountability mechanisms, and how to seek redress from unfair, arbitrary, incorrect, or discriminatory outcomes and improper use of public powers. Access to justice services has been improved through supporting UAGO to produce the Manual on Fair Trial Standards, which sets out the fundamental rights for persons accused of crimes.②

Furthermore, United Nations Development Programme (UNDP) builds the capacity (systems, behaviors and skills) of law officers, lawyers, judges, law students and the police to promote access to justice. UNDP also supports the development of a comprehensive long-term training framework for UAGO and training facility for UAGO through Judicial Training Center (JTC).③

---

① The Law Relating to the Application of Writ, 2014.

② https://www.mm.undp.org/content/myanmar/en/home/projects/SARL.html, last visited on Fer. 25, 2021.

③ https://www.undp.org/.../Fast_Facts_Rule_of_Law.pdf, last visited on Fer. 25, 2021.

3.3 Anti-corruption in Myanmar

Rule of Law is generally based upon reduction in corruption. Corruption occurs not only in developed and developing countries but also in public and private sectors. Myanmar faces problems of corruption in every sector such as the political, administrative and judicial sector. Among the various types of corruption in the country, administrative corruption is at the highest level and judicial sector is at the fourth highest level according to the Myanmar Anti-Corruption Commission (ACC) Annual Report 2018.①

Around the beginning of the transition to democracy, the government of Myanmar started campaigns to institute Good Governance and Clean Government. Since that time anti-corruption has become a national priority. The government has worked towards implementing an anti-corruption framework. In 2012, Myanmar ratified the UNCAC. In 2013, the anti-corruption law was adopted and an anti-corruption commission was constituted. This anti-corruption law is a basic legal framework for preventing, countering and punishing corruption and the anti-corruption commission is the primary anti-corruption framework. ② Other relevant laws are the Penal Code, Public Property Protection Act and the Anti-Money Laundering Law.

Corruption is multi-faceted in Myanmar. The government of Myanmar is endeavoring to develop domestic businesses and also inviting foreign investments for the development of the national economy. It is also needed for reducing the corruption.③ Corruption concerns everyone from people at the grassroots level to national authorities with power. Bribery is found in both public and private sectors in Myanmar. Although the government is trying to

---

① The Rule of Law And Access to Justice Reform in Myanmar, Research Project Summaries, 2019-2020, Supported by the Denmark-Myanmar Programme on Rule of Law and Human Rights.

② Overview of corruption and anti-corruption in Myanmar, Mathias Bak, https://knowledgehub. transparency. org/assets/uploads/kproducts/Myanmar-country-profile-amended_U4-reviewed, last visited on Aug. 28, 2021.

③ Development of the Anti-corruption Mechanism in Myanmar, Ngwe Zaw Aung, https://www.unafei.or.jp/publications/pdf/GG11/18_GG11, last visited on Aug. 27, 2021.

combat and prevent corruption, some officials are ignoring the dignity of the state and their reputation by breaking the law. Therefore, Myanmar's corruption rank went down to 137 in 2020 from 130 in 2019. Transparency International's corruption rank of Myanmar averaged 154.11 from 2003 to 2020.[①]

Corruption is endemic in Myanmar, presenting companies with high risks. Many businessmen believe that corruptions, weak rule of law and complex and opaque licensing systems constitute serious obstacles to investment and trade in Myanmar.[②] Corruption is common in issuing permits or licensesing, processing applications or offering various forms of public services. According to Transparency International's Global Corruption Barometer—Asia Picific (2017), 40 percent of people in Myanmar paid a bribe when accessing a basic service. Another reason is low wages of government officials. The extraction of bribes is a common adaptation mechanism for low-wage officials, providing them with a significant source of income to supplement their salaries. [③]Furthermore, judicial corruption can impact the rule of law and the whole process of fair trials. Most people in Myanmar tend to have little trust in the ability of the justice sector to be fair. Many people do not trust its neutrality and the majority do not take legal action through statutory courts.

In order to reduce judicial corruption, the courts need greater transparency. Due to the lack of legal knowledge, a fear of going to court and a strong desire to win the case, Many people become the victims of brokers, who persuade the parties to commit corruption. Therefore, the courts have to promote the role of public relations department through which the court can provide information (both online and offline) to the public, listen to the public, receive complaints including those concerning judicial corruption and

---

① https://tradingeconomics.com/myanmar/corruption-rank, last visited on Apr. 28, 2021.

② Myanmar Corruption Report, September 2020, https://www.ganintegrity.com/portal/country-profiles/myanmar, last visited on Aug. 26, 2021.

③ Mathias Bak, Overview of Corruption and Anti-corruption in Myanmar, https://knowledgehub. transparency. org/assets/uploads/kproducts/Myanmar-country-profile-amended_U4-reviewed, last visited on Aug. 28, 2021.

negotiate issues between the court and the parties.

Myanmar is highly corrupt in every sector. So, Myanmar government needs to provide adequate salaries, facilitate for all staff, upgrade the basic infrastures for government officials, revise the complex processing for obtaining permits or licenses, and raise legal awareness of reducing corruption.

3.4 Performance of the Union Attorney General's Office for the Rule of Law and Anti-corruption

The Rule of Law is very important to implement the principles of political, economic, social and judicial matters. Law officers, judges, the police, lawyers and all legal professionals are very important persons for the implementation of rule of law. At present, courts and law offices are established under the new 2008 Constitution. As to the formation of courts, the Supreme Court of the Union (SCU) is the highest court and under it, there are High Courts of the Region or State, the District Courts and Township Courts. Law offices also law office and offices of Advocate General of the Region or State, are formed at the same levels of the court. The UAGO which if the head office is the highest law office.

The UAGO is an important organization in Myanmar as it serves as a legal advisory body to the Government of Myanmar. The UAGO's mandated require to interact with the legislative, the executive and the judicial power. The UAGO is the only one institution that involves all three pillars by supporting and balancing these three sectors. ① Therefore, the UAGO plays a very important role in the functions of the government. And in the same way the role of the law officer at every level is also crucial in implementing and promoting the Rule of Law in the country.

The UAGO upgrade the Rule of Law; it has well-planned strategies, which are "Moving Forward to the Rule of Law 2015-2019" and " Providing Legal Service for Justice 2020-2024". The UAGO's strategy is "moving forward to the Rule of Law"; its vision is "safeguarding the principles of the Rule of Law in Myanmar"; its mission is "to advance the government policy

---

① Constitution of the Union of Myanmar, 2008

of strengthening the Rule of Law". Under "Moving Forward to the Rule of Law", many goals are achieved such as publishing Fair Trial Standard, Guideline for Scrutinizing Joint Venture (JV), Land Lease Agreement, and Legislative Drafting Guidebook, establishing Myanmar Law Information System, and Union Coordinating Body (UCB) for the Rule of Law Centers and Justice Sector Affairs. Current strategic plan 2020-2024 contains five goals under which the UAGO is implementing fifteen objectives.

In regard with Rule of Law, the UAGO has been actively involved in the Rule of Law implementing activities under the strategic plan of UCB, 2019-2023. So far it has established several pilot law offices at township levels, which are conducting their duties to be in line with the fair trial standards in order to obtion public trust.

In addition, law officers shall scrutinize the corruption cases for sound construction before prosecuting at the relevant court by the prosecuting body in accordance with the law and appear in that cases on behalf of the Union under Section 36 of the Attorney-General of the Union Law. Besides, Union Attorney General's Office is also participating in public talk by sharing the legal knowledge about the anti-corruption Law. Therefore, the UAGO plays an important role in upholding the Rule of Law and combatting corruption in Myanmar.

4. Comparison of Anti-corruption in Myanmar and Singapore

Myanmar and Singapore were former British colonial countries. The Penal Code was originally based on Indian Law in these countries. Furthermore, both countries are practicing Anti-corruption Law. Singapore came third for its absence of corruption under the ASEAN countries' index. Although Myanmar formulated Anti-corruption Law for reducing corruption, its rank went down to 137 in 2020 from 130 in 2019. Therefore, this chapter deals with the comparison of Myanmar and Singapore in terms of the fight against corruption.

Effective laws provide the basis for the fight against corruption. Moreover, the other three related areas of enforcement, adjudication and government administration are very important in anti-corruption. If one part is inef-

fective, the whole is ineffective. Therefore, these four points must be balanced for combating corruption. Singapore has achieved sucess in keeping the country clean, preventing and controling corruption, and upholding a high standard of transparency, which would not have been possible without capitalizing on the four pillars of anti-corruption, namely, are strict laws, enforcement, tough punishment from the Courts and effective government administration. Although Myanmar has anti-corruption Law, the other three areas are still corrupt. Myanmar government can't arrange the effective administration for corruption. That's why the problem of corruption can't be controlled by the government of Myanmar.

The e-government system is one of the keys for reducing corruption. Because of the eGAP, people in Singapore can access government services from homes. Therefore, Singapore can control corruption. Myanmar started its e-government plan in 2016. ①But all ministries and the public can't well use that system. Because of this, people in Myanmar still pay a bribe when accessing basic services such as obtaining permits or licenses, filing applications or receiving various forms of public services. To address this problem, Myanmar government needs not only to develop the e-government system but also to revise the complex process of obtaining permits or licenses.

Another fact or is low wages of government officials. The two countries have increased the salaries for reducing corruption. But Singapore managed to reduce the gap between salaries of the private sector and the public sector. Myanmar government can't check and balance these two sectors. So, Myanmar government still needs a good plan to reduce corruption.

Furthermore, judicial corruption can impact the rule of law. Singapore's efficient, transparent and extremely sound legal system has been a key to the country's significant growth over the past few years. In contrast, judicial corruption still occurs in Myanmar. The government needs to raise legal awareness about corruption and promotes negotiation of issues between the

---

① Second Myanmar E-governance Master Plan to Include Systems for Cyber Crime, E-payments, https://www.mmtimes.com/news/second-myanmar-e-governance-master-plan-include-systems-cyber-crime-e-payments.html, last visited on Aug. 24, 2021.

court and the parties to curb corruption. The government need to review and revise the laws of Myanmar inconsistent with the present situation.

Myanmar and Singapore do not provide protection of whistle-blowers. Corruption offenses are particularly difficult to resolve. Unlike general crime where there is a victim who tells us everything that happened, in corruption offenses, both the giver and the receiver are guilty parties who possess the motivation to hide the truth. It makes investigations and the collection of evidence more difficult. Therefore, whistle-blowers should be protected under the Anti-Corruption Law.

Corruption attacks the foundation of democracy, the institution and the Rule of Law. Corruption is committed not only within one country but also in connection with other countries; therefoe, anti-corruption cannot be done by one country. Therefore, countries need to share information with and learn from each other. And we all have a common duty to fight the disease of corruption and make the world a better place to live in.

5. Lessons Learned From Singapore

ASEAN and ASEAN Member countries develop and implement policies to more effectively deter and combat corruption. All countries have laws aimed at fighting corruption, but very few governments apply such laws as strictly and consistently as Singapore.

One of the most important steps towards this achievement was the elimination of corruption for Rule of Law in Singapore's history. Singapore applied the anti-corruption measures consistently across the board, regardless of the degree of corruption. It is a cornerstone of the Rule of Law that no person should be above the law. Government officials are subject to the same laws as citizens, limited by checks and balances, and punished for corruption. Therefore, Singapore formulated strict rules and regulations which govern the conduct of public officers for combating corruption. Besides, Singapore can reduce the gap between salaries of the private and the public sectors.

Effective laws provide the basis for the fight against corruption. Rigorous enforcement is also significant. Government administration must be improved.

All these provide the impetus for Singapore's transformation from a corrupt city-state to the present state. Singapore enjoys a good reputation around the world. As a result, Singapore became the third for its lack of corruption in the world.

Myanmar has learned a great deal from Singapore regarding the fight against corruption. There is much more reform required for combatting corruption in Myanmar. The law must be strengthened. In order to prevent and reduce corruption, the government of Myanmar is taking action not only through the Anti-Corruption Law but also through other related laws. As society and the environment changes all the time, it is necessary to review the law periodically to ensure that it is up to date. Myanmar needs to fight corruption as written in the constitution and strengthen enforcement. Moreover, Myanmar should focus on strengthening accountability and competency within justice and government sectors for combatting corruption.

The experience of Singapore may not be replicated exactly anywhere else as every country has its unique character and circumstances. Nonetheless, corruption is a universal problem amongst mankind. Therefore, we have to promote cooperation in the fight against corruption with other countries and international organizations.

Conclusion

The Rule of Law is a term that can mean different things in different contexts. The Rule of Law is an essential part of every democratic society, because a country cannot be stable, peaceful and tranquil without the Rule of Law. The Rule of Law requires that the government exercise its authority in accordance with well-established and clearly written rules, regulations and legal principles. The laws should be consistent with government policy and public policy. Besides, all citizens need to follow and respect the laws for the Rule of Law.

Especially, the Rule of Law is based upon reduction in corruption, protection of economic rights and good governance. Reduction of corruption is one of the most important factors for the establishment of the Rule of Law.

Corruption undermines democratic institutions, slows economic development and contributes to governmental instability. Nowadays, corruption is becoming more widespread as a culture in society. Every country has laid down its priority in policy agendas to promote Rule of Law and combat corruption. We have the same commitment to fight corruption at all levels because it is taking place in the public and private sectors. Thus, the problem cannot be solved with a single initiative or institution.

In conclusion, corruption is a major obstacle to the Rule of Law. Although Myanmar is fighting against corruption, cases of corruption are still accurring in Myanmar. Therefore, Myanmar still needs to reform corruption-related sectors, which are the justice sector, administrative sector, government sector and public sector. The government has a major responsibility to improve the rules and practices to reduce opportunities for corruption, enforce laws and regulations against corruption, and prosecute and punish people who are found guilty of corruption. All citizens have the duty to fight against corruption for the Rule of Law.

Influences of the Regional Comprehensive Economic Partnership to Trade Rules in Lao PDR

Sengphet Bounmixay*

Abstract: Through multiple attempts of negotiating the Regional Comprehensive Economic Partnership (RCEP) agreement since 2012, the Agreement ultimately entered into force in November 2020. Laos is an active member country that has signed the said Agreement but never ratifies. The problem that comes to mind is how this mega trade policy could positively impact Less Developed Country (LDCs) such as Lao PDR? As a result of this, the study examines the impact of trade policy under that Agreement qualitatively. The study additionally highlights comparatively how Laos would enforce the Agreement, while several existing trade policies have been enforced in Laos. As a result, this research specifically addresses the RCEP trade policies in Goods and Trade in service and other substantial aspects to show significant implications for the trade legal system in Laos. The study's objective is to reveal the challenges that Laos may face and analyze how to overcome these challenges for efficiently implementing the Agreement. It is found that the Country's legal system, which may hinder the Agreement, requires substantial reforms.

Keywords: RCEP, Laos, Importance, Challenges

Introduction

RCEP agreement is an agreement proposed by the ASEAN countries with its partners during the 19th ASEAN meeting, held in November 2011. Its negotiations were started in 2012 during the 21st ASEAN meeting in

* Ph.D. candidate, the deputy director of National Institute of Justice, Laos.

Cambodia.[①] Over the time, the Agreement was signed by 15 countries, namely, Brunei, Cambodia, Indonesia, Laos, Malaysia, Myanmar, the Philippines, Singapore, Thailand, Vietnam, China, Japan, South Korea, Australia, and New Zealand and entered into force in November 2020.[②] Before entering into force of the Agreement, Initially, the 16 countries, including India, had negotiated the RCEP together. They account for a third of the world's gross domestic product (GDP) and almost half of the world's population, with the combined GDPs of China and India alone making up more than half of that. RCEP was aimed to create an integrated market with 16 countries, making it easier for products and services of each of these countries to be available across this region. The negotiations were focused on the following: trade in goods and services, investment, intellectual property, dispute settlement, e-commerce, small and medium enterprises, and economic cooperation, yet India has given up signing the Agreement because it protected its domestic economy, which may be impacted by the developed countries although the Agreement previewed and set out this risk to developing and LDCs countries. Despite India's withdrawal, the 15 countries left have insisted on concluding the Agreement with objectives of forming a modern, comprehensive, high-quality, and mutually-beneficial economic partnership. The countries involved have asserted that every signatory welcomes efforts to advance market access and text-based negotiations while remaining mindful of the considerable work that lies ahead. While acknowledging the complexities of the Agreement during the negotiations and the diversity of the Participating Countries, including differences in the level of development, the member countries resolve to find appropriate ways to address the various sensitivities and interests of each Participating Country to arrive at balanced, high-quality, and mutually-beneficial outcomes. The countries look for-

---

① The Agreement Entered into Force in November 2020, and 15 Countries Officially Constitute it, Namely, the ASEAN Countries with its FTA Partners. https://www.business-standard.com/about/what-is-rcep, last visited on Jun. 6, 2020.

② Joint Leaders' Statement on the Regional Comprehensive Economic Partnership (RCEP) September 8, 2016, Vientiane, Lao PDR.

ward to continued progress, including positive and constructive responses to market access requests. They have also reaffirmed the potential of an RCEP agreement to boost business confidence, benefit consumers, enhance contribution to global growth and regional economic integration, and equitable economic development for all Participating Countries.

Every Country in RCEP will benefit from the Agreement since they positively hope that the Agreement is prolific in adjusting all existing Free Trade Agreement (FTAs) and reducing the economic domination of western countries in the Asia Pacific region. Due to a confuse on about the Agreement in Laos and other countries, it's important to conduct empirical research. To determine the main objectives of the topic expressly, the author examines the theme of research by analyzing, interpreting, and comparing every concerning trade policy in Laos. Lao PDR has been supporting the said Agreement since the ASEAN countries' first attempts of negotiation. Accordingly, it proposed to improve and widen the ASEAN plus-one; meanwhile, the Lao government has been holding a strong belief since the commencement of the Agreement that it would increase the flexibility of its domestic trade policies. In referring to dispositions of the Agreement, Laos has more benefits in the Agreement through loose access to the international market and reaffirmed that RCEP membership would give the three LDCs countries with significant economic benefits in the form of access to the large regional market, including the Chinese market on preferential market access, since they have no available access to a market of the EU and that of the US, especially on preferential market access. That means that preferential access of LDCs to RCEP is crucial advantages. ①

In this research, to determine the RCEP agreement policy implication to Lao PDR to demand a deep and more focused analysis on specific issues that will be a positive and negative impact of the Agreement in its Policy with various parallel rules of international organization national Laos' law relating to Trade. Consequently, it is indispensable to analyze the legal policy on trade

① https://oecd-development-matters.org/2021/01/29/regional-comprehensive-economic-partnership-why-should-it-involve-the-excluded-ldcs, last visited on Jun. 6, 2020.

agreement which contains trade in goods, trade in service, trade facilitation, and rule of origins. These agreements are the main parts of the trade agreement in RCEP which are deemed to bring large changes to members like Lao PDR. Enforcement of those trade agreements is relatively determined through the country's economic level to avoid an inequitable interest to every member because the main objectives of the Agreement in trade are to benefit the developed, developing, and underdeveloped countries equally.

In addition, this research highlights the improvement of trade policy in Laos through the enforcement of RCEP, and the capability of the country for good implementation of the Agreement so that it can be prolifice conomically. In fact, it is challenging for Lao as an LDC to enforce and implement the Agreement fully; however, it is stipulated as a commitment that every country member should follow their economic capacity to attain balanced interest with accord to sustainable development.

The RCEP agreement faces challenges for being in parallel with other policies between Laos and other countries, even including the RCEP members, and it is not easy for Laos to determine the full implementation of RCEP agreement whether it is prolific or not, because the rules may be overlapped and confusion may also arise. Therefore, it is indispensable to forward more proper research on what RCEP agreements face parallel implementation, what are their differences?, and whether RCEP is important to improve the previously-existing Agreement or not.

1. RCEP Trade Policy

1.1 Trade Policy in Goods

The Trade in Goods chapter of RCEP contains key elements that govern the implementation of goods-related commitments to achieve a high trade liberalization among the Parties. These include granting national treatment to the other Parties' goods, reduction or elimination of customs duties, temporary duty-free admission of goods, and the reaffirmation of commitments in the World Trade Organization (WTO) Ministerial Decision on Export

Competition, including the elimination of scheduled export subsidy entitlements for agricultural goods. It also sets out rules for determining the applicable tariff treatment in cases of different tariff preferences applied by a Party. In addition, it contains provisions on non-tariff measures that complement tariff liberalization outcomes. Finally, this Chapter also sets out a process for Parties to conduct technical consultations on non-tariff measures that adversely affect trade between them and also provides for the possibility of future work to be undertaken on sector-specific initiatives to facilitate greater trade.

1.2 Trade Facilitation

The Trade Facilitation chapter aims to ensure predictability, consistency, and transparency in applying customs laws and regulations and promote the efficient administration of customs procedures and expeditious clearance of goods. For express consignments and perishable goods, the Agreement contains an expectation that these goods will be released from the customs control within six hours of arrival of the goods and the submission of necessary documents. The objective is to simplify customs procedures and promotes harmonization of customs procedures with international standards. It also contains enhanced trade facilitation provisions such as advance ruling based on tariff classification, rules of origin, customs valuation, the timeline for the issuance of advance rulings, and the period for the customs clearance of goods (to the extent possible within 48 hours of arrival of goods and lodgment of necessary information); provides additional trade facilitation measures related to import, export, or transit formalities and procedures for operators who meet specified criteria (authorized operators), and a risk management approach for customs control and post-clearance audits. In addition, it allows member countries to implement the policy in different stages.

The Trade Remedies consist of two Sections: Safeguard Measures as well as Anti-Dumping and Countervailing Duties. The Safeguard Measures Section provides the Parties with a transitional mechanism to address serious injury or threat of serious injury to the domestic industry caused by Parties' commitments under the RCEP Agreement, subject to well-defined conditions and requirements, including carrying out a proper investigation as well as early and full notifications to Parties concerned with opportunities for consultations. Besides, the Safeguard Measures Section also reaffirms Parties' rights and obligations provided under the Agreement on Safeguards in the WTO concerning global safeguard measures. The Anti-Dumping and Countervailing Duties Section reaffirms and builds on Parties' rights and obligations provided under the relevant Agreements in the WTO. While no Party can have recourse dispute settlement under the RCEP Agreement for any matter arising under the Section on Anti-Dumping and Countervailing Duties, the applicability of dispute settlement is considered in the general review of the RCEP Agreement.

1.3 Rule of Origin (ROO)

The ROO Chapter determines which goods originate under the RCEP Agreement and are eligible for preferential tariff treatment. The ROO Chapter has two Sections: Rules of Origin and Operational Certification Procedures. The ROO Section lists the minimal operations and processes considered insufficient to confer originating status on goods using non-originating materials. Given the geographic configuration of countries in the RCEP, the Parties ensured that the ROO includes clear, direct consignment rules, so that originating goods do not inappropriately lose their originating status. If a good does not satisfy a change in tariff classification rule in the Product-Specific Rules (PSR), the Agreement lays down certain de minimis rules whereby the good could still acquire originating status. Other elements covering Rules of Origin include the treatment applied to packing and packaging materials, containers for transportation and shipment, and the treatment of accessories, spare parts, and tools. And the Operational Certification Procedures section provides detailed procedures for applying the RCEP proof of origin, claiming preferential tariff treatment, and verifying the originating status of a good. The ROO further contains the Product-Specific Rules, which cover all tariff lines at the HS 6-digit level, and Minimum Information Requirements, listing the required information for a Certificate of Origin or a Declaration of Origin.

1.4 Trade in Services

The Trade in Services chapter aims to open up avenues for greater services trade among the Parties through substantial removal of restrictive and discriminatory measures affecting trade in services. This Chapter contains modern and comprehensive provisions, including rules on market access, national treatment, most-favored-nation treatment, and local presence, subject to Parties' Schedules of Specific Commitments or Schedules of Reservations Non-Conforming Measures, as well as additional commitments. Under the provisions, the Parties are to schedule their services commitments using the negative list approach, either on the date of entry into force of the RCEP Agreement or within a defined period after the date of entry into force of the RCEP Agreement. The chapter also includes provisions on the reasonability, objectivity, and impartiality of domestic regulations affecting trade in services, which go beyond equivalent rules in the existing ASEAN Plus-One FTAs.

The Annex on Financial Services promotes the liberalization of financial services in the region while providing a robust prudential safeguard that allows financial regulators to apply measures to preserve the integrity and stability of the financial system. In addition to the obligations established in the Trade in Services Chapter, the Annex prescribes specific obligations on the supply of financial services, and provides an avenue for consultations to discuss or resolve issues related to financial services.

The Annex on Telecommunications Services creates a framework of rules pertinent to trade in public telecommunications services. While all existing ASEAN Plus One FTAs with individual partners include an Annex on Telecommunications Services, additional obligations have been included in the RCEP Agreement about approaches to regulation; international submarine cable systems; unbundling of network elements; access to poles, ducts, and conduits; international mobile roaming; and flexibility in the choice of technology; among others.

The Annex on Professional Services provides an avenue for the Parties to facilitate engagement on the supply of professional services in the region. This includes the prospect of increased dialogue between two or more interested Parties related to the recognition of professional qualifications and encouragement to relevant bodies to negotiate arrangements for mutual recognition of professional qualifications, licensing, or a registration in professional services sectors of mutual interest. It also encourages the Parties or relevant bodies to develop mutually acceptable professional standards and criteria in mutually accepted areas, which may include education, examination, experience, conduct and ethics, professional development and re-certification, scope of practice, local knowledge, and consumer protection.

2. Impact of Enforcing RCEP Trade Agreement in Laos

Enforcement of the RCEP trade agreement in Laos may create large benefits in the field of business.① The Agreement is considered to bring about comprehensive improvement to all existing agreements before RCEP. The Agreement focuses more on improving the existing FTA agreements between the partners in East Asia, such as Improvement of ASEAN plus one FTA among themselves. Not only Laos may benefit from the RCEP trade policy. Yet, all country members, however, this research will figure out in a focused way the impact of enforcing RCEP trade agreement in Laos by studying every opportunity with developed and developing partners in the Agreement, such as the improvement of the trade agreement with China, and new improvement of trade agreement with developed countries.

2.1 Improving Lao PDR Trade Agreement with ASEAN Countries in the RCEP

The ASEAN countries are the pillar of establishing the RCEP agreement and they forecasted that it would be created for improving their existing Free Trade Agreement (FTAs). The Agreement is to serve as an overarching mechanism for bringing together the trading legal system. As envisaged

---

① According to the ranking on the capacity of State on doingbusiness. org, Laos is ranked 154 out of 191 States retrieved at https://www.doingbusiness.org/en/data/exploreeconomies/lao-pdr, last visited on Jun. 6, 2020.

since the commencement of negotiation, all members would benefit from the Agreement in terms of trade policy improvement because the previous existing Agreement, the so-called "ASEAN plus one FTA," shows its weakness in dealing with extensive economic cooperation among them. As a result, every country in ASEAN benefits from new and comprehensive trade policies to enhance the ASEAN plus one, and the country will have free access to the market among them in terms of trade in goods and services.

Therefore, Lao PDR would benefit form the trade system under the Agreement with its ASEAN partners; the Agreement also may enhance the trade policy and economic integration in Laos. Integrally the Agreement may induce improvement to opening business of Laos to other countries involved. The commitment of Laos under the ASEAN plus One FTA would improve. In detail, Laos' export and import to the ASEAN countries would widely extend to more than its performance in ASEAN plus one FTA because the RCEP agreement is specifically targeted at facilitating a complete trading system among its members. Concerning trade policy set by ASEAN charter among Lao's Neighboring Countries. Its partners need to enforce the RCEP because it supposedly creates adjustment to the weakness of the existing trading legal system. For example, the rule of origins (ROOs) is an important part of the RCEP agreement in improving the existing ASEAN FTA. Laos is a member country in ASEAN, which means that it gains and enjoys trade preferences from the Agreement among its partners in ASEAN. Under the said Agreement where the restrictions of the trade barriers diminish, Laos shall have advantages on preferences treatment in the ASEAN countries more than under provisions of ASEAN plus one ROOs. Also, problems of overlapping ROOs among them are reduced by the said Agreement.

Further, the RCEP contributes tremendous economic development to Laos by insuring against rising protectionist assumptions in the global economy on agreements on goods and services. This Agreement is supposed to rebuild changes to economic integration among them. And it is also estimated to help the expansion of sophisticated global chains that will promote East Asia to be the world's largest industry and region conforming to the Agreement scenario up to 2030.

2.2 Improving Laos' Trade Agreement with China

In terms of trade policy, China and Laos have many commitments in trade on goods, service and others alike. However, the nascent RCEP would comprehensively set out all trade climate issues, because the said Agreement encompasses all substantial FTA regulations. China has built a close economic relationship with Laos. Meanwhile, the RCEP of all previous trade rules would be improved largely, especially on facilitating preferential treatment and technical assistance on trade in services. Laos is likely to face the problem of overlapping FTA. Due to the RCEP trade policy, China's imports and exports would increase more than its previous participation. China will have an added incentive to increase business in Laos due to comparative advantages and the preferential market access under the regional arrangement. Many RCEP members are eyeing the lucrative Chinese market. Indeed, there is a high likelihood of trade diversion, and further, China's trade climate is affordable, especially in LDCs such as Laos.

2.3 Establishing Laos' Comprehensive Trade Agreement with Japan, South Korea, and Developing Countries Involved

RCEP agreement is relatively backing up the re-adjustment of trade policy between Laos and developed partners. Laos and Japan as well as Laos and South Korea had bilateral trade agreements before RCEP. Those agreements set out the trade policy to smoothly reach the export, import, and rules of tariffs and trade facilitation, not only, but they also have had tied by the other trade policy in ASEAN. As a result, RCEP would novelize the existing trade policies between Laos and these developed countries; meantime, trade rate exportation, importation, facilitation, and preferential treatment would increase.

It is expressly stated in an ASEAN Briefing that the said Agreement would boost products from the LDCs country like Laos in exporting to developing country partners in RCEP, because its rule of origin policies favor more participation in the international market. Further, a country qualified as lower-cost and lesser-skilled workers like Laos has a special treatment and interest

in the Agreement due to exchanges of experience with manufacturers from Australia, Japan, China, and South Korea. Production costs are higher, etc. In terms of trade, the developed countries help Laos in technical cooperation improvement, the capacity to develop and implement resilient economic development alongside other LDCs countries, the Country required to eliminate tariff rate to 30% of Trade compared to tariff elimination requirement to other developed countries. Laos' SMEs would likely to benefit from technical cooperation with advanced countries like Japan and South Korea by promoting competitive products and enhancing capacity building.①

3. Parallelism between RCEP Trade Policy and Other Trade Policies in Laos before the RCEP Agreement

3.1 WTO and RCEP Trade Rules in Laos

In the context of RCEP, WTO trade policies are amongst an international agreement that has significant roles in ruling trade among members; meanwhile, RCEP recognizes the existence of WTO within its policies. Accordingly, some chapters of the RCEP agreement recognize policies in WTO and allow them to be applied in issues about trade climate among members. As stipulated in Chapter 2 of said Agreement that National treatment on internal taxation and regulation And reduction or elimination of customs duties.

In other words, since both agreements are implemented parallel in Lao PDR, the country must respect both agreement dispositions. Even though RCEP recognizes some parts of WTO policies, it does not mean that they are complementary; they are independent dispute settlement bodies. The two agreements are alternatively applied, and that would risk confusion as to

① Amrita Saha, Saon Ray, Can the RCEP Strengthen Global Cooperation for Trade, Investment, and Sustainable Development? https://www.ids.ac.uk/opinions/can-the-rcep-strengthen-global-cooperation-for-trade-investment-and-sustainable-development/, last visited on Dec. 11, 2020.

which law shall be applied when a dispute occurs. Moreover, as RCEP is a comprehensive Agreement, it contains more than WTO policies and deemed the newest trade policy to supplement all existing FTAs, which face decay and confusion in ruling trade issues in East Asia with Laos' partners.① The said Agreement is more detailed than WTO policies in terms of trade-related investment, including a most-favored-nation treatment clause and commitments on the prohibition of performance requirements that go beyond their multilateral obligations under the WTO Trade-Related Investment Measures (TRIMS) Agreement.②

4. RCEP and Other Trade Policies in Laos

In Laos, there are other trade policies which are overlapped with RCEP, such as bilateral FTAs with various countries, especially with the other member countries of ASEAN; however, apparently, the said Agreement integrates the FTAs in Laos with member countries into one to avoid different branches of rules that may cause altercations. Apart from trade policy, there are many agreements such as Investment and other international FTAs in Laos set out in the RCEP agreement. Therefore, all policies concerning trade and investment among the members are all set out by the Agreement, and it would help Laos to be able to deal with disputes because RCEP dispute settlement organs help facilitation of resolution for disputes targeted in the country, which means that the Agreement not only sets the rules but also mitigate the role of Lao's in dealing with trade and investment matters.

Saying about trade-related investment in Laos that RCEP agreement upholds policies in trade and investment through adjusting equality of member countries in RCEP in making trade in Lao PDR; meanwhile, every member country shall be treated equally before trade and investment targeted in the country because even in investment, Laos has set out this equality of treat-

① Patrick Leblond Digital Trade: Is RCEP the WTO's future? https://www.cigionline.org/articles/digital-trade-rcep-wtos-future, last visited on Nov. 23, 2020.

② See Summary of RCEP Agreement.

ment. Still, this new Agreement helps it to access all partner countries. And other words, laws, and regulations in Laos sometimes lack clarity, and overlap with various related regulations are commonly challenged. It seems that laws are not accessible easily and often lack English translationas well as transparency in regulations and administrative practices. The government of Laos strives to promote its investment to attract foreign trade and foreign direct investment. These are upgraded by RCEP trade policy by regulating affordable customs, taxes, labor, and awareness to protect ownership.

5. Suggestion for Conducive Implementation of RCEP in Laos

As is known, Laos has one of the most structurally-handicapped groups of economies in the world, trying to integrate itself in an accelerated and balanced way in to the international trading system. Henceforth, to implement the RCEP agreement efficiently and equitably in Laos, many internal legal system flaws shall be adjusted. Several lessons can be drawn from the RCEP, particularly for Laos. One key lesson is that negotiating comprehensive partnership agreements is central to sustainable graduation strategies, yet Laos must pursue a proactive legal system conducive to global goods in the country. Before ratifying the RCEP, Laos has to ensure the capability of the domestic policy, institutions, and domestic market. After the Agreement is ratified, the international goods from developed and developing countries will flood the domestic market, so Laos has to accentuate policy to avoid this likely negative impact.

In addition, the country does not have commercial law which is supposed to deal with the issues relating to foreign and domestic traders in the country. This lack of a legal system may hamper the implementation of the Agreement effectively. Therefore, accentuating and even reforming, the rule of law in the country is perceived as a suggestion to make it compatible with trade rules. Accordingly, the country must consider that such partnerships entail a certain degree of reciprocity, commitments, and obligations. As a LDC, Laos enjoys preferential treatment mostly on a non-reciprocal basis. Still, it has demonstrated its readiness to deal with these challenges by undertaking the required economic reforms, policy changes, and institutional strengthening. It has committed to undertaking trade liberalization measures and ensuring compliance with obligations in non-tariff barriers, e-commerce, patents, copyrights, international property rights, labor and environmental standards, and others.①

6. Conclusion and Recommendation

In short, RCEP agreement encompasses all economic agreements akin to trade, investment, and other related sectors among countries in East Asia with its partners. The Agreement contains provisions concerning trade in goods, trade facilitation, trade remedies, rule of origins, sanitary and phytosanitary, trade in services, etc. Not only does the Agreement encompasses all international FTAs, but it further recognizes some agreements of international trade organizations such as the WTO, ASEAN, and other bilateral FTAs between partner countries. In comparing the regulations stipulated in the Agreement with other agreements that novelize the rules profitably use in facing challenges among regions. Accordingly, trade agreements contextualize tariff reduction and elimination of non-tariff measures, regulate preferential treatment for original goods, and facilitate as quick as possible the trade process by types of goods imported.②

The Agreement has tremendous policies and economic implications to every member country, especially the LDCs like Lao PDR. It is deemed that the Agreement brings clarity on overlapping trade policies in Laos and supplements the decaying rules and capability of the government in dealing with trade rules and issues engendering from practices of trade and business-related trade with member countries, and it overlaps with regulations of other international organizations like WTO, ASEAN, and CPPT within its members; however, it works in parallel with most agreements it contains.

① https://oecd-development-matters.org/2021/01/29/regional-comprehensive-economic-partnership-why-should-it-involve-the-excluded-ldcs/, last visited on Jun. 6, 2020.

② See the Chapter of Trade Facilitation in RCEP Agreement.

The issue is that Lao PDR may unbalance treatment for other partner countries which are not parties to RCEP. Therefore, it will undermine the trade climate of those countries in comparison to members in RCEP. Moreover, it contains only little change in the area of intellectual property and enforcement; however, in terms of e-commerce, RCEP does contain new provisions which are intended to support small and medium enterprise engagement with e-commerce and flow of data, promote privacy and consumer protection, and enable electronic authentication and electronic signature.

Even though the RCEP agreement is viewed as a large and well-compiled agreement since it conceptualizes all trade policies, it is complicated to enforce it fully by the fact that every country's economic levels are completely different since there are LDCs that do not have efficient power to implement the trade policy in a good way so that it can benefit them; as a result, they may denigrate the Agreement or relinquish membership. This is why India withdrew from the Agreement. The Agreement may also provoke losses in the trade environment of LDCs significantly. Take Laos as an example. Its trade may face severe negative impact because of large trade caused by countries like Japan, South Korea, Australia, and China. It is not easy to perceive that SMEs in the country may not compete with those from the developed countries installed in Laos.

The implementation of RCEP agreement policies in every country member shall be stringent; every country shall enforce the rules into domestic rules to avoid any confusion among the countries. The existence of the Agreement also shall be known to every person who is doing trade and investment. It always happens to LDCs like Laos that the small business actor has limited pieces of knowledge on the expansion of trade climate and their rights. They should be aware that their country is a member in the Agreement as well, so that they can claim any measures taken by other countries violating the provisions in the Agreement.

The Problems and Counter-measure of the Myanmar Investment Law after the Effective Implementation of the Regional Comprehensive Economic Partnership

Tin Myat Zin*

Abstract: Myanmar has undergone a series of gradual and radical economic reform since the new government came to power in March 2011. Liberalization of trade and foreign investment is an integral part of these economic reforms. The government of Myanmar is actively encouraging export diversification and promoting downstream processing of primary commodities, improving support services in trade financing, market access and trade facilitation as well as removing barriers to inbound foreign direct investment (FDI). Increased economic integration into ASEAN does not really cause trade diversion. The Myanmar government intends to prepare WTO-compatible trade remedy laws and regulations. Technical assistance in preparing the relevant legislation and regulations is needed. Prospect for Myanmar's economic growth for 2019 and 2020 looks positive as the country opens up the retail and wholesale sectors and continues to modernize corporate governance and management.

1. Introduction

The Regional Comprehensive Economic Partnership (RCEP) is a free trade agreement that had been negotiated among the group of 10 ASEAN member

* Ph. D. Candidate of SWUPL, officer of MOLA, Myanmar.

states and its 6 dialogue partners, namely, China, Japan, South Korea, India (In 2019, India opted out of RCEP), Australia and New Zealand since 2012. Myanmar became a member of the world's largest free trade agreement by signing the Regional Comprehensive Economic Partnership (RCEP) Agreement. It covers nearly 30% of the global gross domestic product. RCEP will progressively lower tariffs and aims to counter protectionism, boost investment and allow freer movement of goods within the region. However, India announced on the RCEP summit held in Thailand in November 2019 that it would no longer participate in the RCEP negotiations due to the failure of the other 15 countries to comply with Indian Prime Minister's request on trade and investment issues. Therefore, 10 ASEAN member countries and 5 countries of China, Japan, South Korea, Australia and New Zealand continued the discussions until 2020 and have signed the RCEP Agreement.[①]

Around 2.2 billion people, representing almost 30% of the world's population with a combined GDP of US $26.2 trillion, about 30% of global GDP and 28% of the global trade, make RCEP the world's largest free trade agreement[②]. The signing of the trade deal (RCEP) represents a milestone moment for Myanmar.[③]

Myanmar became a member of the Association of Southeast Asian Nations (ASEAN) in 1997 and has been allowed to participate in ASEAN activities. ASEAN Free Trade Area (AFTA) was established in 2018. As a result, ASEAN countries have become more competitive and have been able to freely invest in goods and services.

After establishing the free trade area within the 10 ASEAN countries, ASEAN will continue to sign free trade agreements with 6 dialogue partners and implemented 5 free trade zones.

---

① http://www.thaibizmyanmar.com, last visited on Nov. 16, 2020.

② U Than Aung Kyaw (Ministry of Investment and Foreign Economic Relations) (MIFER), Myanmar Becomes a Member of the World's Largest Free Trade Area by Signing the Regional Comprehensive Economic Partnership Agreement, Article from "the Mirror" newspaper, last visited on Nov. 16, 2020.

③ THIHA, RCEP Opens up a New Chapter for Myanmar, https://consult-myanmar.com, last visited on Nov. 24, 2020.

All ASEAN countries and its dialogue partners have agreed to sign the Regional Comprehensive Economic Partnership Agreement (RCEP), which is inclusive and beneficial to all Member States with the objective to reap the full benefits of deepening economic cooperation within these free trade countries. And 25 working groups have convened for the 21st ASEAN Summit in Phnom Penh, Cambodia, on November 20, 2012.

Negotiations were coordinated by the Trade Coordinating Committee and 9 sub-working groups and 7 sub-working groups under it. The RCEP Agreement was signed as a signal undertaking.

At the second RCEP Summit in November 2018, all the negotiations were directed to conclude by 2019. It had been almost 6 years from the negotiation to agreement of conclusion.

The Guiding Principles and Objectives for Negotiating the RCEP were approved by the Ministers of participating countries. Consideration was given to the different development levels of the countries involved and the agreement was being negotiated using the provisions for special and differential treatment in accordance with the relevant ASEAN Free Trade Agreement.

As RCEP is a broader regional economic partnership, it will address the status quo between any two member countries and so-called "noodle bowl effect". In addition, the RCEP will open up markets and trade, giving ASEAN countries like Myanmar more choices and opportunities for global value change.

By joining the RCEP, goods, services and investments will be more open to trade, trade barriers reduced, and trade and investment between member countries more transparent.[①]

2. Benefit of Joining the RCEP

Least developed countries like Myanmar will gain positive impact by signing the RCEP agreement. The RCEP agreement takes into account the

① Daw Saw Kalyar (Ministry of Investment and Foreign Economic Relations)(MIFER), Myanmar's Participation in Regional Economic Cooperation which Represents 40% of the World Trading, Article from The New Light of Myanmar Newspaper, last visited on Apr. 23, 2019.

different levels of the development among the signatories; particularity Cambodia, Laos and Myanmar will enjoy more privileges than other countries on tariff elimination. The RCEP member countries will apply duty-free measures to 65% of product lines at the time when the agreement takes effect, but the three countries (Cambodia, Laos and Myanmar) will only need to decrease tariffs by 30%. After ten years, the other countries will have to further eliminate customs tariffs to 80% but Myanmar will be allowed to have fifteen years to do so. Signatories also agreed that the least developed countries would consider the need to implement the commitments under this Agreement effectively and profitably in their efforts to be integrated into interregional and global production and value chains in order to further expand trade and investment opportunities.

As a member of ASEAN, Myanmar is committed to becoming a member of the modern and advanced RCEP. It will provide an opportunity to bring the framework and procedures in line with the international standards, and to increase the capacity of the government and private sector organizations to meet such international standards. The agreement will provide a market opportunity for Myanmar's exports to the developed countries such as Japan, South Korea, Australia, New Zealand and Singapore. Most of the technologically advanced economies in Asia, such as Singapore, are subject to the terms and conditions of the agreement when bringing in the responsible quality investment.

3. How Can Myanmar Get Benefits from Being a Member of the Regional Comprehensive Economic Partnership?

From the very beginning of the RCEP agreement, it considered the various stages of development of the signatories and decided to give special privileges to Vietnam, Cambodia, Laos and Myanmar. The signing of the Regional Comprehensive Economic Partnership (RCEP) among 15 members provides crucial momentum to redouble their strong commitment to pursuing free trade. The members of the RCEP also agreed to provide additional concessions to the least developed countries under the terms of the U-

nited Nations, if necessary, in accordance with the terms of the agreement. In terms of future developments, the agreement also allows on extension of the transition period for Myanmar from a minimum of 3 years to a maximum of 10 years in the implementation of the commitments concerning e-commerce, intellectual property rights and competition.

In the government procurement section, Myanmar will be exempt from contractual obligations and will need transparent cooperation between member countries. As a member of the Association of Southeast Asian Nations (ASEAN), Myanmar will have the opportunity to upgrade its framework and procedures to international standards. Myanmar will also have the right to enhance its trade and investment by becoming a member of the RCEP. RCEP also allows considerable flexibility and includes special provisions for differential treatment, especially for Cambodia, Laos, Vietnam and Myanmar. This ensures that economies at different levels of development, businesses of varying sizes and the broader range of stakeholders have opportunities to maximize the benefits from implementing their commitments.①

Nowadays, trade tensions have risen between some of the world's major powers due to the pursuit of protectionist policies. In this situation, the successful signing of the RCEP agreement, which includes the world's major economies, such as China, Japan, South Korea, New Zealand and Australia, is an opportunity not only for the region but also for the global economy. The RCEP agreement will provide a wider market for Myanmar's exports, which may help to revive Myanmar's economy in the aftermath of the COVID-19 pandemic.

Especially, in the post—COVID-19 era, Myanmar will receive the necessary technology and assistance in accordance with the provisions in the Economic and Technological Cooperation Chapter of this Agreement.

Small and medium enterprises will also have the opportunity to become more economically integrated between the 15 RCEP member states. They

① J.W. Kang (2020) Regional Comprehensive Economic Partnership (RCEP): Overview and Economic Impact. ADB, http://www.adb.org/publications/regional-comprehensive-economic-partnershi-impact, last visited on Apr. 24, 2021.

will also have the opportunity to connect with the global production network. There are chapters that are not included in the previous ASEAN trade agreements, such as the e-commerce, small and medium enterprise (SME), government procurement and intellectual property. These chapters will be essential areas for the establishment of the World Free Trade Area. For example, the inclusion of e-commerce will enable the cross-border e-commerce to be streamlined by enacting the e-commerce legal framework and procedures of each country in accordance with international regulations. In addition, the inclusion of intellectual property rights provisions encourages member countries to innovate, which will help protect and preserve the traditional culture.

4. Post Regional Cooperation and Integration in Myanmar before Signing the RCEP Agreement

Myanmar is a founding member of the WTO and at the regional level, has been a member of the Association of Southeast Asian Nations (ASEAN) since 1997, with current component agreements on goods, services and investment. With other ASEAN member states to the south and east, China to the north-east, and India and Bangladesh to the west, Myanmar borders the countries with more than two billion people and the fastest growing markets in the world. Thus the government of Myanmar attaches a high priority to regional integration and cooperation with ASEAN's member states and its Dialogue Partners, namely Japan, South Korea, China, India, Australia and New Zealand. While the eventual aim of the ASEAN Free Trade Area (AFTA) is to eliminate import barriers to all products within the region by 2015, Myanmar enjoys some flexibility, which allows it to eliminate tariffs and non-tariff barriers by 2018.

The outcome is that Myanmar's trade with ASEAN Member States and its Dialogue Partners accounted for about 95% of total trade in the past few years. In order to ensure the free flow of services, Myanmar was also committed to liberalizing intra-ASEAN trade in its services sectors by 2015. In order to increase intra-ASEAN investment and attract foreign investment

into ASEAN, the ASEAN Comprehensive Investment Agreement (ACIA) was signed in 2009 with the intention of streamlining existing ASEAN Investment Agreements.

One of the potential benefits from further cooperation and integration with neighboring countries is that the government of Myanmar is focused on meeting the requirements for the establishment of the ASEAN Economic Community (AEC), with freer flow of goods, services, capital and skilled labor. Signed by ASEAN Leaders at the 13th ASEAN Summit on November 20, 2007, the AEC Blueprint lays the foundation for realizing the goal of ASEAN as an integrated economic region by 2015. The AEC consists of four pillars: a single market and production base, a highly competitive economic region, a region of equitable economic development, and a region that is fully integrate into the global economy.

Each of the four pillars involves various measures and initiatives that are being implemented to achieve the goals of the AEC. Myanmar plans to address the legislative and regulatory limitations that impede the timely implementation of intra-and extra-ASEAN commitments. It also plans to strengthen the Ministry of National Planning and Economic Development (MNPED), the national coordinating agency for AEC, to effectively coordinate implementation across various focal points and implementing agencies. The government of Myanmar has also informed and engaged the private sector to assess the preparedness and effectiveness of policies and measures. It has also facilitated the establishment by the Union of Myanmar Federation of Chambers of Commerce & Industry (RUMFCCI) of a well-functioning mechanism to monitor the outcomes, analyze the impacts, and address the capacity gaps to ensure that the achievement of the AEC targets will deliver maximum benefits to the private sector. To ensure a timely implementation of the AEC initiatives, ASEAN has established a monitoring mechanism called the AEC Scorecard. As a compliance tool, the AEC Scorecard reports progress in implementing the various AEC measures, identifies implementation gaps and challenges, and tracks the realization of the AEC by 2015. Judging by the latest report issued by the ASEAN Secretariat in 2012, Myanmar's progress is comparable to other ASEAN Members, except re-

garding measures to promote the free flow of capital. However, the AEC Scorecard only states that Myanmar has signed ASEAN-wide agreements and that they have been transposed into national laws; the actual degree of implementation and enforcement of specific initiatives may still lag behind the agreed schedule. Nevertheless, the Government intends to implement all its ASEAN commitments by 2015 or 2018 in accordance with the built-in flexibility. As a consequence of its membership of ASEAN, Myanmar also participates in ASEAN's preferential agreements with China, India, Japan, South Korea, Australia and New Zealand. Moreover, with a view to promoting greater economic integration in the Greater Mekong Sub-region (GMS), Myanmar, Cambodia, Lao PDR, Thailand, Viet Nam, and Yunnan Province of China have been involved in the GMS Program (launched in 1992), whose purpose is to enhance economic linkages across these countries' borders. In 2010, the GMS countries approved a comprehensive medium-term program of Actions for Transport and Trade Facilitation (TTF). Moreover, Myanmar is a member of the Bay of Bengal Initiative for Multi-Sectoral Technical and Economic Cooperation (BIMSTEC), which provides a forum to facilitate and promote trade, investment, and technical cooperation among Bangladesh, Bhutan, India, Nepal, Sri Lanka, and Thailand.

5. Participation in RCEP Will Not Negative Affect Myanmar Domestic Market

Myanmar joined ASEAN in 1997 and is a member of ASEAN free trade area in accordance with the terms and conditions of the ASEAN free trade agreement. In addition, Myanmar joined the ASEAN and China Free Trade Agreement (ACFTA) (2004), ASEAN and Japan Comprehensive Economic Partnership Agreement (2008), ASEAN and India Free Trade Agreement (AITIGA) (2009) and so on. Myanmar has gained experience of more than a decade in participation in free trade area with six countries. According to the above FTAs, sign by Myanmar centered on ASEAN.

6. Entry into Force

All RCEP parties will begin their respective domestic procedures required for implementation. The agreement will enter into force 60 days after six ASEAN Member States and three Dialogue Partners have summited their instruments of ratification to the Secretary-General of ASEAN, who acts as the depository for the agreement. For ASEAN countries, sources within Thailand's Ministry of Commerce (MOC) indicated that it usually takes up to 6-12 months to complete their ratification procedure for each ASEAN FTA. For ASEAN's dialogue partners, it will likely take at least 6 months to complete their ratification procedures. The RCEP agreement is likely to enter into force in late 2021 or early 2022 although it may take business more time to understand how to utilize the agreement and take advantage of its benefits. For new members, RCEP will be open for accession 18 months after its entry into force although the procedures for accession have yet to be adopted by RCEP Joint Committee①.

7. Legal Framework of Investment in Myanmar

In 2014, the new government of Myanmar began to work on the new investment law, intended not only to further liberalize the investment regime but also address the redundancy of two distinct investment laws. A draft consolidated investment was published in early 2015, and the draft revised in early 2016, under the auspices of the new government. The new law aims to simplify and streamline the investment screening and approval processes and liberalize the entry conditions, both intended to attract more foreign direct investment as well as promoting domestic investment.

The Government of Myanmar make known to all a new Myanmar Investment Law (MIL), which combined and replaced the previous Foreign

① https://www. whitecase. com/publications/alert/15-asia-pacific-countries-sign-world-largest-fta-closet-look-rceps-key-outcomes, last visited on Apr. 23,2019.

Investment Law 2012 and the Citizens Investment Law 2013. The MIL came into effect on October 18, 2016. The MIL covers the overall legal framework, including Myanmar Investment Rules 2017, which came into effect on March 30, 2017, as well as two notifications: Notification 13/2017 dated April 1, 2017 (Classification of Promoted Sector) and Notification 15/2017 dated April 10, 2017 (List of Restricted Investment Activities). Together, these represent the body of the current Myanmar foreign investment laws. The Myanmar Investment Commission (MIC) announced the classification of promoted sectors on April 1, 2017, in exercise of the power offered under Section 43 and Sub-section (b) of Section 100 of the Myanmar Investment Law, with the approval of Union Government. Among the promoted sectors, the MIC prioritized manufacturing infrastructure development and agriculture sectors, and gave importance to sectors which provide employment opportunities and offer vocational training to improve the skills of domestic workers.

Regarding prohibited sectors for foreign investment, the MIC defined 15 sectors in February 2017. The prohibited sectors comprise periodical journal publications, freshwater fishing and related services, animal husbandries, food manufacturing and distributing industries, animal regulation and care centers, pet care centers, timber industries in government-owned forest areas, medium-sized mining, testing and producing mineral products in mines, oil drilling, visa stickers, foreigner stay permit printing and distributing business, mini-markets and convenience stores. Nevertheless, some businesses, like fisheries and shrimp forms, veterinary services, and the production of fishnets, accept foreign investments in the form of a joint venture with local business or domestic companies. In addition, the business must follow procedures and restrictions issued by the Department of Fisheries. Moreover, retail-related services such as City Mart and convenience stores will be prohibited from joining foreign firms. Lastly, permission has to be granted if a foreigner wants to enter a joint venture with either Myanmar nationals or local firms. The Investment Rules provide momentous further details and the business activities in which foreigners are permitted to engage; the restrictions applied to application procedures, the use of land, and transfer of shares, foreign currency remittance, the taking of security on land and buildings, and labor relations. The MIL, the Investment Law, Rules, Notifications are the key portions of legislation underpinning the Government's endeavor to attract foreign investment in Myanmar. When doing investment in Myanmar, foreign investors can benefit from significant tax exemptions and other benefits according to the Myanmar Investment Law. To be eligible, the foreign company needs to apply to the Myanmar Investment Commission (MIC) for an MIC Permit or MIC Endorsement.

In the new Myanmar Investment Law, there are new types of approval for an MIC Endorsement for investors whose business does not require an MIC Permit. In this case, the investor can apply for an MIC Endorsement to obtain long-term leases, tax exemption and other incentives. Land lease policy has also been reformed under the new law: foreign investors are competent to lease land directly from private owners and to have longer leases than the 50 + 10 + 10 standard in under-developed regions.

However, Myanmar does not have any legislation pertaining to anti-dumping and countervailing duties or safeguard measures. Myanmar needs technical assistance in preparing the relevant legislation and regulations.

7.1 Form of Investment in Myanmar

According to the Myanmar Investment Law, the certain economic actions are reserved for the State, prohibited from foreign investment, open to foreign investment, open to foreign investment in the form of joint ventures with a local partner, and open to foreign investment with the approval of a Government Ministry (e.g. natural resources). Foreign investors must set up a local company in order to be eligible for the advantages of the MIL. If a joint venture is formed, the ratio of foreign and local capital can be mutually prescribed by both parties.

7.2 Prohibited and Restricted Investment in Myanmar

The prohibited and restricted businesses are the business involving the importation of hazardous or poisonous wastes into Myanmar; business involving technologies, medicines, flora and fauna and/or instruments which are

still being tested and/or not internationally approved, except for investment in research and development; investment that impact upon the traditional culture and customs of Myanmar's ethnic groups; investment in activities which are contrary to the public interest; investment in activities which pose a significant threat to the environment; investment in the manufacturing of products prohibited by Myanmar law.

7.3 Priority Investment Promotion Sectors

At the moment, Myanmar is promoting investment in labor-intensive industries, agricultural-based industries, and infrastructure projects.

7.4 Tax Exemption and Relief

The MIL provides international investors with numerous tax exemptions and reliefs such as exemption from corporate tax for 3-7 years, depending on whether the investment takes place in an "underdeveloped", "moderately developed", or "adequately developed region". The specification of these zones is subject to change from time to time, relying on the development in the respective regions. The tax ememptions and relie include exemption from customs duties or other internal taxes or both on machineries, equipment, instruments machinery components, spare parts, construction materials not available locally, and materials used in the business that are imported as they are actually required, during the construction period, or during the preparatory period of the investment business; exemption or relief from customs duties and/or other domestic taxes on raw materials and semi-finished goods that are imported for the production of export goods by wholly export investment businesses, right to obtain a refund, based on the amount of exported goods, of customs duties and other domestic taxes paid at the time of importation of raw materials and semi-finished goods that are used to manufacture the products in the country and re-export them, if the quantity of investment is increased and the original investment or business is enlarged during the period of investment; exemption or relief from customs duties or other internal taxes or both, on machineries, equipment, instruments, machinery components, spare parts, materials used in the business, and construction materials not available locally, which are imported as they are actually required for use in the business that is being enlarged; exemption or relief from income tax if the profits obtained from the investment business is reinvested in the same business or in a similar type of investment business within one year, right to deduct depreciation for the purpose of income tax assessment, after computing such depreciation from the year of commencement of commercial operation based on an accelerated depreciation rate (which is less than the stipulated lifetime of the asset).

Right to deduct expenses from assessable income incurred for research and development related to the investment activities/business required for the development of the country and carried out in the country. Foreign investors will pay income tax at the rates applicable to citizens residing within the country. Tax incentives are not granted automatically. The Investment Rules make it clear that an investment must be in a promoted sector in addition to the investor being granted an MIC Permit or MIC Endorsement in order for the investor to benefit from the income tax incentive of either 3, 5 or 7 years. Companies engaged in "non-promoted" activities will not receive a tax holiday. If the activity is on the "promoted list", the tax holiday period will be determined based on whether the investment will be located in Zone 1, 2 and/or 3. Companies whose minimum capital is less than US$300,000 will not qualify for a tax holiday.

7.5 Land Usage in Myanmar

An investor who obtains an MIC Permit or an MIC Endorsement has the right to obtain a long-term lease of land or building for an initial period of 50 years with an option to extend the lease by two periods of 10 years.

The investor shall register the land lease contract at the Office of Registry of Deeds in accordance with the Myanmar Registration Act. The Myanmar Government may grant leases for government-owned land on more-favourable terms and conditions.

7.6 Guarantee for Investment

Section 52 of the MIL provides for the "astonishing expropriation" of

assets. According to Section 52 of the MIL, the Government can adopt "non-discriminatory manner" for the benefit of regulating economic or social activity including reasonable measures to protect "citizens' morals" or maintain public interest or national security. "Expropriation clauses" such as Section 52 are commonly used in international investment agreements. Fair and adequate compensation shall be paid equivalent to the prevailing market value at the time of expropriation of the investment. Section 53 clarifies that compensation for the indirect expropriation would normally be equal to an investment's fair market value, but that other factors should also be taken into account.

7.7 Transfer of Shares

The Investment Rules prevent a foreign investor to transfer shares to another foreign investor or Myanmar citizen. In the case of insolvency, the protection of the rights of creditors, criminal offences, financial reporting or records keeping of transfers to help financial regulatory authorities and law enforcement body, ensuring compliance with orders of judicial or administrative proceedings, taxation, social security, public retirement or compulsory savings schemes, severance entitlements of employees, the government can prevent or delay the transfer of funds.

7.8 Foreign Currency Issues

The MIL supplies guarantees for the remittance in foreign currency of imported foreign capital and profits. Such remittance may be made through any bank authorised to perform international banking, at the prescribed exchange rate.

7.9 Dispute Resolution

The MIL comprises dispute-resolution mechanisms. Disputes that cannot be settled amicably are to be resolved in accordance with the dispute resolution provisions in the investment contract. If no such provisions are provided, then Myanmar laws regarding dispute resolution shall apply.

7.10 Insurance

According to Article 73 of the MIL, foreign investors are obligatory to obtain insurance from state-approved insurance companies.

7.11 Appointment of Employees

The MIL contains a number of provisions in respect to employment matters. According to the MIL, an investor may appoint any citizen (foreign or local) to qualified positions such as senior management positions, technical and operational positions, and advisors on the investment project. And then the investors shall provide training and capacity building programs for the citizen. Moreover, the investors shall appoint only Myanmar citizens to unskilled positions. The investor shall ensure that employees are provided with employment contracts in accordance with Myanmar existing law and that employees receive the entitlements and rights offered to them under Myanmar law, including minimum wages, leave, holiday, overtime fee, damages, compensation, social welfare, and other insurance. What is more, the investor shall settle disputes arising among employers, among workers, between employers and workers, technicians or staff in the investment in accordance with Myanmar law.

7.12 Treatment of Investors

The investors are conferred the national treatment, "the treatment no less favorable than it accords to Myanmar citizen investors in respect of the expansion, management, operation and the sale or other disposition of direct investments"①, most-favored-nation treatment, "treatment no less favorable than that it accords to investors of any other country and their direct investments in respect of establishment, acquisition, expansion, management, operation, and the sale or other disposition of direct investments"②, fair and equitable treatment in the matters of prevailing the rele-

---

① Section 47 (a) of Myanmar Investment Law.

② Section 47 (b) of Myanmar Investment Law.

vant information on any measures or decision which has an impact on the investor, and the right to due process and the right to appeal.

Many of Myanmar's investment treaties contain most-favored-nation (MFN) clauses. The effect of these provisions is that any benefit extended to foreign investors from one country under one investment treaty may need to be extended to foreign investors covered by Myanmar's other investment treaties. As a result, Myanmar Investment Law grants a combination of benefits to foreign investors that is more generous than the benefit provided by any one of Myanmar's investment treaties, considered individually.

8. Investment Sector in Regional Comprehensive Economic Partnership

RCEP is relatively comprehensive in coverage①. It involves 20 chapters and includes many areas that ASEAN plus One FTAs did not cover②. The RCEP agreement has specific provisions for trade in goods, rules of origin, customs procedures and trade facilitation, sanitary and phytosanitary measures, standards, technical regulations, conformity assessment procedures, and trade remedies. Its chapters also encompass trade in services including provisions on financial, telecommunication, and professional services as well as the temporary movement of natural persons. The other chapters focus on investment, intellectual property, electronic commerce, completion, small and medium-sized enterprises, economic and technical cooperation, government procurement, and legal and institutional areas, including dispute settlement③.

---

① The full text of the RCEP Agreement.

② ASEAN plus One FTAs include ASEAN's existing bilateral FTAs with Australia, New Zealand, the PRC, India, Japan and the Republic of Korea.

③ Regional Comprehensive Economic Partnership (RCEP): Overview and Economic Impact. ADB. http://www.adb.org/publications/regional-comprehnsive-economic-partnership-impact, last visited on Apr.24,2021.

9. Expropriation

The Expropriation Clause is one of the most fundamental elements in the RCEP Agreement. Article 10: 80 of the investment chapter in the RCEP agreement states that a member state should be involved in privatization, compensation and citizenship of investments other than for public purposes only in accordance with the legal procedures.

In addition to these points, the expropriation has the following two characteristics:

(1) In the matters of land expropriation, compensation to the investor may have to be decided by municipal law rather than international law.

(2) Special attention must be paid to the land laws of the host country regarding land acquisition. In Article 10.13.1 of the investment chapter in the RCEP Agreement, no party shall expropriate or nationalize a covered investment either directly or through measures equivalent to expropriation or nationalization, except for a public purpose, in a non-discriminatory manner, on payment of compensation in accordance with paragraphs 2 and 3 and in accordance with due process of law. The compensation referred to in subparagraph 1(c) shall be paid without delay; be equivalent to the fair market value of the expropriated investment at the time when the expropriation was publicly announced, or when the expropriation occurred, whichever is earlier; not reflect any change in value occurring because the intended expropriation had become known earlier; and be effectively realizable and freely transferable.

Usually guarantees against the expropriation of the foreign investment without payment of compensation are enacted in Foreign Investment Law so as to get rid of any distress of expropriation of foreign investors. According to Article 5 of the Foreign Enterprise Law of China, in every case of expropriation, full compensation will be paid. This guarantee is aimed to eliminate foreign investors' distress of the risk to their investment. Such guarantees are usually convinced by high risk countries to counteract the risk perceptions arising from previous nationalizations.

Together with the bilateral investment agreements which are also entered into huge numbers by the same states, these guarantees have a signaling function. These guarantees can be designated to the foreign investor that previous policies concerning foreign investment have undergo dramatics changes.①

As an opposing aspect, in the matter of revolutionary change of government, guarantee agreed by one government cannot be binding on the following government.② According to the Hans Kelson's theory, in the case of revolutionary change, the basic legal principles or norms changes, qualifying the making of changes to other legal principles in the system. If the coming government has ideological insolences unalike those of the former government, it can be issued that there has been such a fundamental change that the contract made by the previous government cannot be mandatory for the revolutionary government.

On the flip side, although the government changes the guarantees against expropriation do have legal consequences. It can be said that these guarantees have the impact on the state in submitting the foreign investments disputes to an international rather than a national tribunal for settlement. Unilateral guarantee expropriation was supported to transfer foreign investment disputes to the international sphere to consider in shaping the legality of the taking and the quantum of damages.③

In 1974, Southern Pacific Properties (SPP), a Hong Kong company, entered into agreement with the Egypt government of President Sadat to establish a joint venture with the vision to build an international tourist complex near the Egyptian Pyramids. The political issue was arose because of the site, which was adjacent to the historical monuments. After the assassi-

---

① M. Sornarajah, *The International Law on Foreign Investment* (3rd Edit), Cambridge University Press, 2012, p. 99

② Detter Delupis, Ingrid, *Finance and Protection of Investment in Developing Countries*, Gower Pub Co., 1987, pp. 27-32

③ M. Sornarajah, *The International Law on* Foreign *Investment* (3rd Edit), Cambridge University Press, 2012, p. 100

nation of President Sadat, the new government annulled the project effectively cost of parliamentary opposition.

In 1984, the Claimants decided to take the same matter before an International Center for Settlement of Investment Disputes (ICSID) Tribunal, pursuant to Egyptian law, which confined an ICSID arbitration provision. The Claimants advocated that Egypt's actions violated the agreements and amounted to expropriation of the investment, and thus claimed compensation for the value of their investment.

The issue is the liability of the government as a part of the agreement. In finding the liability, the point of arbitral tribunal bank on is the interconnection of the violation of the guarantees for the foreign investor in attracting him to the host country and the liability of the state. According to the Egypt Investment Law referred to by the tribunal, projects may not be nationalized or confiscated. The assets of such projects cannot be seized, blocked, confiscated or sequestrated except by the judicial procedure.

The tribunal found that the decision of Egypt to stop the venture was a lawful expropriation for public purposes that aimed to preserve and protect the antiquities in the area. Nevertheless, the rules of both Egyptian law and international law imposed an obligation to assure parties whose investment had been affected by expropriation. These rights and interests were entitled to the protection of international law and thus compensation for the taking of this right was due.

In its 1992 award based on Egyptian and international law, the tribunal held that Egypt's actions constituted a lawful expropriation of the Claimants' investment and that Egypt was therefore liable to pay "equitable compensation" for the value of the expropriated investment. The tribunal awarded all out-of-pocket expenses incurred by the Claimants with a 5% interest rate, prescribed by Egyptian law, and with an upward adjustment to account for post-1978 US dollar devaluation. In addition, the tribunal awarded the Claimantsthe loss of opportunity to make a commercial success of the project. In total, the tribunal awarded US$ 27.6 million.

The Myanmar Investment Law, replacing the Foreign Investment Law and Myanmar Citizens Investment Law, came into force in 2016 when it was

signed by the President. The Myanmar Investment Law (MIL) was drafted by the Myanmar Investment Commission with the help of International Finance Corporation. The Myanmar Investment Law expressly contains guarantees against expropriation as well as against nationalization. According to Section 55 of the Myanmar Investment Law, is offered the "extraordinary expropriation" of assets. Pursuant to Section 55 of the MIL, the Government can approve "non-discriminatory measures" for the benefit of regulating economic or social activity, including reasonable measures to shield "citizens' morals", or maintain public interest or national security. "Extraordinary expropriation clauses" such as Section 55 are commonly used in international investment agreements.

Fair and adequate compensation shall be paid equivalent to the prevailing market value at the time of expropriation of the investment. Section 53 explains that compensation for the indirect expropriation would normally be equal to an investment's fair market value but that other features should also be considered. Though the Myanmar Government guarantees that it will not nationalize or impose any measures which effectively result in any expropriation except in the case of expropriation for public purpose, the word of "public purpose" is not defined in the law.

Article 53 also stipulates that compensation should reflect the "market value" of the expropriated investment subject to a consideration of quite a few other features with "the public interest", "the interests of the private investor", "the present and past conditions of investment", "the reason for expropriation" and "the profits attained by the investor during the period of investment". These qualifications are different and could credibly conflict with Myanmar's responsibilities under its investment treaties. Article 54 conserves the government's policy space to regulate in the public interest in a manner similar to Annex 2 of the ASEAN Comprehensive Investment Agreement (ACIA) by illuminating that non-discriminatory regulatory measures will not add up to indirect expropriation.

Apart from the guarantee against expropriation, three other investor protections in the MIL have either been introduced for the first time or improved substantially when compared to the previous rule. A general principle

of non-discriminatory treatment is organized in the new law. According to Section 47, foreign investors can expect to be treated in a non-discriminatory manner as national treatment and most-favored-nation treatment. These guarantees was not included in the former rule.

Fair and equitable treatment is defined to cover two types of treatment in Section 48, namely, the right to acquire information on measures or decisions that impact an investor or investment and the right to due process and appeal in respect of government measures, including any changes to terms of investment licenses or permits approved by the government. This newly-introduced guarantee therefore seems to be more restricted and limited than the fair and equitable treatment provisions in almost all of Myanmar's investment treaties.

Chapter 15 of the Myanmar Investment Law and Chapter 21 of the Myanmar Investment Rule guarantee free transfer of funds from investment activities in Myanmar. These provisions are more sophisticated than those under the former law. They start with better precision regarding the types of financial rights protected by the guarantee and present special rules during balance-of-payments and other financial crises.

In Chapter 16 of Myanmar Investment Law and Chapter 20 of the Myanmar Investment Rule, the investor protections are an advanced set of investor obligations, the likes of which are scarce in investment treaties in the region and the world, which largely need investors to abide by domestic laws, abide by the terms of licenses and permits issued to them, respect labor rights enjoyed by their local employees and follow international best practices to avoid environmental damage. Myanmar Investment Commission is authorized to make enforcement and have a supervisory role for some of these responsibilities according to the Myanmar Investment Rule. Security-connected exceptions in Chapters 21 and 22 preserve the government's right to regulate a range of issues in the public interest and also the investor protections are susceptible a field of general.

The new Investment Law does not cover a unilateral, binding undertaking by the government to submit future investment disputes with investors to international arbitration like investment laws in many other ASEAN

member states. An investor grievance mechanism was introduced in the law.[①]

10. Conclusion

RCEP is set to boost intra-Asian trade, influence the direction of global value chains, and determine the future trajectory of the Asia-Pacific's economic architecture. In the case of RCEP, while the economic benefits are more modest and may take years to materialize, the symbolic messing inherent in RCEP, being the world's largest regional trade agreement. Myanmar's economic growth was expected to pick up in 2021 and 2022 because of the higher foreign direct investment (FDI) and positive response to the government's economic policy reform. With the new Foreign Investment Law and lifting of economic sanctions by Western countries, Myanmar is opening rapidly to the global market economy. Anticipations for Myanmar's economic growth for 2021 and 2022 look positive as the country come up with the retail and wholesale categories and go on to rejuvenate corporate governance and management in Myanmar. Myanmar needs to open markets, allow for foreign direct investment inflows, and put up the infrastructure required by the quality investor. And also Myanmar needs to prioritize two main facts in managing foreign investment. One is developing a targeted FDI strategy led by a high-performance agency and improving Myanmar's business environment. The other is in order to provide more specific guidance to potential foreign investors, some types of activities have been specified as open to foreign investment. In conclusion, there are still challenges for Myanmar's economic situations. Specific policies need to be set for the implementation of the broader goals and guidelines outlined above.

---

① OECD Investment Policy Reviews, http://www.oecd-ilibrary.org/sites/Od414646-en/index.html? itemId=/content/component/0d414646-en, last visited on Apr. 24, 2021.

Legal Issues of Lancang-Mekong Cooperation Mechanism: Case Study on Human Trafficking in Myanmar

Win Win Mar*

Abstract: The main purpose of the research is to focus on the role of the Lancang-Mekong Cooperation (LMC) and to explore current status and challenges of human trafficking in Myanmar. The LMC intends to be strong cooperation to mitigate human trafficking issues in the individual country of the sub-region and it is necessary to fully strengthen co-operation and effective support in line with policy and mechanism of the LMC. The LMC as a community of shared future needs to enhance partnership in tackling human trafficking, which is a serious non-traditional threat to all countries in the region. Myanmar has incorporated the international and regional anti-trafficking principles into its national legal framework and has taken measures to combat human trafficking. The problem of human trafficking in Myanmar cannot be addressed without taking into consideration the cross-border problem and the concrete plans and actions of the LMC. According to LMC mechanism, the uniform standards of Mutual and Legal Assistance (MLA) requests and the right to effective remedies for human rights will mitigate the crisis of human trafficking in Myanmar. This paper will find out how the LMC tackled human trafficking and analyze national measures in Myanmar and international cooperation to solve human trafficking issue.

Introduction

The human trafficking issue has existed in the Mekong region since the 1980s and been recognized by the governments, civil society organizations and international organizations. Nowadays, trafficking in person is endemic

* Ph. D. Candidate of SWUPL, judge of Township Court of Myanmar.

all over the world and Mekong sub-region countries in particular have confronted the issue seriously.

Myanmar has ratified eight international conventions relating to anti-trafficking in persons and has cooperated with international and regional organizations and neighboring states to combat trafficking in persons. Myanmar is obliged to prevent and combat trafficking in persons, especially women and children; to protect and assist the victims of human trafficking, with full respect for their human rights; and to promote cooperation among State Parties to combat human trafficking. To meet these objectives, Myanmar is protecting the victims of trafficking in persons by ensuring national law or administrative system.

However, Myanmar has several weak points in combating the human trafficking offences and it also has insufficient mechanism to operate the programmes of human trafficking internally and internationally. These insufficient regulations affect data collection, monitoring system, preparation long-term support, estimate of budgets and human resources, anti-trafficking programs design and implementation areas. And also, it has lack of coordination between the government and enforcement agencies, which results in inadequate responses in policy making, cooperation, prevention, prosecution, protection and capacity building.

The Lancang-Mekong Cooperation (LMC) framework, comprising six countries (China, Thailand, Cambodia, Laos, Myanmar, and Vietnam), was created in 2015 (launched in March 2016) to promote Mekong cooperation at the sub-regional level. along the Mekong River. LMC aims at economic and social development of the sub-regional countries, enhancing the wellbeing of their people and narrowing the development gap among regional countries.

Human trafficking has been one of the serious threats in the Mekong countries in recent decades and is essential to tackle in the sub-region. The LMC stated that it would strengthen cooperation to mitigate the urgent human trafficking issues in LMC is surely the most important and suitable mechanism which is both active and tailored to the specific needs of LMC countries. Through international and regional cooperation, Myanmar will get and share information on human abducting and trafficking, build databases of information related to potential victims and suspected human traffickers, and launch joint investigations, crackdowns on major criminal cases by applying MLA and finally get the effective remedies.

This paper is composed of three parts. The first part explains current status of human trafficking, requirements of action taken in cases and implementation of anti-trafficking in person programs. The second part focuses on LMC mechanism on fight against human trafficking and how to support member countries under the LMC. The third part presents national policy against human trafficking and its implementation in Myanmar; international, regional and bilateral cooperation to reduce human trafficking cases; and the effective remedies.

1. Current Status and Challenges of Human Trafficking in Myanmar

Myanmar has two different destinations for human trafficking—internal and external. Most victims are trafficked by a middle man or broker, who can be a friend and family member. Some victims return by running or are recused by authorities. The external trafficking mainly akes the form of forced marriage, forced labor and sexual exploitation.

The successive governments have outlined policy and implemented programs and cooperation with international organizations, regional countries and regional organizations. Coordination with non-governmental organizations has been established. The government measures include four strategies: prevention, prosecution, repatriation, return and reintegration, but Myanmar has still been facing the human trafficking issue as a threat.

1.1 Current Status of Human Trafficking in Myanmar

Human trafficking has been one of the major issues in Myanmar since 1990s. The main reasons for human trafficking in Myanmar include socio-economic conditions, natural disasters and internal armed conflicts. In Myanmar, five major types of human trafficking cases are forced marriages,

forced prostitution, forced labor, trafficking in children and debt bondage.

The country's human trafficking cases in 2020 were found to be 78.38 percent in forced marriages, forced prostitution 11.7 percent, forced labor 9 percent, surrogacy 0.9 percent. By countries of destination, 76.58 percent of the cases were related to China, 1.8 percent to Thailand, 1.8 percent to Malaysia and 19.8 percent in Myanmar. Myanmar's anti-human-trafficking police force handled 111 human-trafficking cases in 2020, in which 167 (male-15, female-113, child (female)-39) victims were trafficked, according to Myanmar Anti-Human Trafficking Police Force. The victims were trafficked to China, Thailand and Malaysia as well as inside the country, with the majority of victims sent to China for forced marriage, according to the Anti-Human Trafficking Police Force. Among the 111 cases of human trafficking, 83 were related to forced marriage to Chinese men, 1 to forced marriage to Thailand, 3 to forced marriage in the country, 1 to forced prostitution to Thailand, 12 to forced prostitution in the country, 7 to forced labor in the country, 2 to forced labor in Malaysia, 1 to forced labor in China and 1 to surrogacy in China.①

The Anti Trafficking in Persons Law was enacted in Myanmar in 2005, in which acts of human trafficking are criminalized. According to the law, Myanmar has been taking various measures against the trafficking in persons, treating it as a national duty, and drawing up a five-year plan which includes four sectors in cooperation with relevant ministries, namely, United Nations (UN) bodies, international organizations, International Non-Governmental Organizations (INGOs) and social communities. Prevention and protection activities including legal proceedings are also carried out.

According to the law, the Myanmar government formed the Central Body for Suppression of Trafficking in Persons in February 2006. The Central Body for Suppression of Trafficking in Persons (CBTIP) and its working units have been reformed, while the Anti-Trafficking in Person Division of Myanmar Police Force has been expanding its units for effective work. The Minister for Home Affairs led the Central Body, which organized

① Myanmar's Anti-Human-Trafficking Police Force.

three work committees for the implementation: one for the prevention of human trafficking led by the Deputy Minister of Home Affairs, one for the legal framework and criminal prosecution under the guidance of the Deputy Attorney-General, and another one for the reintegration and rehabilitation of victims chaired by the Vice Minister of Social Welfare, Relief and Resettlement. The Anti-Human Trafficking Police Force from the Ministry of Home Affairs (MOHA) and the Department of Social Welfare of the Ministry of Social Welfare, Relief and Resettlement (MSWRR) took main responsibilities practically. The Department of Rehabilitation was separately formed in 2018 to focus on the extended rehabilitation activities which have been carried out as a division under the MSWRR since 1993.①

Myanmar outlined five key points for anti-trafficking in persons, including policy and cooperation, prevention, prosecution, protection, and capacity building. The five-year national plan was started to realize the five key points. The first National Plan of Action (NPA) started from 2007 to 2010 and its functions included three grand strategies, four strategies, and four functions. The second NPA were from 2011 to 2016. The third five-year NPA were carried out from 2017 to 2021.

1.2 Challenges of Human Trafficking in Myanmar

Myanmar has insufficient mechanism to combat human trafficking. Lack of effective monitoring and comprehensive data of trafficking based on the experience and perceptions of those working on site, lack of data of the identified young women and men likely to be trafficked, and lack of proposals to tackle the problem:② Several factors contribute to the invisible nature of trafficking and an absence of on-site agencies to collect and report data to gov-

---

① http://myanmarhumantrafficking.gov.mm/, last visited on Aug.22,2021.

② UN Women, *The Gendered Dynamics of Trafficking in Persons Across Cambodia*, Myanmar and Thailand, 2020, p.57.

ernment departments. ①

Lack of long-term support for reintegration and the ability to follow up with survivors were further cited as a gap in reintegration programming by an Non-Governmental Organizations (NGO) representative in Myanmar: Current reintegration programs are short-lived, and merely based on donors' funding. Long-term programs are instead needed to ensure that the trafficked persons have enough time to start anew.②

At both the national and sub-national levels, limited budgets and human resources constrain the design and implementation of anti-trafficking programs, while lack of coordination between the government and law enforcement agencies results in inadequate responses. There are also very few civil society organizations in Myanmar that specifically focus on this complex issue.③

The government is not providing enough funding for anti-trafficking initiatives, particularly victim support and law enforcement. The government agency responsible for victim support, the Department of Social Welfare (DSW) is doesn't have enough staff at the township level.

Lack of significant efforts, the government continued to prosecute and convict traffickers, and it identified more victims than the previous year. But government officials were complicit in both sex and labor trafficking, by hindering law enforcement efforts against the perpetrators.

Like most developing countries, Myanmar is also challenged by a lack of public awareness of the dangers of trafficking. To raise the awareness, the government should educate young people and establish community-level organizations. The local community is a vital means of disseminating informa-

---

① Mi Ki Kyaw Myint, Can Myanmar's Libraries Help Combat Human Trafficking? https://asiafoundation. org/2018/03/28/can-myanmars-libraries-help-combat-human-trafficking/, last visited on Aug. 22, 2021.

② UN Women, The Gendered Dynamics of Trafficking in Persons Across Cambodia, Myanmar and Thailand, 2020, p.57.

③ Mi Ki Kyaw Myint, Can Myanmar's Libraries Help Combat Human Trafficking? https://asiafoundation. org/2018/03/28/can-myanmars-libraries-help-combat-human-trafficking/, last visited on Aug. 22, 2021.

tion, as well as a key provider of support and shelter to victims.[①]

The 2005 Anti-Trafficking in Persons (ATIP) Law criminalizing all forms of labor trafficking and some forms of sex trafficking is inconsistent with international law, which requires a demonstration of force, fraud, or coercion to constitute a child sex trafficking offense, and therefore does not criminalize all forms of child sex trafficking.

Apart from penalty of human trafficking in the Penal Code and the ATIP Law, Myanmar does not set up any realistic mechanisms for potential prey to gain access to the substantive and procedural right to remedies. The ATIP Law refers to a little bit of restitution, compensation and satisfaction but they are not sufficient to allow room for the victims to gain access to the system.

Chapter Five of the ATIP Law titled "Safeguarding the Rights of the Trafficked Victims" does not address the legal rights of the trafficked victims to an effective remedy from the human rights perspective. The UN Guideline suggests that the right to an effective remedy must reflect a victim-centered and human rights—based approach that empowers victims of trafficking in persons and respects fully their human rights.[②] Limiting open trials and publications regarding human trafficking cases to deter the adverse effect on the victims and vesting power in the Central Body to make arrangements for the preservation of the victims' dignity, physical and mental security and for repatriation and resettlement alone are not adequate remedies from the viewpoint of a victim-centered and human rights—based approach.

The Anti-Trafficking in Persons Division (ATIPD) maintains dedicated anti-trafficking task force (ATTF) police throughout the country and continues to increase the number of officers among regional offices. ATIPD leadership traveled throughout the country for trafficking investigations. AT-

---

① Mi Ki Kyaw Myint, Can Myanmar's Libraries Help Combat Human Trafficking? https://asiafoundation. org/2018/03/28/can-myanmars-libraries-help-combat-human-trafficking/, last visited on Aug. 22, 2021.

② Summary of the consultation in the UN Guideline paragraphs 3, 15, 16 & the UN Basic Principles 3.

TF officers continued to consult and cooperate with law enforcement agencies in China, Laos, and Thailand as part of formal dialogues on trafficking issues; however, ATTF officers were prevented from participating meaningfully in some of these cooperative mechanisms.①

Current governmental plans to address these problems include focusing on victims, building partnerships between government and civil society, and producing results in taking action against human traffickers. While the government pledges to increase arrests and prison sentences to address the trafficking problems, widespread governmental corruption remains an obstacle to progress in putting criminals away.② Thus Memorandum of Understanding (MoU) is ineffective in practice: it is a slow process for allowing legal migration, and it has not reduced trafficking. Moreover, it is not clear how effective these MoUs are in terms of providing adequate remedies to the victims.

The court may order to pay damages to the trafficked victim from money confiscated from the offender, from the proceeds of sale of property of the offender or from a fine.③ Under the special protection scheme of trafficked victims, including women, children and youth, CBTIP shall carry out programs of security and other protection for trafficked women, children and youth victims during the period of instituting a suit for compensation for tort by the trafficked victim for the trafficking in persons.④But the difference among criminal justice systems is one of the challenges to eliminate human trafficking in Myanmar and collecting the evidence is also difficult.

Myanmar has provided an effective remedy which encompasses both "the substantive right to remedies and the procedural rights necessary to secure access to them." However there is also no guideline, either at the formal level or at the implementation level, which focuses on the victim cen-

① United States Department of State, 2018 Trafficking in Persons Report -Burma, https://www.refworld.org/docid/5b3e0b8a7.html, last visited on Aug. 22, 2021.

② Allison Meade, Human Trafficking in Myanmar, 2013, https://borgenproject.org/human-trafficking-in-myanmar/, last visited on Aug. 22, 2021.

③ Section 33 of the ATIP Law,2005.

④ Section 17 of the ATIP Law,2005.

tered and human rights—based approach to addressing the victims' rights.

There are several key points to settle the current situation. The first is economic development and welfare of people should be promoted. The second is that education level and awareness of human trafficking need to be increased for more effective implementation of programmes in at-risk communities. The third point is that the existing network comprising schools, universities and club can be used to share anti-trafficking messages. The fourth is sufficient funding for anti-trafficking measures. The fifth point is understanding of authorities from source and destination countries about the true nature of human trafficking. The sixth point is cross-border collaboration on repatriation that can lead victims to come back home safely. Among these, closer cooperation among regional countries is very important.① The last and the most important point is adequate funding for the reintegration and rehabilitation of victims.

2. Policy Frameworks of Lancang-Mekong Cooperation and National Regulations for Anti-trafficking in Persons

International, regional and sub-regional organizations have strived to combat the issue of human trafficking for many years. Without concrete principles and deeper cooperation, these issues cannot be solved effectively. LMC is surely the most important and suitable mechanism which is both active and tailored to the specific needs of LMC countries.

The human trafficking issue has been a concern in the Mekong region since the 1980s. The rising trend and scope of human trafficking in the subregion have been recognized by the governments, civil society organizations, and international organizations in recent years. Poverty and irregular migration cause human trafficking and exploitation of migrants that cause slavery,

① http://www.myanmarisis.org/publication_pdf/human-trafficking-by-kmmm-1-ssboco-asIsRR.pdf, last visited on Aug. 22, 2021.

forced prostitution, forced marriage, and child labor.[①] Nowadays trafficking in persons is endemic all over the world and Mekong-region countries in particular have confronted the issue seriously. Trafficking in persons can take place within and from the region. The most vulnerable factor is that source and destination countries of human trafficking are usually in the sub-region.[②]

2.1 Mechanism of Lancang-Mekong Cooperation (LMC)

LMC will be conducted within a framework featuring leaders' guidance, all-round cooperation, and broad participation, follow a government-guided, multiple-participation and project-oriented model. It aimed at building a community of shared future of peace and prosperity among LMC countries and establishing a new form of international relations featuring win-win cooperation.

LMC has three areas in practical cooperation, which are political and security issues, economic affairs, and social and cultural cooperation. The first area, political and security issues, includes non-traditional security cooperation in human trafficking, organized illegal crossing of national border, transnational crime, drug trafficking, cybercrime.[③]

LMC has identified the three cooperation pillars of political and security issues, economic and sustainable development, and social, cultural, and people-to-people exchanges as well as the five key priority areas, namely, connectivity, production capacity, cross-border economic cooperation, water resources, agriculture, and poverty reduction, and implemented many projects beneficial to people for all-round and long-term cooperation among LMC countries.

In the political and security area, non-traditional security cooperation will be

---

① The Vulnerability Report-Human Trafficking in Mekong Sub-region, Australia, World Vision, 2014.

② https://www.myanmarisis.org/publication_pdf/human-trafficking-by-kmmm-1-ssboco-asIsRR.pdf, last visited on Aug. 22, 2021.

③ Five-year Plan of Action on Lancang-Mekong Cooperation (2018-2022), http://www.lmcchina.org>eng>hzdt, last visited on Aug. 22, 2021.

deepened in issuse including human trafficking, smuggling of firearms and ammunition, organized illegal crossing of the national border, terrorism, and cyber-crime. LMC focuses on the Five-year Plan of Action since Mekong area has faced these threats.①

The Ministers agreed to promote dialogues among political parties and exchanges on governance, and step up cooperation on non-traditional security issues including human trafficking. The Ministers also agreed to promote exchanges and dialogues among local/regional governments of border areas as well as border management departments of the six countries in line with the spirit of Maritime Labour Convention (MLC) and domestic rules and regulations of each member country.

The Coordinated Mekong Ministerial Initiative against Trafficking (COMMIT) is a high-level policy dialogue in the Greater-Mekong Sub-region (GMS) and is implemented with the six national COMMIT Task-forces and United Nations Action for Cooperation against Trafficking in Persons (UN-ACT) as the Secretariat. COMMIT signed Memorandum of Understanding (Moll) against Trafficking in Persons and received the government's response to human trafficking to meet international standards and to highlight the need for multilateral, bilateral and government-NGO cooperation for fight against human trafficking. The MoU also called for the creation of a national task force to cooperate with the United Nations Inter-Agency Project on Human Trafficking in the Greater Mekong Sub-region (UNIAP).

During the operation, the relevant countries will share information on human abducting and trafficking, build databases of information related to potential victims and suspected human traffickers, and launch joint investigations and crackdowns on major criminal cases.②LMC is surely the most important and suitable mechanism which is both active and tailored to the specific needs of LMC countries. Compared with other cooperation mecha-

① https://www.myanmarisis.org/publication_pdf/human-trafficking-by-kmmm-1-ssboco-asIsRR.pdf, last visited on Aug. 22, 2021.

② Lancang-Mekong Countries Launch Joint Crackdown on Human Trafficking, htp://xinhuanet.com/english/2019-09/03/c_138362117.htm, last visited on Aug. 22, 2021.

nisms, the LMC is more practical and more effective to solve the human trafficking issue.①

The governments of the Lancang-Mekong region have individually adopted laws combating human trafficking and have jointly adopted Memoranda of Understanding and a regional agreement to combat human trafficking. Moreover, bilateral agreements have been a common tool for addressing human trafficking in both source and destination countries.

2.2 Legal Frameworks of Anti-Trafficking in Persons in Myanmar

Myanmar has incorporated the anti-trafficking principles into its national legal framework according to the international agreements which it has acceded to and has taken measures to combat human trafficking. Despite these measures, the authorities and the government institutions have the responsibilities to effectively protect the victims and provide adequate remedies.

In 2005, the Anti Trafficking in Persons (ATIP) Law was enacted in Myanmar and the government has been taking various measures against the trafficking in persons, treating it as a national duty, and drawing up a five-year plan which includes four sectors in cooperation with relevant ministries, namely, UN bodies, international organizations, INGOs and social communities. Prevention and protection activities including legal proceedings are also carried out.

According to the Anti Trafficking in Persons Law, 2005, exploitation includes receipt or agreement for receipt of money or benefit for the prostitution of one person by another, other forms of sexual exploitation, forced labor, forced service, slavery, servitude, debt bondage or the removal and sale of organs from the body.②

According to Section 3 of the ATIP Law, the consent of the victim is irrelevant. The explicated act of the trafficker was taken action under Section

---

① http:// www.myanmarisis.org/publication_pdf/human-trafficking-by-kmmm-1-ssboco-asIsRR.pdf, last visited on Aug. 22, 2021.

② Section 3 explanation (1) of the Anti Trafficking in Persons Law, 2005.

24 in the case of Ma Aye Aye San vs Ma Yan Maik Yi.[①]

One of the aims of the ATIP Law is to "enable effective and speedy investigation to expose and take action against persons guilty of trafficking in persons and to prevent further trafficking in persons by passing effective and deterrent punishment."[②]

Sections 24 and 25 of the ATIP Law prescribes that:"Whoever is guilty of trafficking in persons especially women, children and youth shall be punished with imprisonment for a term which may extend form a minimum of 10 years to a maximum of imprisonment for life and may also be liable to a fine[③] and whoever is guilty of trafficking in persons other than women, children and youth shall, on conviction be punished with imprisonment for a term which may extend form a minimum of 5 years to a maximum of 10 years and may also be liable to a fine."[④]

Daw Ji Taung Vs Naw Hsaing[⑤], Muse District Court with the prior sanction of the Central Body. Subsequently, the accused was prosecuted under Section 24 for selling the victim to a Chinese businessman. Police officer Aye San Vs Kyaw Myo Tun[⑥] and two offenders were sentenced to rigorous imprisonment for a term which may extend to 14 years for forced marriage to Chinese men. Police officer Aye San Vs Nu Nu Khaing[⑦] and Police officer Hla Myint Vs Ma Sai Ra and one [⑧]Accused was sentenced to 14 years for offence of forced labor in China. Police officer Thet Tin Oo Vs Aung Kyaw Theik (a) Kyaw Kyaw and one,[⑨]and Police officer Aye Aye Win Vs Nyan Tun and Three [⑩], offenders were punished with rigorous imprisonment of

---

① (New Light of Myanmar Newspaper dated on 26 August 2006)

② Section 4 (c) of Anti Trafficking in Persons Law, 2005.

③ Section 24 of the Anti Trafficking in Persons Law, 2005.

④ Section 25 of the Anti Trafficking in Persons Law, 2005.

⑤ New Light of Myanmar Newspaper dated on 26 August 2006.

⑥ Mandalay District Court, Criminal Case, No. 47 / 2007.

⑦ Mandalay District Court, Criminal Case, No. 47 / 2007.

⑧ Mandalay District Court, Cirminal Case, No. 84/2009.

⑨ Mandalay District Court,, Criminal Case, No. 103 / 2008.

⑩ Pyin Oo Lwin District Court, Criminal Case, No. 5 / 2010.

10 years for abducting the victims to work at a beauty salon in Muse and to sell them in Kyae Khaung in China. Police officer Tun Tun Naing Vs Ma Aye Khaing that and Ma Aye Chan Moe ①and Police officer that Win Tun Vs Ma San Lwin (a) San San Lwin②in this case the offence is prostitution and other forms of sexual exploitation, and the accused shall be sentenced to imprisonment for a term which may extend to 12 years, each with hard labor.

Section 26 (a) of the ATIP Law prescribes that:"Whoever is guilty of any acts of adopting or marrying fraudulently shall, on conviction be punished with imprisonment for minimum of 3 years to a maximum of 7 years and may also be liable to a fine."③

In the cases of Police officer Aye Aye Win Vs Tin Tin Khaing and four,④ Police officer Tun Tun Oo Vs May Thet Htun (a) EiEi Than and two,⑤ Police officer Aye Aye Win Vs Ma Zar Zar (a) Ta Yoke Ma and one,⑥ Ma Thiri Tun Wai (a) Ma Thandar Vs Khin Mg Oo (a) Kalar (a) Soe Paing and one,⑦ Police officer Myint Thein Vs Daw Khin San Myint (a) Daw Khin Than Myint (a) Daw Myint Myint⑧, the accused took victims to China and sold them to Chinese men as their wives by forced marriage and 4 of the accused were found guilty according to Section 26 and were sentenced to imprisonment for 20 years.

Therefore, in the above-mentioned cases, the most used routes by the trafficker are from Mandalay to Lashio and Muse and then to Shwe Li. The most usual forms of trafficking in persons are abduction, induced forced marriage and forced labor.

Plans were under way to update the 2005 Anti Trafficking in Persons Law, together with adopting its Bylaw. The CBTIP and its working units

---

① Mandalay District Court, Criminal Case, No. 106 / 2016.

② Mandalay District Court, Criminal Case, No. 140 / 2016.

③ Section 26 (a) of the Anti Trafficking in Persons Law, 2005.

④ Mandalay District Court, Criminal Case, No. 103 / 2008.

⑤ Mandalay District Court, Crimminal Case, No. 122 / 2007.

⑥ Mandalay District Court, Criminal Case, No. 126 / 2007.

⑦ Mandalay District Court, Cirminal Case, No. 5/2007.

⑧ Mandalay District Court, Criminal Case, No. 166 / 2011.

have been reformed, while the Anti-Trafficking in Persons Division of Myanmar Police Force has been expanding its units for effective work.[①]

Addressing human trafficking cases can be very difficult and complicated. The lack of uniform legislation in countries and weak cooperation among stakeholders make the prosecution of crimes and the protection of victims even more challenging. Indeed, investigating crimes of human trafficking requires close cooperation between countries of origin, transit and destination. The Mekong region is one of the most vulnerable areas where home and destination countries for trafficking are closely connected in economy, culture, history, and geography.

3. Reducing the Crime of Human Trafficking in Myanmar

Myanmar is a primary country of origin for trafficked persons. In reality, many women and youth are in the illegal trade due to sex, unemployment, poverty and low level of education and it is very easy for them to become victims under the sex trading agents, organized criminal networks, businesses and individual traffickers. Suppression plans of human trafficking are set out as a national duty to the pride and pedigree of Myanmar. The penalties for the traffickers and effective remedies to victims are methods for reducing crimes and contributing to prevention and prosecution of human trafficking, and repatriation, return and reintegration of victims.

3.1 International and Regional Cooperation to Combat Human Trafficking

As for implementation to combat human trafficking, Myanmar is in cooperation with the International Organization for Migration (IOM) and the United Nations Inter-Agency Project (UNIAP) on Human Trafficking in the Greater Mekong Sub-region (GMS), the latter of which was established in 2000. The Government of Myanmar has also been cooperating with the UNIAP actively in the counter-trafficking sector through the national plan of

---

① http://myanmarhumantrafficking.gov.mm/, last visited on Aug. 22, 2021.

action on human trafficking. Myanmar established a comprehensive framework including legislation, the plan of action, bilateral and multilateral cooperation in anti-human trafficking.

The International Organization for Migration (IOM) has been working together with the Myanmar government for protection of the displaced persons and preparation of Standard Operation Procedure (SOP). It has also funded the rehabilitation of victims and conducted the survey to evaluate rehabilitation and reintegration for life of former victims. The establishment of the shelter is provided by UNIAP and IOM. International non-governmental organizations (INGO), civil society organizations (CSO), UN agencies and local NGOs have also cooperated with the Myanmar government.

Mekong Delta Regional Trafficking Strategy 2 (MDRTS-2) Project is being conducted in five countries simultaneously—Cambodia, Laos, Vietnam, Thailand, and Myanmar. The goal of MDRTS-2 is to reduce vulnerability to trafficking in both source and destination areas and to provide trafficking survivors with the support they need to start a new life after the trafficking experience. It also seeks to synergize country-level operations to create a united response to the issues of human trafficking.

The Action against Trafficking (AAT) Project is to reduce the number of vulnerable people trafficked for sexual labor and other forms of exploitation within Myanmar and from Myanmar to Thailand. New opportunities to remain within home villages reduce forced migration and the risk of trafficking, and increase the ability of those who still choose to migrate to protect themselves from exploitation on arrival. The project builds on knowledge and understanding among local partners contributing to the developing of national and regional advocacy strategies.

The Children in Crisis, Laboratory of Learning Project (CIC-LOL) Projectaims to reduce the number of children being trafficked or subjected to any form of exploitation within Myanmar and from Myanmar to Thailand, and to empower the populations at risk to effectively protect themselves from falling victim to organized crime groups.

The Regional Advocacy Anti-Child Trafficking Project (RACTP) flows across Cambodia, China, Laos, Myanmar, Thailand, and Vietnam. Its main

goal is to improve the policy environment towards eliminating trafficking in persons, especially children, in GMS. Strategies include the strengthening of local advocates on trafficking issues and partnering with governments to encourage real action to effectively combat human trafficking at the community, national and regional levels.①

Myanmar has also been tackling the problems of human trafficking with cooperation of the GMS countries. On October 29, 2004, the first Inter-Ministerial Meeting (IMM) of the GMS countries signed the MoU on Coordinated Mekong Ministerial Initiative against Trafficking (COMMIT) in Yangon. The countries attended the meeting and discussed the design and implementation of their COMMIT National Plan of Action. The Myanmar Government approved its COMMIT National Plan of Action on December 26, 2007. The bilateral arrangements to mitigate the problem of human trafficking are carried out with neighboring countries.

As a member of ASEAN, Myanmar is joining multilateral efforts within the ASEAN context to combat human trafficking issues. The ASEAN Declaration against Trafficking in Persons Particularly Women and Children was signed in November 2004, at the 10th ASEAN Summit in Laos. At the summit the declaration of eight points of cooperation among the ASEAN member countries was issued.

Myanmar hosted the 19th Senior Officials Meeting on Transnational Crime (SOMTC) and its related meetings, the 16th ASEAN SOMTC Working Group, and the 34th Special Senior Officers Meeting on Anti-Trafficking in Persons. The country was cooperating with other member countries on the implementation plan for the ASEAN Political-Security Community (APSC)(2009—2015), the future plan for ASEAN Convention Against Trafficking in Persons, Especially Women and Children (ACTIP) and Bohol Trafficking in Persons Work Plan (2017—2020).

Like Myanmar, other Mekong countries have similar factors necessary to combat trafficking in persons. Under the circumstances, Lancang-Mekong Cooperation is the best mechanism to tackle the problem. It is characterized

① http:// www.wvasiapacific.org/, last visited on Aug. 22, 2021.

by high efficiency, great resource and focus on concrete projects. Besides, it aims at bolstering economic and social development of members and enhancing well-being of people. LMC as a community of shared future needs to enhance partnership in tackling the issue of human trafficking, which is a serious nontraditional threat to all countries in the region.

3.2 Mutual Legal Assistance in Human Trafficking

International cooperation plays an important role in handling criminal matters, especially in transnational crime. Criminal offenders shield themselves from different legal systems in their crimes and are taking advantage of these differences. Criminal offenders are mobile, and they can evade detection, arrest, and punishment by operating across international borders. In that sense, international cooperation in criminal matters with Mutual Legal Assistance (MLA) becomes necessary in extradition by covering negotiated treaties, agreements, and other instruments applied to specific regulatory areas and respective jurisdictions or statutory procedures. Mutual Legal Assistance is "a process by which States seek and provide assistance in gathering evidence for use in criminal cases."

In the United Nations Convention against Transnational Organized Crime (UNTOC), Article 18 is devoted to Mutual Legal Assistance in investigations, prosecutions and judicial proceedings in relation to the transnational organized crime covered by this Convention. Myanmar acceded to this Convention on March 31, 2004. To be in line with and to implement the provision of MLA, Myanmar enacted the Mutual Assistance in Criminal Matters Law in 2004 and promulgated the Mutual Assistance in Criminal Matters Rules in 2004.

The countries of the Greater Mekong Sub-region, in cooperation with UNTOC, took the first step to increase cross-border information sharing through the establishment of the Border Liaison Office (BLOs) mechanism. This PATROL project aims to assist countries in the Greater Mekong Subregion in their fight against transnational organized crime (TOC) by helping them strengthen border control and expand cross-border cooperation. The PATROL project has made significant progress in the training of law enforcement and border officials associated with BLOs. Their main goal was to establish the state of training and infrastructure at different border sections and measure officer's perception of the intensity and direction of criminal flows.①

Most member states of the Lancang-Mekong region have adopted domestic legislation to deal with mutual legal assistance, while member states depend upon MLA to enact their own domestic law. Currently, laws and practices relating to MLA in criminal matters in member states are at different levels of development.② Due to the difference of legal system, laws and regulations, MLA and extradition process is hard. So basically it depends on assistance of other countries. Political will is a key factor.③

The Central Authority (CA) for MLA in Myanmar is Ministry of Home Affairs. The Central Authority in Myanmar has the power to grant or refuse the MLA Request, has the right to carry out the mutual legal assistance immediately, and can perform immediate duties. It may delegate the power to any members of CA or anybody who is a member of the CA. The Focal Point of Myanmar to receive the request for rendering Mutual Legal Assistance is Head of Department of Transnational Organized Crimes. The requesting State may, in urgent circumstances, make a request orally by telephone, facsimile, electronic mail or other electronic means including computer networks. In making such requests, the original letter of request shall be sent to the Central Authority without delay.④

In Cambodia, procedures of MLA start from the requesting country's approaching Cambodia through diplomatic channels, usually through Embassy or Ministry of Foreign Affairs. It forwards the request to the Ministry of Justice, and makes a determination on what types of assistance has been requested and assesses the request.

In Lao PDR, according to Article 271 of the code of Criminal Procedure, a request for legal assistance in criminal matters shall be imple-

---

① Border Control in the Greater Mekong Sub-region, UNODC, 2013.

② MLA and Extradition in East Asia and the Pacific Working Paper, UNODC, 2016.

③ MLA and Extradition in East Asia and the Pacific Working Paper, UNODC, 2016.

④ Section 13 of The Mutual Assistance in Criminal Matters Law, 2004.

mented in two ways: (1) treaties (2) criminal law. In Lao PDR, MLA requests must be submitted in writing to the Ministry of Justice.

In Thailand, under the 1992 MLA Act, competent authorities to provide MLA are Royal Thai Police, Attorney General, and Department of Corrections. For Human Trafficking/ Migration Smuggling, competent authorities are Royal Thai Police, and Ministry of Social Development and Human Security. Office of Attorney General is the main responsible agency. The Department of Corrections is responsible for transferring persons who makes a testimony.

In China, Ministry of Justice is the main central authority for MLA. The second central authority is Ministry of Foreign Affairs, sometimes called liaison authority. Ministry of Foreign Affairs is the central authority for bilateral extradition law if the request was submitted through diplomatic channels. The third one is Supreme People's Procuratorate. The Fourth one is Ministry of Public Security. It is one of the central authorities under UNTOC, and Ministry of Public Security was designated as the central authority together with Ministry of Justice in about three bilateral mutual leagal assistance treaties.

According to the 2007 Law on Mutual Legal Assistance of Vietnam, the central authority for Mutual Legal Assistance is Supreme People's Procuracy. It handles requests for mutual legal assistance in criminal matters. Ministry of Public Security of Vietnam handles the matters of extradition and transfer of sentenced persons, and Ministry of Justice of Vietnam handles requests for mutual legal assistance in civil matters.

According to the information mentioned above, it can be found that in procedures for MLA requests of Mekong countries, particularly for the central authority, there are so many difference ways such as a lack of understanding with regard to another country's legal system and tradition, including the legal requirements for executing MLA requests; a lack of a standard format for outgoing requests; the complicated process for submitting and executing requests; the lack of a standard language and weak communication both domestically and amongst partner countries; and a lack of a designated focal point or central authority in some cases.

The absence of unified procedures for granting MLA or extradition results in a cumbersome and delayed process with no guarantee of successful execution of requested assistance. Effective execution of MLA and extradition requires well-trained staff and practices. In that sense, additional financial resources will be necessary to ensure continued implementation towards achieving sustainable impact of the project in supporting regional criminal justice cooperation mechanisms in the region.

The suggestions are that uniform standards for submitting, receiving and processing MLA requests should be provided or implemmented in domestic law, or bilateral treaties and regional agreements concluded between Lancang-Mekong countries. All member states agree on the importance of further developing their capacity to engage in cross-border criminal justice cooperation. In this regard, it is recognized that there is a need to address common challenges faced by all countries in the region.

3.3 Legal Remedies for Trafficked Victims

The overall analysis of the relevant national laws shows that effective remedies for the victims of human trafficking in persons include restitution, compensation, rehabilitation, and guarantee of non-repetition by sanctioning the traffickers. States must encompass both the substantive rights to remedies and the procedural rights necessary to secure access to victims.

The UN Trafficking in Persons Protocol and the United Nations Convention against Transnational Organized Crime (UNTOC) oblige States Parties to provide trafficked people with the legal possibility of obtaining compensation and restitution for victims of offences.

Article 6 (6) of the UN Trafficking in Persons Protocol Prescribes that each State shall "ensure its domestic legal system contains measures that offer victims of trafficking in persons the possibility of obtaining compensation for damage suffered."

Basic Principles and Guidelines on the Right to a Remedy and Reparation for Victims of Gross Violations of International Human Rights Law and Serious Violations of International Humanitarian Law were adopted by the UN General Assembly in 2005 to clarify the rules on remedies and reparation appli-

cable to human rights violations committed by or implicating States. They also confirm that the rights to a remedy for gross violations of human rights, a term that would incorporate the most serious cases of trafficking, include the right of access to justice, the right to reparation for harm suffered and the right of access to information concerning violations and reparation mechanisms.

The overall objective will be to help anti-trafficking responders in the LMC region, including through the commit process, collectively identify and address high-priority challenges with a rights-based anti-trafficking response. These three areas are prioritized:

1. trafficking victim protection systems and policies, including shelter systems and victim/witness treatment;

2. informed consent and privacy for trafficking-affected persons in the media and public awareness raising activities;

3. impacts in source communities.

Traffickers and exploiters of sex, labor, and marriage trafficking rob trafficking victims of their fundamental rights to dignity, freedom, and security. The anti-trafficking community should be focusing its energies on immediately reinstating dignity, freedom, and security for trafficking-affected persons. Government and non-government commitment to improving the ethical conduct of anti-trafficking responders would be a strong step in the right direction, with a focus on truly appreciating the meaning and value of a rights-based approach. ①

In the Lancang-Mekong region, there are Memoranda of Understanding (MoUs) between Myanmar and Thailand, and Myanmar and China, as these two neighboring countries are the common channels for human trafficking to and from Myanmar. However, it is not clear how effective these MoUs are in terms of providing adequate remedies to the victims.

Myanmar Anti Trafficking in Persons Law (2005) provides the right to the remedy for victims of trafficking in persons. Enactments of legal

① Lisa Rende Taylor and Melinda Sullivan, Raising the Standard of Ethics and Human Rights Among Anti human Trafficking Responders in the Mekong Region, p.68.

remedies include protection of privacy and identity[①], counseling and legal rights[②], medical treatment[③], and protection of physical safety[④] taking into account age, gender and special needs of victims.

The type of remedies for restitution and rehabilitation provided in Myanmar may not be adequate as the only restitution found in the ATIP Law is the repatriation of the victims to their original place of residence and the availability of damages for the trafficked victim from money confiscated from the offender, from the proceeds of sale of property of the offender or from a fine. Therefore, the right to the effective remedy in the human right perspective should be clearly implemented or provided in MoUs concluded between Lancang-Mekong countries and national laws.

Under international legal framework, Myanmar is responsible to provide appropriate remedies. There is little evidence that Myanmar has provided an effective remedy which encompasses both the substantive rights to remedies and the procedural rights necessary to secure access to them. International law dictates that the form of the remedy should reflect and advance the obligation on the offending State to, as far as possible, wipe out the consequences of the breach and re-establish the situation that existed prior to its occurrence.

Conclusion

Addressing human trafficking problems can be very difficult and complicated. The Mekong region is one of the most vulnerable areas where home and destination countries for trafficking are closely connceted in terms of economy, culture, history, and geography. The lack of uniform legislation in countries and weak cooperation among stakeholders make the prosecution

---

① Sections 11 (a), (b) and (c); Section 16 (f), and Section 19 (e) of the Anti Trafficking in Persons Law (2005).

② Sections 19 (c) and 19 (d) of the Anti Trafficking in Persons Law (2005).

③ Sections 16 (e) and 19 (f) of the Anti Trafficking in Persons Law (2005).

④ Sections 14, 16 (a) and 17 of the Anti Trafficking in Persons Law (2005).

of crimes and the protection of victims even more challenging. Indeed, investigating crimes involving human trafficking requires close cooperation between countries of origin, transit and destination.

Human trafficking is undoubtedly a major threat to rule of law and governance. The problem has global dimensions, and transnational crime organizations have shown a great level of sophistication in their criminal activity. Responses to this phenomenon need to be coordinated if it is intended that they should have any real impact. International judicial cooperation, particularly MLA and extradition agreements, is the global response to this phenomenon.

In terms of procedures for MLA requests of Mekong countries, particularly for the central authority, there are so many difference ways such as a lack of understanding with regard to another country's legal system and tradition, including the legal requirements for executing MLA requests; a lack of a standard format for outgoing requests; and the complicated process for submitting and executing requests. Therefore, the uniform standards for submitting, receiving and processing MLA requests should be clearly provided or implemented in domestic law, or bilateral treaties and regional agreements concluded between Lancang-Mekong countries.

The Member States are bound by international human rights conventions that they have ratified and by customary international law, so they have the duty to fulfill their obligations under international law and provide victims with the right to effective remedy. One of the most important principles of access to the right to an effective remedy is that the State must make sure that the victims have access to remedies that is not dependent upon their capacity or willingness to cooperate in legal proceedings. The State must encompass both the substantive rights to remedies and the procedural rights necessary to secure access to them.

The Impact of the Regional Comprehensive Economic Partnership Trade Rules on the Rule of Law in Myanmar and Its Response

May Thiri Aung*

Abstract: The Regional Comprehensive Economic Partnership (RCEP) was signed in November 2020 between ASEAN members and their five trading partners. This agreement includes many new chapters to improve important policies for future trading systems. The RCEP agreements provide for the reduction of import duties in accordance with the rules governing the trading of goods and services, regional trade, investment, intellectual property, e-commerce, dispute resolution, small and medium enterprises, and business cooperation. In 2020, Myanmar also signed the agreement and became a member country of the RCEP. In this situation, Myanmar needs to modify the national laws so that it can accelerate the adaptation to the RCEP trade standards and harmonization between the RCEP trade rules and practical implementation of national laws in Myanmar. The RCEP includes lots of provisions that explore new areas of trade-related matters. Therefore, this paper emphasizes some newly-developed areas of the RCEP and the impact of RCEP on Myanmar in some new trade-related matters, such as intellectual property, e-commerce, and non-tariff measures.

Keywords: Regional Comprehensive Economic Partnership (RCEP), E-Commerce, Intellectual Property, Non-Tariff Measures

1. Introduction

The Regional Comprehensive Economic Partnership (RCEP) is an agreement

* Ph. D Candidate of SWUPL, officer of MOLA, Myanmar.

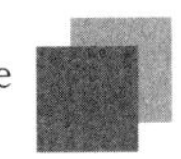

on the creation of a free trade area between the ASEAN members and their 5 negotiating partners: China, Japan, South Korea, Australia, and New Zealand.[①] Prior to the RCEP, there was the US-led Trans-Pacific Partnership (TPP), free trade agreement negotiated in 2008. The TPP included Brunei Darussalam, Malaysia and Thailand. Later, Singapore, Vietnam, Australia, New Zealand, Japan, Canada, Chile, Mexico, Peru, and the United State participated in negotiation. After the TPP negotiation, the agreement was signed in 2016. In 2017, the United States withdrew from the TPP. After the withdrawal of the United States, the TPP was renamed as the Comprehensive and Progressive Agreement for Trans-Pacific Partnership (CPTPP), and that Agreement came into force in December 2018. Since then, the impact of the TPP trade rules have steadily weakened and the RCEP have become stronger than TPP in the trade sphere. Both the CPTPP and the RCEP are multilateral free trade agreements dominating the Asia-Pacific countries. However, the 2 free trade agreements differ in their memberships, orientation and aspirations. The RCEP Agreement had been discussed by representatives from 16 member countries since 2012. In November of 2019, on the third RCEP Summit held in Thailand, the Prime Minister of India wanted no longer to participate in the RCEP negotiations because the other 15 countries had not followed India's demands of the negotiated agreement on trade and investment. Therefore, the 10 ASEAN members and China, Japan, South Korea, Australia and New Zealand continued discussion and signed the RCEP Agreement in November 2020.

The RCEP Agreement contains both great coverage and seriousness of commitment. The RCEP consists of 20 chapters and covers various sections, which are rules of origins, customs clearance and trade facilitation, human and animal health, pest control programs, standards, technical procedures and quality assurances, trade remedies, and specific trade regulations. It also includes provisions on trade in financial services, professional services, and temporary movement of natural persons. In addition, it also includes lots of chapters related to investment, intellectual property, e-commerce, competi-

① http//www.mofa.go.jp/mofaj/files/100114908.pdf, last visited on Apr. 3, 2020.

tion, small and medium enterprises, electronic cooperation, government procurement, and dispute resolution.

In the RCEP agreement, the intellectual property (IP) chapter, the e-commerce chapter and the small and medium enterprises chapter is a new statement for the trade area. There are current laws in place in Myanmar regarding these sections, but there are no laws for certain sections. Myanmar enacted a new legal framework regarding four IP issues (Industrial Design Law, Patent Law, Trade mark Law and Copyright Law) in 2019 to cope with current economic trends and development in the IP field. These IP laws were adopted very recently and also badly needed to difficult enforce or implement the impact of those laws in the practical sectors within a short period. On the other hand, the purposes of these laws are to help the free flow of literary and artistic work, foods, and services in the RCEP region, to facilitate access of Myanmar goods to international markets, and to promote free trade and foreign direct investment. Between various aims of those laws and the practical situation of the nation, Myanmar will still have many questionable difficulties and gaps for its own national interests and trade environment in the future. Myanmar has not yet enacted a legal framework for e-commerce. So, this paper focuses how Myanmar might benefit from RCEP and what are the commitments to fulfill after signing them.

2. Related Trade Sectors in Regional Comprehensive Economic Partnership

The 15 countries currently participating in the RCEP have a population of 2.2 billion, representing 30% of the world's population. Production value is US $26.2 trillion, accounting for 30% of global production. In addition, trade between the RCEP countries accounts for about 28% of world trade making. Therefore, the RCEP is one of the world's largest free trade agreements. The RCEP will create an extensive trading bloc as an ASEAN-centered regional free trade initiative. It might also be used as a tool to re-

move complexities in the present RTAs.[①] The RCEP provides special privileges for the least developed countries, so there are more advantages for Myanmar than disadvantages.

The RCEP Agreement is designed to contain provisions for special and differential treatment as appropriate, additional flexibility for the least developed Parties like Cambodia, Lao PDR, Myanmar, and Vietnam. In addition, the RCEP Agreement includes technical cooperation and capacity building that will be available to support the implementation of commitments made under the RCEP Agreement. The Regional Comprehensive Economic Partnership, which includes countries stretching from Japan to Australia and New Zealand, aims to reduce tariffs, strengthen supply chains with common rules of origins, and codify new e-commerce rules. It aims to counter protectionism, boost investment and allow freer movement of goods within the region.

2.1 Trade in Goods

The RCEP agreement includes key plans to implement trade-related commitments, to increase trade liberalization between member countries and to achieve a higher level in relation to trade in goods. It also includes granting other member states the same rights as citizens', easing or removing tariffs on goods, providing temporary tariffs on imports, and reaffirming World Trade Organization (WTO) ministerial commitments on export competition. It also includes non-tariff measures to facilitate customs clearance. These measures include general removal of quantitative restriction, greater transparency on non-tariff arrangement, management of import license procedures and the use of fees and procedure for import and export. Finally, this chapter discusses the technical negotiation of the effects of non-tariff arrangements on trade between member countries. It also states that future

---

① Rajan S. Ratna, H. jing, Regional Comprehensive Economic Partnership (RCEP) FRA: Reducing Trade Cost Through Removal of Non-tariff Measures, *Korea and the World Economy Journal*, 2016, Vol. 17, No. 2, pp. 213-242.

plans will be made for facilitating trade-related areas.[①]

2.2 Trade in Services

The trade in services section aims to open the door to better service trade between member countries and to eliminate the barriers and discrimination that affect trade in services. This section covers laws relating to market access, equal rights as citizens', and equal access to all member states. These sectors include additional commitments and arrangement that are inconsistent with the member state's detailed commitments or permissible lists. This chapter states that all Member States shall abide by the specified schedule of their respective services on the date of the entry into force of the RCEP Agreement. The negative list related to service commitments under the RCEP Agreement will provide greater security for service providers by obtaining information on the policies and procedures. This chapter also deals with the impartiality of domestic regulations that affects trade in services beyond the provisions of the current ASEAN+1 Free Trade Agreements.[②]

So, the RCEP Agreement asks for establishing a single trade market for goods and services in the Asia-Pacific region. The agreement is aimed at boosting regional economy, facilitating regional investment and trade, and promoting equitable development among member states. With the increase of tariff reduction, relaxation of investment and services in member countries, transparency of rules and regulations, and improvement of customs procedures, local investors will have more trade opportunities. The establishment of the ASEAN Economic Community 2015 leads to the elimination of tariffs on goods, services and capital, and facilitated regional trade.

2.3 The Role of Custom Procedures and Trade Facilitation

The customs procedures and trade facilitation chapter aims to promote

---

① Summary of RCEP, http//www.mdn.gov.mm/en/rcep-opens-new-chapter-myanmar, last visited on Apr.4,2020.

② Summary of RCEP, http//www.mdn.gov.mm/en/rcep-opens-new-chapter-myanmar, last visited on Apr.4,2020.

uniformity and transparency in the application of customs laws and regulations, and to improve the effective management and clearance of goods for customs procedures. With regard to the sector of express delivery and perishable goods, the goods are to be picked up within 6 hours from the time of arrival, so that the goods are free from any damage. The RCEP is formed with countries of different levels of development, but they have to perform beyond the provisions of the World Trade Organization (WTO) Trade Facilitation Agreement, by giving appropriate level of responsibilities for each and every country. The RCEP agreement includes provisions predetermining the types of customs of duties, determining the rules of the country of origin, determining the customs value, and setting a time for customs clearance. It can promote the area of facilitating trade, import and export procedures in accordance with the standards, facilitating trade, customs control and management.①

2.4 Trade Remedies

The trade remedies chapter consists of two sections: RCEP safeguard measures, and anti-dumping and countervailing duties. In the section of safeguard measures, the parties with a transitional mechanism to address serious injury or threat of serious injury to the domestic industry caused by a partner's commitments under the RCEP Agreement, are subject to well-defined conditions and requirements, including carrying out a proper investigation as well as early and full notifications to parties concerned with opportunities for consultations. The safeguard measures section also reaffirms the rights and responsibilities of the parties to the Agreements of safeguard in the WTO with regard to global safeguard measures. The anti-dumping and countervailing duties section reaffirms and builds on parties' rights and responsibilities provided under the relevant agreements in the WTO. This chapter also contains a supplementary provision relating to anti-dumping and countervailing duties proceedings which are practiced by some parties and

① Summary of RCEP, http//www.mdn.gov.mm/en/rcep-opens-new-chapter-myanmar, last visited on Apr.4,2020.

may promote the goals of transparency and due process in trade remedy proceedings. While no party has the right to dispute settlement under the RCEP Agreement for any matter arising under the section of anti-dumping and countervailing duties, the applicability of dispute settlement to this section will be considered in the general view of the RCEP Agreement.①

3. Current Status of Myanmar Trade Law

Myanmar has been undergoing economic reforms since 2011 to promote economic growth. The Myanmar Government is imporving the services sector, including export promotion, market access, and the trade facilitation, as well as promoting foreign direct investment. As Myanmar transitioned to a market economy, it began to undergo structural reforms and adopted new legal policies for a market economy. International trade practices were also adopted to enable the private sector to actively participate in foreign trade. Myanmar's export policy is to extend the foreign markets by exploring natural resources effectively and to promote value-added products, and the import policy is to allow imported capital goods to support public interest. Therefore, the government of Myanmar is encoring export and import sectors including trade financing, market access and trade facilitation.②

3.1 Substantive Trade Laws and Trade-Related Laws in Myanmar

The Ministry of Commerce (MOC) is a focal ministry in Myanmar to draft trade-related laws and necessary regulations, rules and procedures. The existing trade-related laws in Myanmar are as follows:

(1) the Sea Customs Act, 1878;

(2) the Tariff Law, 1992;

(3) the Land Customs Act, 1924;

---

① Summary of RCEP, http//www.mdn.gov.mm/en/rcep-opens-new-chapter-myanmar, last visited on Apr.4,2020.

② Trade Policy Reforms in Myanmar, http//: www.unescap. org> sites>default file, last visited on Apr.4,2020.

(4) the Export and Import Law, 2012;

(5) the Essential Supplies and Services Law, 2012;

(6) the Foreign Exchange Management Law, 2012;

(7) the Central Bank of Myanmar Law, 2013;

(8) Consumer Protection Law, 2014; and

(9) Competition Law, 2015.

Regarding import and export of goods, the Sea Customs Act (1878), the Land Customs Act (1924), the Export and Import Law (2012), and the Tariff Law (1992) are existing laws that are administered by the Ministry of Commerce. The new Export and Import Law enacted in September 2012 replaces the Control of Imports and Exports (Temporary) Act (1947). The main purposes of the new law are:

(a) to enable to implement the economic principles of the State successfully;

(b) to enable to lay down the policies relating to export and import that support the development of the State;

(c) to ensure the policies relating to export and import of the State and activities are to be in conformity with the international trade standards;

(d) to be streamlined and speedy in carrying out the matters relating to export and import.

The new law describes basic regulations regarding export/import control and detailed procedure supplemented by regulation, rules etc. The Ministry of Commerce (MOC) has authority to publish necessary regulations, rules, and procedures by obtaining the approval of the Union Government, and can release notifications, orders, instructions, and procedures. The Ministry also enacted the Foreign Exchange Management Law in 2012 to liberalize the import/export restrictions.

According to the Export and Import Law of 2012 and related Notifications, the Ministry of Commerce implemented export/import licenses in 2011, and automatic licensing was introduced for some products. The Ministry started an online application for licenses in 2014 and changed its license control from a positive list system to a negative list of products related to import/export licenses. Nevertheless, in the trade sector it needs to abolish import and export licensing requirements to improve the functioning of the capital market and facilitate trade and investment.

Myanmar promulgated the Competition Law in 2015 and the law came into force in 2017. This law has lots of aims: to prevent actions that endanger fair competition in economic activities through monopolization or manipulation of prices by any individuals or group; in line with the development of national economy, to control unfair trade the market competition on the internal or external trade and economic development; to prevent the abuse of dominant market power; and to control the restrictive agreement and arrangements among businesses.

The Foreign Exchange Management Law of 2012 is a law governing foreign exchange control and abolishing multiple exchange rates in the market to manage the floating-rate system. The Myanmar government had initially allowed only state commercial banks to run foreign exchange businesses, but with this law, private banks have also been allowed to perform foreign currencies exchange business and banking services, if they are qualified to do it.

3.2 International Trade Sector

The Myanmar Government has been pursuing trade liberalization and trade facilitation for many years. Import and export regulations have also been improved. Myanmar is a member of WTO. Myanmar believes that a multilateral trading system can bring many opportunities for exports. Myanmar's trade policy influences free trade agreements with third parties of ASEAN countries in cooperation with ASEAN countries.

Myanmar continues to be an exporter of primary products and an importer of manufactures and capital goods under unfavorable trade conditions. Myanmar's foreign trade is mainly related to Asian countries. The main trading partners are China, Thailand, Singapore, India, Japan, and South Korea. In accordance with the Government's objective of remodeling Myanmar from a centrally-planned into a market-oriented and more open economy, the role of the state in trade, production, and prices setting has been reduced. International trade has been largely dominated by private sector activities.

Several steps are taken to encourage the active participation of the private sector in international trade. In particular, state trading monopolies were largely abolished in November 2011 so that private enterprises and individuals import and export almost all products.

The export policy of Myanmar is to extend and explore the foreign markets by utilizing the natural and human resources effectively and also to promote the export of traditional and value-added products. Myanmar's import policy is to import such primary products as state-required capital goods, raw materials for production, other important goods and the goods which support the public interest and promoto export. Myanmar's business promotion strategies can be outlined as follows:

(1) to export all exportable surplus and diversify foreign markets by using natural and human resources;

(2) to increase and diversify exports and improve the quality of products;

(3) try to reduce the trade barriers and simplify export/import procedures;

(4) to encourage the private sector participation in the foreign trade;

(5) to establish Export Processing Zones and Special Economic Zones at suitable places;

(6) to organize training, seminar, workshop, business matching, trade fairs;

(7) To disseminate trade-related information through websites, journals, and bulletins.

3.3 Intellectual Property Issue in Myanmar

The chapter Intellectual Property (IP) in RCEP Agreement provides that each party shall be free to determine the appropriate method of implementing this chapter within its own legal system and practice. Myanmar joined WIPO in 2001. Myanmar has promulgated several laws and regulations with regard to IP rights, such as Myanmar Patents and Designs Act of 1945, Myanmar Patents and Designs (Emergency Provision) Act of 1946, Myanmar Merchandise Marks Act, Myanmar Copyright Act of 1914.

These laws are outdated and are inconsistent with international IP treaties and agreements. Therefore, Myanmar created a new legal framework regarding four IP issues (Industrial Design Law, Patent Law, Trademark Law and Copyright Law) in 2019 to cope with the current economic trend and development in the IP field. These IP laws were adopted very recently and are actually difficult to enforce in practice within a short period. The said, the laws help the free flow of literary and artistic works, foods and services throughout the RCEP region, facilitate access of Myanmar to international markets and promote free trade and foreign direct investment.

Before promulgating these IP laws, copyright problems were solved under the Sea Customs Act, the Land Customs Act, and the relevant legislation. Myanmar Customs is responsible for detecting illegal imports of IPR-related goods and other goods, collaborating with national enforcement bodies such as the police force, the local, and the legal authorities. At the international level, Myanmar Customs has cooperation with the WCO, WIPO, the Regional Intelligence Liaison Office, and the International Criminal Police Organization.

In accordance with the Sea Customs Act, any import or export of goods having applied counterfeit trademarks (within the meaning of the Penal Code), or false trade description (within the meaning of the Merchandise Marks Act), are subjected to detention and confiscation. Persons involved in any such offence are liable to pay a fine. According to the sections 170 and 171 of the Sea Customs Act and the section 9 of the Land Customs Act, customs officers and police officers are authorized to stop and search any person vessels and vehicles of goods, on responsible sufficient grounds for suspicion.

3.4 E-Commerce and Myanmar

E-commerce is a key factor in the global digital economy and it is outlined in Chapter 12 of the RCEP Agreement with the aim to facilitate paperless trading, e-signature, e-authentication, personal information protection, online consumer protection, unsolicited commercial electronic messages, domestic regulatory framework, customs duties and cyber security. Cross-bor-

der activities including trade are changed as a new digital style and it would be likely to bring benefits for all trade partners as well as promote a digital trade environment in the region. The global e-commerce sector seems to leverage the developing countries to increase their export and import by using those technologies and innovative digital platforms.

Considering the disadvantages or things to be prepared for the future after participating in RCEP, Myanmar has not yet enacted a legal framework for e-commerce. This is a new chapter of this regional agreement and all signatory countries should prepare to fulfill the Agreement's commitments within the designated time frame, especially the developing countries.

E-commerce is prioritized in financial services and it requires secure and fast payment systems. Traditional banking transactions have some negative effects on customers such as time constraints and costs. Most e-commerce transactions are now conducted through electronic payment systems by using the major international credit cards, Visa and MasterCard, and specialist online exchanges or transactions platforms such as KBZPay, wave money, OK, and so on, especially in Myanmar. Myanmar started these e-payments and e-banking systems very recently. Both Myanmar business owners including SMEs and customers have not fulfilled capacity and awareness building regarding the electronic transaction, e-payment system, Internet, and IT technology. China and other trade partners and investors have such knowledge in advance when doing their business in the e-commerce platforms.

The legal framework for e-commerce, including regulating online business registration and operating, is still in the drafting process by the Ministry of Commerce. Myanmar is a Facebook fast country, and now online shopping and Facebook live sale are rapidly developing among Myanmar people. However, due to the lack of those required laws and regulations for e-commerce in Myanmar, the government may lose the revenue from taxes and besides, both sellers and customers may face difficulties in their online selling and buying process and money transactions on digital platforms.

3.5 Non-tariff Measures in Myanmar

SPS measures and Technical Barriers to Trade (TBT) are legitimate tools to achieve public interest goals. Their trade-restricting effects can be minimized by reducing procedural costs through good design and efficient implementation. The Ministry of Commerce of Myanmar is the focal ministry to initiate the trade-related legislation and is responsible to adopt and implement trade policies. The ministry increases the number of Non-tariff Measures (NTMs) by, for example, issuing licenses for products in positive or negative lists; providing regulations or restrictions on imports of heavy industry products, construction machinery and transport vehicles; removing import prohibition on certain agricultural products and relaxing restriction of trading rights for foreign-invested companies. Some regulations can be liberalized in trade but some still remain controversial, for example, rigid regulation on car imports. The Ministry of Commerce issued instructions and notifications on vehicles, machinery, construction materials and petroleum products to meet TBT requirements, including labeling and packaging, production and post-production, product quality and safety, and conformity assessment.①

Other government ministries issue regulations and notifications to maintain NTMs especially SPS and TBT standards. Regarding TBT, the Ministry of Health regulates cosmetics, cigars and tobacco, medicines, and chemicals. Several regulations of/under the Ministry of Agriculture, Livestock and Irrigation also contain TBT, such as the regulation on new seed variety registration, the Pesticide Law, the National Food Law, and the Fertilizer Law.

The Ministry of Livestock, Fisheries and Rural Development stipulates the regulation for importation and exportation of animals and animal products in accordance with the Animal Health and Development Law. The Myanmar Marine Fishery Law regulates many NTMs related to the trade activities of animal, animal products and fishery products. The Ministry of Agriculture, Livestock and Irrigation issues regulations under the Pesticide Law, the Plant Pest Quarantine Law, and the Fertilizer Law, and ranks sec-

---

① Non-tariff Measures in Myanmar, in Ha Thi Thanh Doan and S. Rosenow(eds), *Non-tariffs Measures in ASEAN*. Jakarta: ERIA, pp. 120-136.

ond in terms of the number of NTMs issued.[①]

The Ministry of Natural Resources and Environmental Conservation issues the NTMs on vegetable and animal products along with international standards such as the Convention on International Trade in Endangered Species of Wild Fauna and Flora (CITES), regarding the rules of export and import permits for CITES species. Therefore, the Protection of Wildlife and Conservation of Natural Areas Law of 1994 and the Environmental Conservation Law of 2012 were enacted under the CITES standard to cover many sectors such as exporting animal and animal products and transporting them in local areas.[②]

Notifications of the Myanmar Petroleum Products Enterprise issued by the Ministry of Energy contain many TBT measures and licensing for economic reasons. The National Food Law issued by the Ministry of Health and notifications from the Ministry of Home Affairs also regulate NTMs. The Ministry of Science and Technology is in the process of drafting the law related to TBT. It is also the focal ministry for the responsibility of the Chemical Weapons Convention (CWC), where Myanmar is a member. This Ministry is also in the process to notify the CWC. The Ministry of Science and Technology enacted the Law on Standardization in 2014 and the Ministry would take the leading role in coordinating with the relevant ministries in order to promote the TBT standard in the future.

4. Newly-Developed Chapters in RCEP

4.1 Intellectual Property in RCEP

The WTO Agreement on Trade-Related Aspects of Intellectual Property

---

① Cho Cho Thein, Zin Zin Naing, 'Report on Non-tariff Measures in Myanmar', in Ing, L.Y, S. F. de Cordoba and O. Cadot (eds), *Non-Tariff Measures in ASEAN*. ERIA Research Project Report 2015-1, Jakarta: ERIA, pp. 103-112.

② Report on Non-Tariff Measures in Myanmar. "In L. Y, S.F de Cordoba and O Cadot (eds), *Non-tariff Measures in ASEAN. ERIA Research Project Report* 2015-1, Jakarta: ERIA, pp. 103-122.

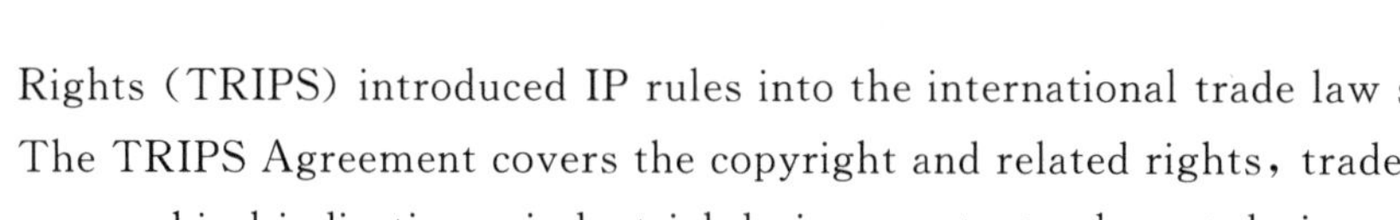

Rights (TRIPS) introduced IP rules into the international trade law system. The TRIPS Agreement covers the copyright and related rights, trademarks, geographical indications, industrial designs, patents, layout-designs and undisclosed information.

Intellectual property is covered in one chapter in the RCEP agreement and it protects intellectual property rights beyond the level of the TRIPS Agreement. The provisions in this chapter cover protection and enforcement of IP rights, promotion of technical innovation, national treatment, criminal procedures and penalties against infringement of IP rights, streamlined procedures to establish e-applications, public health and fulfillment of international and national legal frameworks. This agreement also designates member countries to be entitled to set up an appropriate legal IPRs system and to upgrade those systems in practice.

4.2 E-Commerce in RCEP

The WTO Agreement on Trade-Related Aspects of Intellectual Property Rights (TRIPS) aims to protect and achieves the development of local investment and knowledge for small and underdeveloped countries through digital industrialization. In 1998, WTO General Council agreed to establish a Work Programme on E-Commerce to examine all trade-related issues associated with global e-commerce.

Regarding the digital economy, as an example, China has embarked on a systematic programme related to the e-commerce system for cross-border trading and the Internet regulation for the Belt and Road Initiative (B&R). The historical trade routes can be changed to the "digital Silk Road", with digital operators from private sectors creating an ecosystem which includes fundamental digital and physical infrastructure for the future of commerce.

At present, the effect of the corona virus is spreading through out the world and people are changing their lifestyle especially in the sectors of selling, buying and also trading, which moves towards a style of electronic transaction. Along with the terrible outbreak of COVID-19 pandemic, the e-commerce sector expands to customers and producers.

In the RCEP agreement, the parties negotiated and included the e-com-

merce chapter, which aims to enhance and promote cooperation of the digital economy among them. This chapter sets out provisions that encourage the Parties to improve trade administration and processes by using electronic means. This chapter requires the Parties to adopt or maintain a legal framework which creates a conducive environment for development of e-commerce, including protection of personal information of e-commerce users. The e-commerce chapter also addresses some data-related issues, through provisions on location of computing facilities and cross-border transfer of information by electronic means. The Parties also agreed to maintain the current practice which does not impose customs duties on electronic transmission, in accordance with the WTO Ministerial Decision.

Governments need to be encouraged to improve e-commerce and digital economy during the global crisis. But it can be a challenge or barrier when they cannot adopt policy and specific regulations effectively regarding e-commerce in the practical sectors. Governments also need to adopt fair and sufficient measures for competition in the retail sector, communication services, and trade for a well-functioning environment for e-commerce.①

4.3 Non-tariff Measures (NTMs)

The implementation of Non-tariff Measures (NTMs) has several purposes, including to protect human health and to maintain ecosystems and the environment. In order to achieve the Sustainable Development Goals (SDGs), NTMs are also imposed in international trade for economic growth and poverty reduction.② These measures can be classified as technical and non-technical measures. Technical measures include regulations, standards, testing and certification, primarily sanitary and phytosanitary (SPS) and Technical Barriers to

---

① OECD Policy Responses to Coronavirus: E-commerce in the Time of Covid-19. Organization for Economic Co-operation and OECD, http:// www. OECD. Org// coronavirus/policy-responses/e-commerce-in-the-time-of-covid-19-3a2b78e8, last visited on Apr. 4, 2020.

② Muhamad Rias K. V. Zainuddin, Sustainable Production, Non-tariff Measures, and Trade Performance in RCEP Countries, *Sustainability Journal*, 2020, Vol. 12.

Trade (TBT) measures. Non-technical measures involve quantitative restrictions, price measures, forced logistics or distribution channels, and so on.

As an international agreement on NTMs, the SPS Agreement entered into force in 1995. The agreement allows countries to adopt scientifically-based measures in order to protect human, animal and plant life or health. It recognizes the sovereign rights of WTO Members to provide the level of health protection they deem appropriate, and it ensures that NTMs are not disguised restrictions on international trade and encourages Members to base their measures on international standards such as those of FAO or WHO. The TBT Agreement was signed in 1980. This agreement is replaced by the 1995 WTO Agreement. This agreement is to promote the use of international standards and the mutual recognition of requirements and of conformity assessment procedures between WTO Members.

Some scholars argue that NTMs have a positive impact on trade by increasing consumer confidence in and the technical capabilities of exporters and NTMs also help increase the quality of imported goods. However, NTMs in various export markets, for example, European Union, Japan and ASEAN, can face different effects of harmonization of standards. One region can increase exports because of the harmonization of regional standards.

Therefore, not all countries would get a benefit from such harmonization and it would both significantly increase exports from developed countries and decrease exports from low-income countries. The reason is that many low-income countries can export only to countries applying lax standards and not having production processes.

NTMs may include inconsistent standards, expensive testing and unclear regulations. Significantly, there will be higher costs for the consequences of NTMs and those costs may be borne by consumers and companies. RCEP members discussed reducing or eliminating NTMs; however, a number of NTBs are enacted by RCEP including SPS and TBT measures with some guiding principles, such as using international standards, eliminating double testing, discussing and allowing standard issues by the RCEP SPS and TBT Committee.

5. Impact of RCEP on Myanmar

The Regional Comprehensive Economic Partnership (RCEP) includes lots of provisions that are not contained in the ASEAN +1 Free Trade Agreement, such as the e-commerce chapter, small and medium enterprise chapter, the government procurement chapter, and the intellectual property chapter. These chapters will be the essential areas for future free trade agreements.

For example, the inclusion of e-commence will facilitate the cross-border e-commence and enable it to be more systematic by enacting the framework and procedures of each country's e-commence law in accordance with international rules and regulations. In addition, the inclusion of provisions of intellectual property rights encourages member countries to innovate and to protect the traditional culture.

In the IP chapter in RCEP, member countries shall ratify or accede to the IP-related international treaties if they are not parties to it. So, Myanmar needs to fulfill these requirements and the correspending ministry (Ministry of Education) shall arrange to complete the domestic procedure of acceding to the international agreement. Myanmar ensures a comprehensive and effective IP protection system for promoting foreign investment and technology transfer as well as for boosting industrial development. Strengthening the protection of intellectual property rights in Myanmar will be a catalyst for economic growth, encouraging foreign direct investment, and also will reap rewards in terms of greater domestic innovation and increased technology diffusion in the long run. It is also important to enhance awareness of IPR in all sectors to make sure that Myanmar can gain benefits by introducing a new IP system. Developing human resources and promoting the capacity of the workers are important matters for establishing the IP Office in Myanmar. Technical assistants are also needed in setting up the IP infrastructure in Myanmar for collaborating with local and international organizations.

Myanmar ratified the ASEAN E-Commerce Agreement in 2018 and then the government set up the Digital Economy Road map (2018—2025) to promote Myanmar's digital platform for the highest potentials of e-commerce growth in the region. Therefore, the government needs to create a strong policy or legal framework in accordance with the international standards for e-commerce and to establish infrastructure for supporting and creating innovative e-commerce business models that ensure flexible accommodation for both online and offline business. Building sufficiently strong domestic digital industries and capabilities are essential for Myanmar to engage effectively and create value in the digital economy.

In addition, least developed countries are working to integrate regional and global manufacturing in order to expand trade and investment opportunities. In doing so, these requirements will be taken into account, if necessary, to ensure the effective implementation of the commitments under this Agreement and its profitability. The implementation of the commitments made in the e-commerce and intellectual property chapters included in the RCEP agreement is expected to a change in the future with a minimum transition period of 3 years to a maximum of 10 years; in the services trade sector, the transition period is up to 15 years for Myanmar.

Myanmar is one of the Least Developed Countries (LDCs). So, while some members are committed to removing tariffs on 65% of trade in goods according to the Agreement, Myanmar needs only to remove tariffs on 30%, so Myanmar business is in a strong and competitive position. The country can increase investment, get more labor opportunities and in some areas such as intellectual property, competition policy and e-commerce, there are transition periods ranging from 3 to 10 years. During this period, the government can ensure that it is ready to implement all provisions, including building human and institutional capacities in both public and private sectors, in line with the relevant international standards.

Through participation in the RCEP, Myanmar businesses will also gain greater market access (65%) for a growing range of unique and in-demand Myanmar exports. Unified rules of origin regulations, including those covering goods requiring labor-intensive attention to detail such as garment finishing, can be expected to encourage greater foreign investment into Myanmar's expanding manufacturing sector.

In RCEP, businesses will grow and more markets will be available for

Myanmar's export. The biggest difference for Myanmar in the RCEP is the rule of origin. This is not a trade facilitation process but a matter of determining the country of origin of the goods. Under the Trade Agreement, businesses are required to adhere to different methods and standards for national recognition. For example, under a trade agreement, exporters are required to meet certain requirements for each trade item. According to other ASEAN +1 Free Trade Agreements, trade many forms and includes different countries to ratify the country of origin.

Myanmar's participation in the RCEP is also consistent with its longer-term strategic development priorities outlined within the Myanmar Sustainable Development Plan, including a commitment to ensure that Myanmar's private sector can take full advantage of new market conditions and opportunities. Myanmar can get benefit from participation in RCEP. Besides, the agreement also opens the door to a range of opportunities to forge closer ties with the development partner community.

The Regional Comprehensive Economic Partnership (RCEP) agreement includes countries with different levels of development. Appropriate concessions and privileges are granted to the least developed countries. Trade-related commitments to further improve trade liberalization among member states include granting other member states the same rights as those of citizens, reducing or eliminating tariffs, and granting temporary tariff exemption on goods. It also sets out the rules for proper customs action if a member state conducts a tariff classification.

6. Conclusion

In the current global trade platform, RCEP brings opportunities for the liberalization of trade barriers by supporting open markets and creating a free trade area in the region. This regional trading system can also bring a wide range of economic benefits for Myanmar through trade and investment cooperation. Myanmar can promote trade in the region through harmonization of non-tariff measures, trade and investment facilitation measures, etc. It will also achieve benefits in other areas such as conducting government and private sector capacity-building, supporting the growth of SMEs, developing job opportunity, increasing skilled labor, IT and technology sharing, and so on. According to the RCEP Agreement, it gives a transition period of up to 15 years to Myanmar and thus the government has time to prepare to fully integrate into the trade sector, including some new development areas such as e-commerce, intellectual property, government procurement, competition sectors and so on. It is also important to prepare for the drawing up of a plan and implementation of new markets for local products and to enhance the capacity of the government and private-sector organizations.

RCEP focuses on economic benefits among member countries by cutting tariffs and increasing market access even though it also requires member countries to consider labor rights and environmental issues. Therefore, it is also a good chance for Myanmar to participate in RCEP as a member of ASEAN and build bilateral relationships with other developed countries such as Australia, New Zealand, etc. The developed countries have strong trade policies and the largest export market but they will also make trade liberalization which would accrue to be a party in the RCEP agreement. Because the signatories of RCEP have been committed to lower their tariff to 0% within 10 years for more than 90% of their products and each liberalization consists of the complete removal of import taxes, export taxes and subsidies, Myanmar can gain suitable market access in the Asia-Pacific region and the government needs to prepare all required matters such as policy, regulations, and domestic procedures to fully participate in the RCEP.

Investment and Dispute Settlement Procedure of the Regional Comprehensive Economic Partnership Agreement

Su Wah Htwe*

Abstract: On 15 November 2020, the Regional Comprehensive Economic Partnership (RCEP) agreement was concluded with ASEAN and five Asia-Pacific countries to liberalise, promote, protect and facilitate the trading system. It states twenty chapters and four annexes. The RCEP agreement brings many opportunities for ASEAN to meet its Sustainable Development Goals by reducing barriers to trade, services, and investment. It covers national treatment, most-favoured-nation (MFN) treatment, and fair and equitable treatment for members, but MFN treatment has some exceptions. One of the distinctive features of RCEP is no special and differential treatment in investment. The dispute between members may be resolved in accordance with the provision of the RCEP dispute settlement mechanism but this mechanism does not provide a dispute for an investor-member state. The RCEP agreement allows the parties to choose the forum in which to resolve the dispute. Moreover, the parties may appoint panelists and change the time limit with the consent of the Parties. A unique characteristic of the RCEP dispute settlement system is that it does not approach compulsory jurisdiction.

Keywords: Regional Comprehensive Economic Partnership (RCEP) Agreement, Association of Southeast Asian Nations (ASEAN), Investment, Dispute Settlement Mechanism

Introduction

A regional trade agreement (RTA) is one of the major parts of a

---

* Second-year doctoral candidate of the School of International Law, Southwest University of Political Science and Law (SWUPL) and deputy director of the Constitutional Tribunal of the Union of Myanmar.

country's development because it is a useful tool in promoting the growth of many sectors. Consequently, countries have been concluding RTAs between two or more governments for many years. The economy of a country may change with the effects of RTA, particularly that of the least developed countries. Moreover, this can be influenced by a variety of aspects which include economic, political, and security considerations. According to the list of World Trade Organisation (WTO), there are 348 regional trade agreements in the international community.①

After the East Asian Financial Crisis, the Association of Southeast Asian Nations considered creating a comprehensive regional free trade area. Two regional agreements were proposed for ASEAN-centred regional economic integration: a 2001 proposal to establish an ASEAN + 3 (China, Japan and South Korea) East Asia Free Trade Area (EAFTA), and Japan's 2006 proposal to establish an ASEAN+6 Comprehensive Economic Partnership in East Asia (CEPEA), which would include Australia, India and New Zealand. A comparison of EAFTA and CEPEA was analysed to determine which agreement was more comprehensive and which contain greater benefits. According to the analyses, CEPEA will promote facilitation and liberalisation, and the estimated potential GDP for East Asian countries will increase by 2.1 percent. The benefits of East Asian countries are large in the CEPEA compared with other alternatives in the region. In 2009, a joint study group of representatives from ASEAN, Australia, China, India, Japan, South Korea, and New Zealand recommended to Leaders that work towards CEPEA should proceed.

The objectives of the Comprehensive Economic Partnership in East Asia (CEPEA) are: to deepen economic integration, narrow development gaps and achieve sustainable development. At the Fourth East Asia Summit in October 2009, officials were tasked to consider the recommendations of both the East Asia Free Trade Area and Comprehensive Economic Partnership in East Asia studies. In November 2011 ASEAN ended the debate by proposing

① https://www.wto.org/english/tratop_e/region_e/region_e.htm, last visited on Jun.20,2020.

its own model for an ASEAN-centred regional free trade agreement—the Regional Comprehensive Economic Partnership (RCEP).

In November 2011, the RCEP concept was initially endorsed by ASEAN leaders. ASEAN's invited officials from Australia and ASEAN's five other FTA partners (China, India, Japan, South Korea and New Zealand) participated in preparatory discussions in the latter half of 2012 to develop Guiding Principles and Objectives for Negotiating the RCEP. The Guiding Principles and Objectives for Negotiating the RCEP were considered by ministers in August 2012.①

A ceremony to launch negotiations for the Regional Comprehensive Economic Partnership (RCEP) was held in Phnom Penn, Cambodia on 20 November 2012. At the ceremony, the ASEAN countries and the FTA partners announced the launch of RCEP negotiations. The leaders of each relevant country endorsed the Guiding Principles and Objectives for Negotiating the Regional Comprehensive Economic Partnership.

The first and second round of RCEP negotiations were held in Brunei from 9 to 13 May 2013, and in Australia on 23 to 27 September 2013 respectively. The third round, fourth round, fifth round and sixth round of RCEP negotiation and related meetings were held in 2014 at Malaysia, China, Singapore and India. The RCEP negotiations were held four times in 2015 and six times in 2016. Then, several rounds of RCEP negotiations were held from 2017 to 2020.

As the result of the negotiations, the Regional Comprehensive Economic Partnership (RCEP) agreement can be signed by fifteen countries except India. The RCEP agreement becomes the newest development of regional trade agreement. At the annual summit of the Association of Southeast Asian Nations (ASEAN), China, Japan, South Korea, Australia, New Zealand and the ten members of the Association of Southeast Asian Nations (Brunei, Vietnam, Laos, Cambodia, Thailand, Myanmar, Malaysia, Singapore, Indonesia and the Philippines) signed the RCEP agreement on 15 November 2020, via teleconference.

---

① Background to the Regional Comprehensive Economic Partnership (RCEP) Initiative.

1. The Structure and Content of the Agreement

The Regional Comprehensive Economic Partnership (RCEP) agreement includes twenty chapters and spreads over trade in goods, trade in services, temporary movement of natural persons, investment, intellectual property, electronic commerce, competition, small and medium enterprises (SMEs), economic and technical cooperation, government procurement and institutional provisions.

Firstly, the agreement sets out the establishment of the RCEP, definitions, and objectives of the agreement. The type of RCEP is a free trade agreement and it was enacted in accordance with the General Agreement on Tariffs and Trade (GATT, 1994) and the General Agreement on Trade in Services (GATS).① This agreement states thirty-five definitions② and the terms of both 'least developed country party'③ and 'least developed country' are described in detail.④ The objectives of the RCEP agreement are stated in Article 1.3 of the RCEP agreement.

Chapter 2 'Trade in Goods' states the rules of the trade in goods with intent to achieve a high level of trade liberalisation between the members of RCEP. These rules are national treatment to the goods of the other Parties, reduction or elimination of customs duties, acceleration of tariff commitments, tariff differentials, classification and shipment of goods, temporary

---

① Article 1.1 of the Regional Comprehensive Economic Partnership Agreement provides that The Parties, consistent with Article XXIV of GATT 1994 and Article V of GATS, hereby establish the Regional Comprehensive Economic Partnership as a free trade area in accordance with the provisions of this Agreement.

② Article 1.2, Regional Comprehensive Economic Partnership Agreement.

③ Article 1.2(o) of the Regional Comprehensive Economic Partnership Agreement provides that Least Developed Country means any country designated as such by the United Nations and which has not obtained graduation from the least developed country category.

④ Article 1.2(p) of the Regional Comprehensive Economic Partnership Agreement provides that Least Developed Country Party means any Party that is a Least Developed Country.

admission for goods, containers and pallets. In addition, it includes duty-free temporary admission of goods; and the reaffirmation of commitments in the WTO Ministerial Decision on Export Competition, including the elimination of scheduled export subsidy entitlements for agricultural goods and rules for determining the applicable tariff treatment in cases of different tariff preferences applied by a Party. Section B contains the provisions for non-tariff measures, which are the general elimination of quantitative restrictions, greater transparency on the application of non-tariff measures, administration of import licensing procedures, and the application of fees and formalities connected with importation and exportation.①

The third chapter describes the requirements for determining originating status of goods. The list of the minimal operations and processes are set out in Article 3.6 to confer originating status on goods using non-originating materials. The members ensure the direct consignment rules so that originating goods do not inappropriately lose their originating status. If a good does not satisfy a change in tariff classification rule in the Product-Specific Rules, this chapter lays down certain *de minimis* rules whereby the good could still acquire the originating status. Section A includes the treatment applied to packing and packaging materials and containers for transportation and shipment, and the treatment of accessories, spare parts and tools. Further, Section B provides detailed procedures for applying the RCEP proof of origin, claiming preferential tariff treatment, and verifying the originating status of a good.

The Customs Procedures and Trade Facilitation Chapter provides for enhanced trade facilitation provisions, such as advance ruling based on tariff classification, rules of origin, customs valuation and the timeline for the issuance of advance rulings; time period for the customs clearance of goods; additional trade facilitation measures related to import, export, or transit formalities and procedures for operators who meet specified criteria (authorised operators); and a risk management approach for customs control and post-clearance audits. The details of the staged implementation of the com-

---

① Chapter 2, Regional Comprehensive Economic Partnership Agreement.

mitments are provided in an Annex.

Next chapter is 'Sanitary and Phytosanitary Measures (SPS)', which sets out the basic framework for developing, adopting and applying SPS measures for the purpose of protecting human, animal or plant life or health as well as for facilitating trade by minimising the negative effects of SPS measures on trade. These provisions highlight the importance of transparency, cooperation, capacity-building, and technical consultations in addressing SPS matters under the objectives of this chapter. The rules on Dispute Settlement do not apply to this chapter at the entry into force of the RCEP Agreement but the non-application of dispute settlement is subject to review 2 years after the entry into force of the RCEP Agreement.①

The chapter of 'Standards, Technical Regulations, and Conformity Assessment Procedures' shall apply to the standards, technical regulations, and conformity assessment procedures of central government bodies that may affect trade in goods among the Parties, whereas it shall not apply to any sanitary or phytosanitary measure, and purchasing specifications prepared by governmental bodies for production or consumption requirements of governmental bodies.② Similar to the SPS chapter, this chapter also underscores the need for cooperation, designation of contact points, and technical discussions to resolve issues related to the implementation of this chapter. The Dispute Settlement procedures do not apply to this chapter, although non-application of dispute settlement is subject to review two years after the entry into force of the RCEP Agreement.

The chapter of 'Trade Remedies' consists of two Sections: (i) RCEP Safeguard Measures; and (ii) Anti-Dumping and Countervailing Duties. Moreover, it also includes an Annex on Practices Relating to Anti-Dumping and Countervailing Duties Proceedings, which are practised by some Parties and may promote the goals of transparency and due process in trade remedy proceedings. This chapter contains modern and comprehensive provisions including rules on market access, national treatment, most-favored-nation treat-

---

① Chapter 5, Regional Comprehensive Economic Partnership Agreement.

② Chapter 6, Regional Comprehensive Economic Partnership Agreement.

ment, and local presence, which are subject to Parties' Schedules of Specific Commitments or Schedules of Reservations and Non-Conforming Measures, as well as additional commitments.①

The regulation of 'Temporary Movement of Natural Persons' sets out commitments that facilitate the temporary entry and temporary stay of natural persons engaged in trade in goods, supply of services or conduct of investment. It does not concern natural persons seeking access to the employment market of a Party and not apply to measures regarding nationality, citizenship, residence or employment on a permanent basis. This chapter establishes rules for the Parties in granting such temporary entry and temporary stay, including for the expeditious processing of complete applications, and a party shall ensure that any fees imposed are reasonable in that they do not represent an unjustifiable impediment to the temporary movement of natural persons covered by this chapter.②

The next part of the RCEP contains the provisions covering the four pillars of investments—protection, liberalisation, promotion, and facilitation. It aims to create an enabling investment environment in the region. This chapter provides for improved investment facilitation provisions which also address investor aftercare, such as assistance in the resolution of complaints and grievances that may arise.③

Relating to Intellectual Property, the RCEP agreement states a balanced and inclusive approach to the protection and enforcement of intellectual property rights in the region. These rules provide for the protection of intellectual property rights beyond the level of the WTO Agreement on Trade-Related Aspects of Intellectual Property Rights (TRIPS), including provisions relating to technological protection measures and enforcement in the digital environment. Besides, it also includes provisions to streamline and align procedures for the establishment of certain intellectual property rights such as those relating to electronic filing of applications and making

---

① Chapter 7, Regional Comprehensive Economic Partnership Agreement.

② Chapter 9, Regional Comprehensive Economic Partnership Agreement.

③ Chapter 10, Regional Comprehensive Economic Partnership Agreement.

relevant information available online for intellectual property right holder.[①]

The chaptar of 'Electronic Commerce' sets out the rules of trade administration and processes by using electronic means. The Parties also agreed to maintain the current practice of not imposing customs duties on electronic transmissions, in accordance with WTO Ministerial Decision. In the event of any differences in the interpretation and application of this chapter, the Parties agreed to first engage in consultations in good faith and make every effort to reach a mutually satisfactory solution.[②]

To promote competition in markets and enhance economic efficiency and consumer welfare, RCEP provides obligations for the Parties to adopt or maintain competition laws and regulations that proscribe anti-competitive activities and to establish or maintain authorities to implement its competition laws, and RCEP requires that the Parties recognise the sovereign rights of each Party to develop and enforce its own competition laws and policies and allowing for exclusion or exemptions based on grounds of public policy or public interest. This part not only includes provisions on exchange of information and allows for the coordination in enforcement actions, but also prescribes that Parties shall undertake technical cooperation activities to build necessary capacities to strengthen competition policy development and competition law enforcement.[③]

The RCEP members recognise that SMEs, including micro enterprises, contribute significantly to economic growth, employment, and innovation and therefore seek to promote information sharing and cooperation in increasing SMEs' ability to utilise and benefit from the opportunities created by the RCEP Agreement in order to strengthen cooperation in the areas of e-commerce, intellectual property rights, access to markets, and innovation, among others.[④]

The chapter of 'Economic and Technical Cooperation' provides a

---

① Chapter 11, Regional Comprehensive Economic Partnership Agreement.

② Chapter 12, Regional Comprehensive Economic Partnership Agreement.

③ Chapter 13, Regional Comprehensive Economic Partnership Agreement.

④ Chapter 14, Regional Comprehensive Economic Partnership Agreement.

framework for realising the development dimension of the RCEP Agreement. The Parties agreed that the economic and technical cooperation in the RCEP context aims to narrow the development gaps and maximise mutual benefits among the Parties. Economic and technical cooperation under this chapter will support the inclusive, effective and efficient implementation and utilisation of the RCEP Agreement. Priority will be given to activities that provide capacity building and technical assistance to developing country Parties and least developed country Parties, that increase public awareness, and that enhance business' access to information.[①]

The Government Procurement provisions aim not only to promote the transparency of laws, regulations, and procedures but also to develop cooperation among the Parties. Each Party shall publish information on government procurement in the Annex to this chapter consistent with the objective of promoting transparency in government procurement.[②]

Chapter 17 'General Provisions and Exceptions' creates an appropriate review and appeal mechanism in respect of each Party's administrative proceedings; provides for the protection of confidential information and the geographical scope of application of the RCEP Agreement; affirms Parties' rights and responsibilities under the Convention on Biological Diversity; and commits Parties to take appropriate measures, in accordance with their laws and regulations, to prevent and combat corruption regarding matters covered by the RCEP Agreement. This chapter provides that a decision on whether or not to approve or admit a foreign investment proposal, and the enforcement of any conditions or requirements for such approval or admission, are not subject to dispute settlement under the RCEP Agreement.[③]

The part of 'Institutional Provisions' establishes the institutional arrangements for the RCEP Agreement and the structure for the meetings of the RCEP Ministers; the RCEP Joint Committee; four Committees, namely, on Goods, Services and Investment, Sustainable Growth, and the Business Environ-

① Chapter 15, Regional Comprehensive Economic Partnership Agreement.

② Chapter 16, Regional Comprehensive Economic Partnership Agreement.

③ Chapter 17, Regional Comprehensive Economic Partnership Agreement.

ment; and other subsidiary bodies established by the RCEP Joint Committee. The RCEP Joint Committee is established to consider any matter relating to the implementation and operation of the RCEP Agreement. The RCEP Joint Committee also reports to the RCEP Ministers and may, as appropriate, refer matters to the RCEP Ministers for consideration and decision.①

Dispute Settlement mechanisms are stated in Chapter 19, which aims to provide effective, efficient, and transparent rules and procedures for settlement of disputes arising under the RCEP Agreement. The RCEP dispute settlement process includes: (i) choice of forum; (ii) consultations; (iii) good offices, conciliation, or mediation; (iv) establishment of a panel; and (v) rights for interested third parties. Another important provision in this chapter is on Special and Differential Treatment involving the Least Developed Country Parties.②

The last chapter is 'Final Provisions' and sets out the relationship between the RCEP Agreement and other international agreements, a general review mechanism, procedures to amend the Agreement, and an accession provision. The RCEP Agreement is open for accession by any State or separate customs territory 18 months after its entry into force, although this Agreement is open for accession of India, as an original negotiating State, from the date of its entry into force, without waiting for 18 months. The provision on Entry into Force provides that the RCEP Agreement would need signatory States, including at least six ASEAN and three non-ASEAN signatory States, to deposit their instruments of ratification, acceptance or approval for the RCEP Agreement to enter into force.③

The characteristics of RCEP are the rules on intellectual property and electronic commerce. These rules will provide for the digitalisation of businesses in international trade and improve consumer confidence in online business. The agreement will provide the Sustainable Development Goals of the Association of Southeast Asian Nations with the cooperation of member countries.

---

① Chapter 18, Regional Comprehensive Economic Partnership Agreement.

② Chapter 19, Regional Comprehensive Economic Partnership Agreement.

③ Chapter 20, Regional Comprehensive Economic Partnership Agreement.

2. Studying on the Investment Provisions

Chapter 10 of the Regional Comprehensive Economic Partnership Agreement deals with investment. The 'Investment' chapter includes eighteen provisions and two annexes. It aims to create an enabling investment environment in the region. This Chapter contains provisions covering the four pillars of investments—protection, liberalisation, promotion, and facilitation. These provisions upgrade and enhance the existing ASEAN Plus One Free Trade Agreements.

According to the RCEP agreement, the word 'investment' means every kind of asset that an investor owns or controls, directly or indirectly, and that has the characteristics of an investment, including such characteristics as the commitment of capital or other resources, the expectation of gains or profits, or the assumption of risk.[①] 'Covered investment' means an investment in its territory of an in-

---

① Article 10.1(c) of the Regional Comprehensive Economic Partnership Agreement states that 'investment means every kind of asset that an investor owns or controls, directly or indirectly, and that has the characteristics of an investment, including such characteristics as the commitment of capital or other resources, the expectation of gains or profits, or the assumption of risk. Forms that an investment may take include: (i) shares, stocks, and other forms of equity participation in a juridical person, including rights derived therefrom; (ii) bonds, debentures, loans, and other debt instruments of a juridical person and rights derived therefrom; (iii) rights under contracts, including turnkey, construction, management, production, or revenue-sharing contracts; (iv) intellectual property rights and goodwill, which are recognised pursuant to the laws and regulations of the host Party; (v) claims to money or to any contractual performance related to a business and having financial value; (vi) rights conferred pursuant to the laws and regulations of the host Party or contracts, such as concessions, licences, authorisations, and permits, including those for the exploration and exploitation of natural resources; and (vii) movable and immovable property, and other property rights, such as leases, mortgages, liens, or pledges. The term "investment" does not include an order or judgment entered in a judicial or administrative action or an arbitral proceeding.'

vestor of another Party.[①] The RCEP agreement grants national treatment[②], most-favoured-nation treatment[③], treatment of investment.[④] According to

---

① Article 10.1(a) of the Regional Comprehensive Economic Partnership Agreement provides that 'covered investment means, with respect to a Party, an investment in its territory of an investor of another Party in existence as of the date of entry into force of this Agreement or established, acquired, or expanded thereafter, and which, where applicable, has been admitted by the host Party, subject to its relevant laws, regulations, and policies'.

② Article 10.3 of the Regional Comprehensive Economic Partnership Agreement states that '1. Each Party shall accord to investors of another Party, and to covered investments, treatment no less favourable than that it accords, in like circumstances, to its own investors and their investments with respect to the establishment, acquisition, expansion, management, conduct, operation, and sale or other disposition of investments in its territory. 2. For greater certainty, the treatment to be accorded by a Party under paragraph 1 means, with respect to a government other than at the central level, treatment no less favourable than the most favourable treatment accorded, in like icircumstances, by that government to investors, and to the investments of investors, of the Party of which it forms a part.'

③ Article 10.4 of the Regional Comprehensive Economic Partnership Agreement states that '1. Each Party shall accord to investors of another Party treatment no less favourable than that it accords, in like circumstances, to investors of any other Party or non-Party with respect to the establishment, acquisition, expansion, management, conduct, operation, and sale or other disposition of investments in its territory. 2. Each Party shall accord to covered investments treatment no less favourable than that it accords, in like circumstances, to investments in its territory of investors of any other Party or non-Party with respect to the establishment, acquisition, expansion, management, conduct, operation, and sale or other disposition of investments. 3. For greater certainty, the treatment referred to in paragraphs 1 and 2 does not encompass any international dispute resolution procedures or mechanisms under other existing or future international agreements.'

④ Article 10.5 of the Regional Comprehensive Economic Partnership Agreement states that '1. Each Party shall accord to covered investments fair and equitable treatment and full protection and security, in accordance with the customary international law minimum standard of treatment of aliens. 2. For greater certainty: (a) fair and equitable treatment requires each Party not to deny justice in any legal or administrative proceedings; (b) full protection and security requires each Party to take such measures as may be reasonably necessary to ensure the physical protection and security of the covered investment; and (c) the concepts of fair and equitable treatment and full protection and security do not require treatment to be accorded to covered investments in addition to or beyond that which is required under the customary international law minimum standard of treatment of aliens, and do not create additional substantive rights. 3. A determination that there has been a breach of another provision of this Agreement, or of a separate international agreement, does not establish that there has been a breach of this Article.'

the above mentioned, the 'Investment' chapter of the RCEP agreement contains three principles: national treatment, most-favoured-nation treatment, and fair and equitable treatment. However, CLMV countries have no obligation to comply with the most-favoured-nation treatment. In return, they are not entitled to these rights. The RCEP agreement does not promulgate the special and differential treatment in investment which allows special rights to the least developed countries. For example, the WTO agreements have special and differential treatment which includes longer time periods for implementing agreements and commitments or measures to increase trading opportunities for developing countries. Although the RCEP agreement does not permit special and differential treatment in investment to the three least developed country members, this treatment is allowed at all stages of the determination of the causes of a dispute and dispute settlement procedures involving a least developed country.

3. Reservation and Non-conforming Measures

The provisions of National treatment, Most-Favoured-Nation Treatment, Prohibition of Performance Requirements and Senior Management and Board of Directors shall not apply to: any existing non-conforming measure maintained by a Part at different levels of government (central, regional and local government); the continuation or prompt renewal of any non-conforming measure; and an amendment to any non-conforming measure. The amendment does not decrease the conformity of the measure: (i) for Cambodia, Indonesia, Lao PDR, Myanmar, and the Philippines, as it existed at the date of entry into force of this Agreement; and (ii) for Australia, Brunei, China, Japan, Korea, Malaysia, New Zealand, Singapore, Thailand, and Viet Nam, as it existed immediately before the amendment, with the aforementioned points.

Article 10.3, Article 10.4, Article 10.6 and Article 10.7 of the RCEP agreement shall not apply to any measure that a Party adopts or maintains with respect to sectors, subsectors, or activities, as set out by that Party in List B of its Schedule in Annex III. In addition, Article 10.3 and Article 10.4

of the RCEP agreement shall not apply to any measure that falls within Article 5 of the TRIPS Agreement, and any measure that is covered by an exception to, or derogation from, the obligations imposed by Article 11.7 of the RCEP agreement, or imposed by Article 3 or 4 of the TRIPS Agreement.①

Restricted investments of the Republic of the Union of Myanmar.

The restricted sectors of Myanmar will be described according to the existing laws of Myanmar. The following types of investment businesses shall be stipulated as a restricted investment:

(a) investments allowed to carry out by the Union;

(b) investments not allowed to carry out by foreign investors;

(c) investments allowed only in the form of joint venture with any citizen owned entity or any Myanmar citizen;

(d) investments carried out with the approval of the relevant ministries.②

According to Myanmar Investment Law, Myanmar Investment Commission issued the list of restricted investments with the approval of the Union Government. The following kinds of investment can only be carried out by the Union:

(a) manufacturing of products for security and defence being specified by the notification of the Government from time to time;

(b) manufacturing and related services of arms and ammunition for the national defence;

(c) issuing the national postage stamps; establishment and hiring of post office and post boxes which are only to be performed by the post office operator on behalf of the Union;

(d) air traffic services;

(e) pilotage services;

(f) management of natural forest and forest area except the business relating to reduction of carbon emission;

(g) feasibility study and production of radioactive metals such as urani-

---

① Article 10.6, Chapter 10, Regional Comprehensive Economic Partnership Agreement.

② Section 42, Myanmar Investment Law, the Pyidaungsu Hluttaw Law No. 40/2016.

um and thorium;

(h) administration of electric power system;

(i) inspection of electrical business.

In Myanmar, foreign investors are not allowed to invest in the following sectors:

(a) publishing and distribution of periodicals in ethnic languages including Myanmar;

(b) fresh water fisheries and relevant services;

(c) establishment of quarantine station for exportation and importation of animals;

(d) pet care service;

(e) manufacturing of forest products from forest area and government administered natural forest;

(f) prospecting, exploring, performing feasibility study and developing mineral for small-and medium-scale businesses in accordance with the Mines Law;

(g) refinement of minerals by medium-scale and small-scale businesses;

(h) performing shallow oil wells up;

(i) printing and issuing sticker for visa and stay permit for foreigners;

(j) prospecting, exploration and production of jade/gem stones;

(k) tour-guide service;

(l) mini-market, convenience store [floor area must be below (100 ft. × 100 ft.) 10,000 square feet or 929 square metres].

The following investments are only allowed to be made by a joint venture with a local citizen or a national-owned enterprise: construction for fishing harbour, fish auction market, and fish landing site and fisheries research, which shall be carried out in accord with the law, procedure, directive and regulation of the Fishery Department; veterinary clinic, which shall be carried out in accord with the law, procedure, directive and regulation of the Livestock Breeding and Veterinary Department; cultivation of crops in agricultural land, distributing them to the local market, and exporting them; manufacturing and domestic distribution of plastic products, chemicals based on natural resources, flammable solid, liquid, gaseous fuels, aerosol, oxidants, compressed gases, corrosive chemicals, industrial chemical gases; value-added production and domestic distribution of cereal products such as biscuits, wafers, all kinds of noodles and vermicelli; manufacturing and domestic distribution of all kinds of confectionery including those of sweet, cocoa and chocolate; processing, canning, production and marketing of food products except milk and dairy products; manufacturing and domestic distribution of malt and malt liquors and non-aerated products; manufacturing, distilling, blending, rectifying, bottling and domestic distribution of all kinds of spirits, alcohol, alcoholic beverages and non-alcoholic beverages; manufacturing and domestic distribution of all kinds of purified ice, purified drinking water, and all kinds of soap; manufacturing and domestic wholesale of all kinds of cosmetic products; development, sales and lease of residential apartments and condominiums; local tour service; and transportation agency for patients to overseas hospitals.

The notification states that investments are not allowed to be made without the permission of the relevant ministries. Production and distribution of medicines that are produced by using narcotic drugs and psychotropic substances need the approval of the Ministry of Home Affairs. Ministries of the Union of Myanmar are issuing permits to invest in certain types of businesses in accordance with the law.[①]

Foreign investors are allowed to carry out the investment activities in the above-mentioned sectors only in the form of a joint venture with any Myanmar citizen-owned enterprise or Myanmar citizen. The foreign equity ratio shall not be more than 80 percent in the joint venture company under the Myanmar Investment Rules.[②] The investor carrying out investment business restricted by Section 42 of the Investment Law shall notify the Office of the Investment Commission or the branches of the Region or State Office of the Directorate of Investment and Company Administration[③] within 3 months

① Myanmar Investment Commission Notification No. 15 /2017.

② Rule 22, Myanmar Investment Rules, 2017.

③ Rule 23, Myanmar Investment Rules, 2017.

from the commencement of implementation of the investment activity.[①]

According to Section 3 of the State-Owned Economic Enterprises Law 1989, exploration and extraction of natural gas and petroleum are restricted activities to be carried out solely by the Government of Myanmar.[②] However, an investor who wants to engage in these activities shall complete the international bidding round when it is announced. The Management Committee shall consist of a total of seven members in total, four from the Myanmar side, one of whom shall act as Chairman, and three from the investor side according to the agreement between the Ministry of Electricity and Energy and the investor.[③]

The RCEP agreement will reduce barriers to trade, services, and investment. Most international investment agreements have a dispute settlement mechanism between an investor and a State, but the RCEP 'Investment' chapter does not include an investor-State dispute settlement mechanism. If an investor of the right of a RCEP member is violated under the RCEP 'Investment' chapter, he could request his home country to support his claim/claims by way of diplomacy and subsequently, the home State may bring a claim against the host State according to the provisions of the RCEP agreement.

Myanmar will gain more trust of investors from ASEAN member countries as well as developed countries such as Japan, New Zealand, Australia, South Korea and attract more investment in Myanmar. As a result, Myanmar will be able to access world markets through RCEP member countries. Myanmar government should be aware of the competition for some enterprises in Myanmar. Manufacturing capacity, worker skills, and the business environment need to be improved in Myanmar. On the other hand, the government should amend or repeal the outdated laws and enact the required laws.

---

① Rule 24, Myanmar Investment Rules, 2017.

② Section 3, the State-Owned Economic Enterprises Law, 1989.

③ State-Owned Economic Enterprises Law Related Directives.

4. Dispute Settlement Procedure

Dispute settlement procedure shall apply to a dispute arising under the RCEP agreement.① The 'Dispute Settlement' Chapter grants the complaining Party the choice between a dispute settlement panel or tribunal under international multiple agreements. The choice of forum provision shall not apply if there is a written agreement that this provision does not apply to a particular case.② Another exception to the dispute settlement procedure of RCEP is that Most-Favoured-Nation Treatment does not encompass any international dispute resolution procedures or mechanisms under other existing or future international agreements.③

Notifications, requests and replies contained in the RCEP dispute resolution must be made in writing. The panel shall consider the reports of the WTO panels and appellate body but the panel cannot change the rights and obligations under the RCEP agreement. In order to reach a mutual agreement for a dispute, the Parties involved in the dispute are encouraged to make effort through cooperation and consultations. The time limitation involved in the procedure for dispute settlement can be modified by the mutual agreement of the Parties to the dispute without prejudice the third Parties. The RCEP dispute settlement mechanism resolves some issues immediately.④

---

① Article 19.3 of the Regional Comprehensive Economic Partnership Agreement provides that '1. Unless otherwise provided in this Agreement, this Chapter shall apply: (a) to the settlement of disputes between Parties regarding the interpretation and application of this Agreement; and (b) when a Party considers that a measure of another Party is not in conformity with the obligations under this Agreement or that another Party has otherwise failed to carry out its obligations under this Agreement. 2. Subject to Article 19.5 (Choice of Forum), this Chapter shall be without prejudice to the rights of a Party to have recourse to dispute settlement procedures available under other agreements to which it is party.'

② Article 19.5, Regional Comprehensive Economic Partnership Agreement.

③ Article 10.4(3), Regional Comprehensive Economic Partnership Agreement.

④ Article 19.4, Regional Comprehensive Economic Partnership Agreement.

5. Dispute Settlement Methods of the RCEP Agreement

Parties to a dispute can make a consultation, undertake an alternative method of good offices, conciliation, or mediation before the establishment of a dispute settlement panel in accordance with the RCEP agreement. A consultation can be requested by any Party with the reasons for the request that includes identification of the measure at issue and an indication of the factual and legal basis for the complaint. At the same time, the complaining Party shall give a copy of the request for consultation to the responding Party. Reciprocally, the responding Party shall notify its receipt of the request for consultation to the complaining Party. The consultations is intended to be confidential without prejudice to the rights of any Party to the dispute. The consulting Parties shall make every effort to get the mutual agreement through their consultation and they must be in good faith.[①] The Parties may begin and terminate the procedures for an alternative method of dispute resolution, including good offices, conciliation, or mediation. The alternative methods of dispute resolution are confidential.[②]

6. Dispute Settlement Panel

If the responding Party does not consent to choose these resolution ways as mentioned above or the consultations cannot resolve a dispute during the time limitation, the complaining Party can request for the establishment of a panel.[③] When there are multiple complainants with regard to the same matter, a single panel can be established to investigate these multiple complaints relating to the same matter. On the other hand, more than one panel can be established for the same matter in accordance with the RCEP agreement.[④]

---

① Article 19.6, Regional Comprehensive Economic Partnership Agreement.

② Article 19.7, Regional Comprehensive Economic Partnership Agreement.

③ Article 19.8, Regional Comprehensive Economic Partnership Agreement.

④ Article 19.9, Regional Comprehensive Economic Partnership Agreement.

Any Party having a substantial interest in a matter before a panel shall have the rights and obligations of a third party. The RCEP agreement fully provides the third party during the panel process that includes the establishment of a panel, compliance review, compensation, and suspension of concessions or other obligations. A third Party has the right to be present at a panel hearing, submit to the panel, and answer the questions asked by the panel. Moreover, a panel can grant additional or supplemental rights to any third Party to participate in the panel proceedings if the Parties to the dispute agree those rights.①

A panel comprises three panelists② who have the specified qualifications.③ If the Parties to the dispute are not able to negotiate for the procedures of panel composition within 20 days of the date of the request for the establishment of a panel, both the complaining Party and the responding Party shall appoint one member of the panel respectively. The Parties to the dispute shall nominate a maximum of three persons to appoint the third panellist who is the chair of the panel.④ In case of non-appointment, any Party to the dispute may request the Director-General of the World Trade Organisation to choose the remaining panellists.⑤ If the rest members of the panel cannot be appointed in the second way, any Party can request the Secretary-General of the Permanent Court of Arbitration to appoint the remaining panellists promptly.⑥ If a panellist is appointed under Sections 19.11 (7) and (8),

---

① Article 19.10, Regional Comprehensive Economic Partnership Agreement.

② Article 19.11(2), Regional Comprehensive Economic Partnership Agreement.

③ Article 19.11(10) of the Regional Comprehensive Economic Partnership Agreement provides that 'Each panellist shall: (a) have expertise or experience in law, international trade, other matters covered by this Agreement, or the resolution of disputes arising under international trade agreements; (b) be chosen strictly on the basis of objectivity, reliability, and sound judgment; (c) be independent of, and not be affiliated with or take instructions from, any Party; (d) not have dealt with the matter in any capacity; (e) disclose, to the Parties to the dispute, information which may give rise to justifiable doubts as to his or her independence or impartiality; and (f) comply with the Code of Conduct as annexed to the Rules of Procedures.'

④ Article 19.11(4)(5)(6), Regional Comprehensive Economic Partnership Agreement.

⑤ Article 19.11(7), Regional Comprehensive Economic Partnership Agreement.

⑥ Article 19.11(8), Regional Comprehensive Economic Partnership Agreement.

additional qualifications are required more than the above-mentioned qualifications.[①] The Chairman shall not be a citizen and shall not has the usual place of residence of any Party involved in the dispute.[②]

In panel formation according to DSU regulations, the Secretariat shall maintain an indicative list of governmental and non-governmental individuals possessing the specified qualifications, from which panelists may be drawn as appropriate. Panels shall be composed of three panellists unless the parties to the dispute agree, within 10 days from the establishment of the panel, to a panel composed of five panellists. The Secretariat shall propose nominations for the panel to the parties to the dispute. The parties to the dispute shall not oppose nominations except for compelling reasons.[③]

The members of RCEP have the excellent chance to appoint a member of the panel. On the other hand, the RCEP procedure of the panellists' appointment has many sequences and the maximum time period to form a panel is 130 days. There is a suggestion that RCEP should list the panellists like WTO. It may simplify the complicated procedures and reduce the time for the panel establishment. The duty of a panel is making an objective assessment of: the case, the applicability of the provisions of RCEP cited by the Parties, and whether the measure in issue is not in conformity with the obligations, or whether the responding Party has otherwise failed to carry

---

① Article 19. 11 (11) of the Regional Comprehensive Economic Partnership Agreement provides that 'In addition to the requirements of paragraph 10, each panellist appointed under paragraph 7 or 8 shall: (a) have expertise in law including public international law, international trade, and the resolution of disputes arising under international trade agreements; (b) be a well-qualified governmental or non-governmental individual including an individual who has served on a WTO panel or the WTO Appellate Body or in the WTO Secretariat, taught or published on international trade law or policy, or served as a senior trade policy official of a WTO Member; and (c) in the case of the chair of the panel, wherever possible: (i) have served on a WTO panel or the WTO Appellate Body; and (ii) have expertise or experience relevant to the subject matter of the dispute.'

② Article 19.11(13), Regional Comprehensive Economic Partnership Agreement.

③ Article 8, Understanding on Rules and Procedures Governing the Settlement of Disputes, World Trade Organisation.

out its obligations according to RCEP. A panel shall only make the findings, determinations, and suggestions provided for in RCEP.[①]

According to the above-mentioned, the parties to the dispute have the right to appoint each panellist and to modify time without prejudice to the rights of the third party. Besides, the duties of a panel are to make only the findings, determinations, and suggestions. The RCEP dispute resolution mechanism does not approach compulsory jurisdiction.

7. Panel Procedures

A panel shall carry out its duties in accordance with Chapter 19 and the Rules of Procedures[②].[③] The RCEP dispute resolution system recognises the consensus method in making the findings and determinations of a panel. If it does not achieve a consensus agreement, the panel uses the majority vote. When the panel invites all Parties to the dispute to appear before it, they must present themselves at the panel. There shall be no *ex parte* communications with the panel concerning matters under consideration by it. Panel deliberations shall be confidential. All Parties to the dispute, including the third Party, have a duty to fully assist the panel information. The final report of the panel shall be issued to the Parties not exceeding 7 months from the date of formation of the panel. However, the panel shall endeavor to issue its interim report within 90 days for an urgent case which concerns perishable goods.[④] The Parties can suspend or terminate the panel proceedings at any time in accordance with the conditions of the RCEP agreement. Within 12 months from the date of the agreement to suspend, any party can request to resume the suspended panel. But the authority for the establish-

---

① Article 19.12, Regional Comprehensive Economic Partnership Agreement.

② Article 19.1(e) of the Regional Comprehensive Economic Partnership Agreement provides that 'Rules of Procedures means the Rules of Procedures for Panel Proceedings adopted by the RCEP Joint Committee'.

③ Article 19.13 (1), Regional Comprehensive Economic Partnership Agreement.

④ Article 19.13, Regional Comprehensive Economic Partnership Agreement.

ment of the panel shall lapse after 12 months.[①] The findings and determinations are made by the unanimous agreement of the panel and it is final and binding on the Parties to the dispute. But the panel can make suggestions besides the findings and determinations. The RCEP provides the procedures of findings and determinations, whereas it does not legislate on issuing a suggestion of a panel.

8. Implementation of the Final Report

The findings and determinations of a panel shall be final and binding on the Parties to the dispute. If the responding Party does not act in conformity with the obligations or fails to carry out its obligations under RCEP, the responding Party shall be held liable in accordance with the RCEP agreement. The respondent shall notify the complainant about its plan, including the timeline for how the responsibilities of the respondent will be implemented. The respondent must release this notification to the complainant within 30 days of the date of the issuance of the panel's report. If the responding Party is impracticable to comply immediately with the obligation under the panel report, it shall have a reasonable period of time to comply with the panel report. The reasonable period of time shall, whenever possible, be agreed by the Parties to the dispute. Where the Parties to the dispute are unable to agree on the reasonable period of time, any Party to the dispute may request that the chair of the panel determine the reasonable period of time, by way of notification to the chair and the other Party to the dispute.[②]

If the Parties disagree on the implementation of the final report, a Compliance Review Panel can be reconvened to settle it.[③] A Compliance Review

① Article 19.14, Regional Comprehensive Economic Partnership Agreement.

② Article 19.15, Regional Comprehensive Economic Partnership Agreement.

③ Article 19.16 (1), Regional Comprehensive Economic Partnership Agreement.

Panel makes an objective assessment of the matter before it.[①] The report of a Compliance Review Panel describes the summary of the arguments of all Parties to the dispute, both findings and determinations concerning the questions, and the reasons for its findings and determinations.[②] The report of the Compliance Review Panel is difficult to consider as a final and conclusive report because there are no specific rules for implementing the report. Although RCEP does not promulgate an appeal procedure, it allows reconvening of a Compliance Review Panel. If RCEP members have the right to appeal, the Responding Party may delay the implementation of its responsibilities provided in the panel report. It is difficult to conclude that the absence of an appeal procedure leads an incomprehensive dispute resolution system.

9. Negotiations for Compensation and Suspension of Concession or Other Obligations

The complainant has the right to take limited specific actions by negotiating with the respondent for its loss. These are temporary actions that include compensation and suspension of concession or other obligations. Compensation is voluntary and, if granted, shall be consistent with the RCEP Agreement.[③]

If the Parties could not agree on compensation or agree on compensation whereas the respondent has failed to observe the terms and conditions of that agreement, the complainant may thereafter notify the respondent and the

---

① Article 19. 16 (3) of the Regional Comprehensive Economic Partnership Agreement stipulates that 'A Compliance Review Panel shall make an objective assessment of the matter before it, including an objective assessment of: (a) the factual aspects of any action taken by the Responding Party to comply with the obligation under paragraph 1 of Article 19.15 (Implementation of the Final Report); and (b) the existence or consistency with this Agreement of any measure taken by the Responding Party to comply with the obligation under paragraph 1 of Article 19.15 (Implementation of the Final Report).'

② Article 19.16 (4), Regional Comprehensive Economic Partnership Agreement.

③ Article 19.17 (1), Regional Comprehensive Economic Partnership Agreement.

other Parties that it intends to suspend the application to the responding Party of concessions or other obligations equivalent to the level of nullification or impairment and may suspend concessions or other obligations 30 days after the receipt of the notification.① In considering what concessions or other obligations to suspend, the complaining Party shall apply the principles.② The level of the suspension of concessions or other obligations shall be equivalent to the level of nullification or impairment.③

The responding Party may request the reconvening of a panel to examine the level of suspension proposed, the terms and conditions of the compensation agreement, or two principles by notifying the complaining Party. At the same time, the responding Party shall send a copy of the request to the other Parties.④ According to the request, the panel shall reconvene within 15 days of the date of the request, and its determination shall be provided to the Parties to the dispute with in 45 days of the date of its reconvening.⑤ Then, the complaining Party may suspend concessions or other obligations to comply with the panel's determination.⑥

---

① Article 19.17 (3), Regional Comprehensive Economic Partnership Agreement.

② Article 19. 17 (6) of the Regional Comprehensive Economic Partnership Agreement states that 'In considering what concessions or other obligations to suspend, the Complaining Party shall apply the following principles: (a) the Complaining Party should first seek to suspend concessions or other obligations in the same sector or sectors in which the panel has determined that there is non-conformity with, or failure to carry out an obligation under this Agreement; and (b) if the Complaining Party considers that it is not practicable or effective to suspend concessions or other obligations in the same sector or sectors, it may suspend concessions or other obligations in other sectors.'

③ Article 19.17 (7), Regional Comprehensive Economic Partnership Agreement.

④ Article 19.17 (8), Regional Comprehensive Economic Partnership Agreement.

⑤ Article 19.17 (9), Regional Comprehensive Economic Partnership Agreement.

⑥ Article 19.17 (11), Regional Comprehensive Economic Partnership Agreement.

10. Special and Differential Treatment

A Least Developed Country Party[①] to the dispute may enjoy the special and differential treatment. Cambodia, Laos, and Myanmar are the Least Developed Countries under the list of the United Nations.[②] If the Least Developed Country is involved in the dispute, its special circumstances shall be considered when determining the causes of a dispute and the dispute settlement procedures. When the Least Developed Country has a duty to comply with the provision of Article 19.17 or other obligations pursuant to these procedures, a Complaining Party shall exercise due restraint. Where any Party to the dispute is a Least Developed Country Party, the panel's report shall explicitly indicate the form in which account has been taken of relevant provisions on special and differential treatment for a Least Developed Country Party that form part of this Agreement which have been raised by that Party in the course of the dispute settlement procedures.[③]

The provision of Article 19.18(1) of the RCEP agreement is largely similar to paragraph 1 of Article 24 of the WTO Dispute Settlement Understanding (DSU), which provides special procedures involving Least-Developed Country members. As mentioned above, Parties exercise special and differential treatment and due restraint to a Least Developed Country Party in the dispute settlement mechanism. However, the RCEP does not include the interpretation of due restraint and the procedures for due restraint. Therefore, the RCEP members should negotiate to clarify the uncertainty of the term 'due restraint'.

The dispute Parties have the right to choose the dispute settlement

---

① Article 1.2 (p) of the Regional Comprehensive Economic Partnership Agreement provides that 'Least Developed Country Party means any Party that is a Least Developed Country.'

② https://www. un. org/development/desa/dpad/least-developed-country-category/ldcs-at-a-glance.html , last visited on Jun. 6, 2020.

③ Article 19.18, Regional Comprehensive Economic Partnership Agreement.

body: a panel under the RCEP agreement, or a panel or tribunal under another international trade or investment agreement. Unlike the Dispute Settlement Body of the UN, the RCEP agreement allows the Parties to the dispute to appoint their panellist. Parties to the dispute may modify the timetable provided in the dispute settlement procedure without prejudice to the rights of the third Parties. The Parties may begin and terminate the procedures for an alternative method of dispute resolution. Moreover, Parties can also suspend or terminate the panel proceedings at any time in accordance with the conditions of the RCEP agreement. For that reason, the RCEP agreement has found that its members have many options in dispute resolution procedures. It remains to be seen if these options have any effect in practice. According to the provision of Article 19.11 of the RCEP agreement, a panel is not permanent. It shows that RCEP does not include a permanent dispute settlement body.

The RCEP's dispute settlement methods can only be used between member States. If there is a dispute between a member State and an investor of an RCEP's member, how to settle it? Interestingly, no provisions concerning the procedure of appeal are included in the RCEP agreement but the RCEP agreement allows establishing the 'Compliance Review Panel', on which RCEP has detailed regulations. Some dispute settlement provisions of RCEP are similar to the Understanding on Rules and Procedures Governing the Settlement of Disputes (DSU). The dispute settlement mechanism of the RCEP Agreement deserves to be recognised as fruitful except for the absence of an investor-State dispute settlement procedure.

11. Conclusion

The terms of the Regional Comprehensive Economic Partnership (RCEP) cover trade in goods and services, investment, economic and technical cooperation, and there are new rules for electronic commerce, intellectual property, government procurement, competition, and small and medium-sized enterprises. It can upgrade the economy of the Asia-Pacific region by reducing barriers to trade, services, and investment. RCEP will create the world's largest trading bloc, with its Asia-Pacific members accounting for nearly a third of global gross domestic product. In addition, it will contribute not only to a more progressive economy of ASEAN but also to more organised participation of ASEAN in the world economy. The absence of compulsory judiciary, a feature of the RCEP dispute resolution mechanism, is considered to be enshrined in accordance with the ASEAN Charter. The RCEP agreement is expected to contribute to the economic recovery of the region and strengthen confidence in the longer-term economic prospects for the region. It provides the investment and investors between the RCEP members with equal opportunities, mutual protection of investments, facilitated investments, eased investment laws and regulations, investment promotion activities, cooperation on investment issues, and conformity with ASEAN Plus One FTAs. To conclude up, the Regional Comprehensive Economic Partnership Agreement will establish an important trading area in the world throughout the Asia-Pacific region in the future.

Study on the Rule of Law in Myanmar

Si Thu Swe Tun[*]

1. Introduction

The Republic of the Union of Myanmar is the largest state in mainland Southeast Asia. With a land mass of 653,508 square kilometers (about 252,320 square miles) and a total population of around 55 million, the country comprises 7 regions and 7 states, as well as 6 'self-administered areas' and a purpose-built capital at Nay Pyi Taw (which has been directly administered by the president since the government moved there in 2006).① It is officially composed of 135 ethnic groups with 8 major national races,② and is one of the most ethnically diverse countries in the world. Among the 8 major national ethnic races, the Bamar ethnic race is in the majority, which constitutes more than 70% of the country's total population and non-Bamar population is around 30% of the total population. Historically, people in Myanmar has been staying together in peace, ensuring that they lived with unity and diversity.

---

* Ph. D. Candidate of SWUPL, officer of MOLA, Myanmar.

① The Constitution of the Republic of the Union of Myanmar, 2008, Sec. 49-56. The regions are Ayeyawady (Irrawady), Bago (Pegu), Magway, Mandalay, Yangon, Sagaing and Taninthayi (Tenassarim); the ethnic states are Chin, Kachin, Kayin (Karen), Kayah (Karenni), Mon, Rakhine (Arakan) and Shan; the self-administered areas are Naga, Danu, Pa-O, Pa Laung, Kokang, and Wa.

② Eight major national races of Myanmar are Kachin, Kayah, Kayin, Chin, Mon, Bamar, Rakhine and Shan.

Since Myanmar has been transforming towards a democratic system, the development of rule of law must be prioritised. The rule of law establishes the justice, independence and equality as well as providing the emergence of the sustaining peace and development. As the rule of law processes are concerned with all sectors of the legislature, executive and judiciary, the cooperation among all stakeholders is significantly required for its achievement.

Myanmar strongly believes that the rule of law is a foundation for relations among nations. Multilateralism can only succeed if the inter-state relations is based on rules and law. A rule-based international order could be the key platform to bring peace, harmony and development in our world today. In fact, the United Nations (UN) was established to strengthen rule of law at international level to govern the behaviour of states in accordance with the principles enshrined in the UN Charter.①

2. Myanmar Concept of Rule of law

Myanmar has embarked on a process of democratisation that requires reform phase by phase. The rule of law plays a profoundly important role in this process. It serves as a foundation for the prosperity of the nation by safeguarding the security and fundamental rights of the people. It builds on justice values of independence, impartiality, integrity and propriety.②

According to the preamble of the Universal Declaration of Human Rights, human rights should be protected by the rule of law.③ In addition,

---

① Nyan Lin Aung, Statement on the Rule of Law at the National and International Level at the Sixth Committee of the 75th Session of the United Nations General Assembly, p. 1, https://estatements. unmeetings. org/estatements/11. 0060/20201022/lxhF5jnsO6Rw/9m5VSvLqtY6Q_en.pdf, last visited on Jun. 6, 2020.

② Dr. Tun Shin, The Legal Concept of the Rule of Law and Access to Justice, *Law Journal of the Union Attorney General's Office*, 2013, Vol. 10, No. 2, p. 76.

③ Universal Declaration of Human Rights, adopted by the UNGA with resolution 217A (III on 10 December 1948 at the Palais de Chaillot in Paris, France, https://treaties. un.org, last visited on Jun. 6, 2020.

one of the principles of the ASEAN Charter states that ASEAN member States shall act in accordance with 'adherence to the rule of law, good governance, the principles of democracy and constitutional government'.

The Government of Myanmar regards rule of law as a fundamental principle of democratic governance. The government and legislature are seeking to make the laws in Myanmar more transparent and protect the interest of all the people in the country to ensure that each and every one is equal before the law.

People always mention rule of law, but frequently misunderstand it. Rule of law is not simply law and order, following the rules and obeying laws. Rule of law does not mean rule by law; much more than a legal concept, rule of law refers to a wider system of governance that is an essential part of democracy and that forms a framework for the protection of human rights. In the Myanmar language, the term is commonly expressed as 'uba-day baung dwin nay tai gyin bay kin yan kwar seit chan thar'. It means that when people stay and obey the frame of the existing law, they will get security and peace. This phrase does not accurately convey the full sense of what rule of law is and it is sometimes easier to understand rule of law if we first rule out what it is not.①

The Government of the Republic of the Union of Myanmar places great importance on the establishment of stability and prosperity of the community and it hopes that the public understand not only the essence of rule of law but also the impact of rule of law. The rule of law is the cornerstone for strengthening democracy and development of the country. One of the basic principles of the rule of law is to promote the establishment of a rule-based society in the interest of legal certainty and predictability. Strengthening the rule of law is to protect the rights of and provide access to justice for all Myanmar people. Good governance is accountable and responsible to the citizens for their fundamental rights and in consequence, the eternal principles of justice, liberty and equality in the Union will develop and

---

① Richard H.Fallon, Jr., "The Rule of Law" as a Concept in Constitution Discourse, *Columbia Law Review*, 1997, Vol. 97, No. 1.

the citizens can fully enjoy the valuable standards of judiciary.①

In fact, rule of law is a much broader concept. It is a system of governance in which all people are treated equally and without discrimination, where nobody is 'above the law', regardless of their political position or social status, and where, crucially, the exercise of arbitrary power is restrained. The transformative value of rule of law depends upon a broad conception of what it means, which includes a reform agenda that extends beyond laws themselves and to all aspects of governance.

In 2015, 'the rule of law' was referred to twice in the Nationwide Ceasefire Agreement, and the recent, ambitious Strategic Plan released by the Union Attorney General's Office is entitled simply 'Moving Forward to the Rule of Law'. Across sectors, almost every element of the rule of law and the judicial system in Myanmar have been under review and up for debate.

3. Global Concept of Rule of law

The rule of law is an important component of sustaining peace, as advanced by the General Assembly and Security Council in the twin resolutions on the review of the peacebuilding architecture. Sustaining peace requires an integrated and comprehensive approach across the UN system, based on coherence between political, security, development, human rights, gender equality and rule of law activities in support of Member State-led efforts.

Strengthening the rule of law involves respect for the norms of international law, including on the use of force, and recognition of the primary responsibility of States to protect their populations from genocide, crimes against humanity, ethnic cleansing and war crimes. The rule of law is a core element of the humanitarian, and it is crucial to understanding and addressing the reasons for displacement and statelessness. It is the foundation of the hu-

① U Tun Tun Oo, Attorney General of the Union, Speech contained in the Fair Trial guidebook for Law Officers, 2018; Published by the Union Attorney General's Office, the Republic of the Union of Myanmar.

manitarian protection regime.[①]

There is no universal definition of rule of law, but fundamentally, it means that everybody is treated and protected equally under the law; nobody is above the law, and courts, informal tribunals, government institutions and officials must treat each person equally, all of the time. The United Nations' definition of rule of law encompasses its most important components: 'The "rule of law"... refers to a principle of governance in which all persons, institutions and entities, public and private, including the State itself, are accountable to laws that are publicly promulgated, equally enforced and independently adjudicated, and which are consistent with international human rights norms and standards'.

This definition includes the values of transparency, equality, accountability and independence and it stresses that rule of law requires legislation and legal institutions to conform to international human rights standards. Rule of law is a relatively modern concept and linked to the principle of justice. Rule of law requires trust between people and their government. Law applies to everyone and is equally enforced without discrimination and laws are independently and fairly adjudicated.[②] The UN General Assembly (2012) has stated that 'the advancement of the rule of law at the national and international levels is essential for the realisation of sustained economic growth, sustainable development, the eradication of poverty and hunger and the protection of all human rights and fundamental freedoms.'[③]

Rule of law, the mechanism, process, institution, practice, or norm that supports the equality of all citizens before the law, secures a nonarbitrary form of government, and more generally prevents the arbitrary use of

---

① Nyan Lin Aung, Statement on the Rule of Law at the National and International Level at the Sixth Committee of the 75th Session of the United Nations General Assembly, p. 2.

② Rule of Law Centers, https://www.rolcmyanmar.org/en/what-is-rule-of-law, last visited on Jun. 6, 2020.

③ Universal Declaration of Human Rights, Adopted by the UNGA with Resolution 217A (III on 10 December 1948 at the Palais de Chaillot in Paris, France, https://treaties.un.org, last visited on Jun. 6, 2020.

power. In general, the rule of law implies that the creation of laws, their enforcement, and the relationships among legal rules are themselves legally regulated, so that no one including the most highly placed official is above the law. The legal constraint on rulers means that the government and its citizens are subject to existing laws. Thus, a closely related notion is the idea of equality before the law, which holds that no 'legal' person shall enjoy privileges that are not extended to all and that no person shall be immune from legal sanctions. In addition, the application and adjudication of legal rules by various governing officials are to be impartial and consistent across equivalent cases, made without taking into consideration the class, status, or relative power among disputants.

While certain institutional traditions and conventions, as well as written laws, may be important to ensure that judicial decisions are grounded on plausible interpretations of existing laws, no single institutional character of a state should be seen as necessary or sufficient to the rule of law ideal. The rule of law is tied neither to any one national experience nor to any set of institutions in particular, although it may be better served in certain countries and by some institutions. Moreover, the institutional arrangements that ensure the rule of law in one polity might not be easily duplicated in or transplanted to another. Different polities embody their own judgments about how to implement specific rule of law ideals given their particular legal and cultural traditions, which naturally influence the character of their institutions. Nonetheless, the initial sociological condition for the rule of law is shared across cultures: for the rule of law to be more than an empty principle, most people in a society, including those whose profession is to administer the law, must believe that no individual or group should be above the law.

The ASEAN Charter (which Myanmar ratified on 21 July 2008) meanwhile declares it self to be a principle to be honoured by all member states, and the community-building process that is currently under way within the organisation is explicitly designed 'to strengthen democracy, enhance good governance and the rule of law, and to promote and protect human rights and fundamental freedoms'.[①]

As the aspirations expressed by ASEAN suggest, the concept of the rule of law is inextricably linked nowadays to an assumption that arbitrary actions are wrong, and that discretionary powers should always be exercised predictably. The Venice Commission's useful analysis ascribes 6 features to the concept, namely: (i) the supremacy of transparently made laws; (ii) legal certainty; (iii) a prohibition of arbitrariness; (iv) access to justice before independent and impartial courts; (v) procedures that allow for human rights to be protected; and (vi) non-discrimination and equality before the law.[②]

As noted above, the Universal Declaration of Human Rights explicitly linked the rule of law to the protection of human rights more than half a century ago, and its substantive components were emphasised in 2004 by the then UN Secretary-General Kofi Annan:

> The "rule of law"... refers to a principle of governance in which all persons, institutions and entities, public and private, including the State itself, are accountable to laws that are publicly promulgated, equally enforced and independently adjudicated, and which are consistent with international human rights norms and standards. It requires, as well, measures to ensure adherence to the principles of supremacy of law, equality before the law, accountability to the law, fairness in the application of the law, separation of powers, participation in decision-making, legal certainty, avoidance of arbitrariness and procedural and legal transparency."

It is not an effective way to imagine or design rule of law initiatives. Instead, achieving rule of law requires comprehensive justice reform and collaborative, inclusive efforts between local, state, national, and international actors. The rule of law protects and promotes the rights and responsibilities

---

① Charter of the Association of Southeast Asian Nations, Art 1(7) and 2(2)(h), http:// www.asean.org/archive/publications/ASEAN-Charter.pdf, last visited on Apr. 4, 2020.

② Venice Commission, *Report on the Rule of Law*, No. 3, pp. 10-13.

of the government and the people, and therefore necessitates an interconnected approach.[①]

4. Application of Rule of Law in Myanmar

Application of rule of law is important in the case of Myanmar because durable development requires that reforms command moral authority within the country and respect in the world. Neither can be achieved through a legal system that limits justice to the rigid application of commands from above. The rule of law has been used as a synonym for forceful rule by law, and the 2008 Constitution of Myanmar itself contains in English version, Burmese terminology which appeared in the official translation of the previous 1974 Constitution as 'rule of law' is consistently rendered 'prevalence of law and order.'

As the Republic of the Union of Myanmar is transitioning towards a democratic system, development of rule of law must be prioritised. The rule of law ensures justice, independence and equality as well as promotes sustainable peace and development. As the rule of law is concerned with all sections of the legislature, the executive and the judiciary, cooperation among all stakeholders is necessary for its prevalence.

4.1 The Establishment of Rule of Law Centres

In 2013, the first seminar on the rule of law was jointly organised by the Union Attorney General's Office and the European Union. Since then, institutions have developed their own strategic plans and civil society organisations have emerged. A legal aid system is being established and the legal profession has come to recognise the need to modernise. International development partners acknowledge and accept that their support is important for the democratic transformation process as well as the development of the rule of law and the justice sector of Myanmar. Rule of Law Centres were designed and launched with the support of UNDP. Rule of Law Centres currently operate

① UN General Assembly Resolution 67/1, 2012, p.2.

out of hubs in Yangon, Mandalay, Taunggyi and Myitkyina in order to raise legal and civic awareness among the people. The British Council's MyJustice Programme supports Justice Centres in Yangon, Mawlamyine, Taungoo, Hpa-An, Taunggyi and Mandalay with the European Union funding and provides legal aid for the poor who are accused of a criminal offence.

4.2 The Formation of the Union Coordinating Body for Rule of Law Centres and Justice Sector Affairs

In February 2017, the Government of Myanmar established the Union Coordination Body for Rule of Law Centres and Justice Sector Affairs (UCB) to improve cooperation among justice sector institutions and local, regional and international organisations. The Government designated the Attorney General of the Union as the Chairperson of the UCB, with 17 members from institutions including the Hluttaw, Supreme Court of the Union (USC), the Ministry of Home Affairs, the National Human Rights Commission and from civil society organisations, including the Bar Council and educators. Recognising the complexity of its task, the UCB in turn created a Sub-Coordinating Body (SCB) for each of Myanmar's 14 Regions and States. The UCB must strives to develop legal awareness and access to justice for the people, and to advance the rule of law in the country.

As it is important to establish work plans, methods and a strategic plan for achieving its goals, the National Conference on Justice Sector Coordination for Rule of Law (Rule of law for all forum) was held on 7 to 8 March, 2018, at the Myanmar International Convention Centre II in Nay Pyi Taw. This Conference on the Justice Sector coordination for Rule of Law includes the training of a future generation of legal professionals, which would further improve the justice system and encourage young people to consider pursuing public service through a legal career. It was attended by government delegates, the representatives of the UN organisations, national, regional and international experts and representatives from civil society organisations.

The UCB's Strategic Plan, which has been drawn and published based on outcomes of the Conference, will contribute to better judicial services, ensure respect for the rule of law and serve as a vital bridge to better coordination among different justice actors. The UCB is committed to enhancing access to justice for all the people of Myanmar. It will work in collaboration with the relevant departments and organisations, development partners and civil society organisations including those concerned with the relevant sectors for implementing the 4 Goals and Work Plans of this Strategic Plan.

On 15 May 2017, the UCB established the Advisory Group of international technical experts to seek necessary advice for its work. It also set up a secretariat and a working group to achieve its goals effectively. The UCB considered it necessary to establish a Work Programme and Strategic Plan to carry out its work effectively. The UCB invited participants from across the country to the National Conference on Justice Sector Coordination for Rule of Law, held on May 7-8, 2018, in order to obtain advice from relevant institutions, organisations and individuals.

The Strategic Plan was drawn up based on research, the experience of its members and consultation with stakeholders. In particular, this Strategic Plan has been inspired by the Myanmar Sustainable Development Plan (2018 to 2030) and has been prepared in conformity with the coordination framework established by the Development Assistance Coordination Unit (DACU).

The 4 Goals of the Strategic Plan are: 1. justice sector coordination; 2. public trust; 3. justice knowledge; 4. justice sector planning. The 6 Thematic Areas of the Strategic Plan are: 1. access to justice and legal aid; 2. justice for children and other vulnerable groups; 3. the empowerment of women; 4. legal education and the professional development of lawyers; 5. law enforcement and crime prevention; and 6. accountability and efficiency in all justice services.

The aim is to implement this Strategic Plan effectively with the cooperation of local and international organisations working in the area of rule of law and justice. Only when public trust is established, will the rule of law prevail in the country. Extensive cooperation among justice sector institutions is crucial to achieving justice for all. They should engage with the civil society, NGOs and development partners to ensure justice sector development. Myanmar needs a comprehensive plan to establish an effective

justice sector. This plan, when fully developed, should address the people's need for institutions, technology, justice services, as well as outreach to the people.

The following institutions are direct implementation body of Myanmar's rule of law sector: the Ministry of Home Affairs, Supreme Court of the Union, Anti-corruption Commission and Union Attorney General's Office. The following union level offices are vital for enhancing the rule of law sector in Myanmar and connecting Myanmar with other countries, especially those in the ASEAN area.

4.3 Ministry of Home Affairs

Under the Constitution, the Ministry of Home Affairs is formed and Minister of Home Affairs is a member of Union Government. Objectives of the Ministry of Home Affairs are state security, prevalence of law and order, community peace and tranquility, and to carry out social rendering service. The 2 major implementation bodies of rule of law are under the Ministry of Home Affairs. They are General Administration Department (GAD) and Myanmar Police Force.

At present, the General Administration Department has been under the umbrella of the Ministry of Home Affairs for successive governments. Like the Ministry of Home Affairs, the official mandate of the GAD is first and foremost, ensuring the rule of law as well as the peace and prosperity of villages and townships, regional development, and people's welfare. Down to the level of every village in the country, the GAD has a mandate to support government security efforts as well as report relevant information back to Nay Pyi Taw.①

The relevant offices implement the administration sector such as rule of law, politics, society, economy in accordance with the relevant laws. They offer the planning, guidance to the relevant office and stand as the coordination body. These relevant offices have the control to relevant level respective

① Lachlan Mcdonald, https://www.frontiermyanmar.net/en/making-the-most-of-gad-reforms/, last visited on Apr. 4, 2020.

body, i.e. police force, immigration office, municipal and electrical power office and so on. That is why these relevant-level general administrative offices are the focal points in Myanmar's rule of law sector.

The Ministry of Home Affairs manages the administrative matters by giving the duties to General Administration Department and Myanmar Police Force on behalf of State Government as whole Country. Minister gives the policy of Administrative and Secretary arrange to working for succeed to supervise. Therefore, Burma Civil Services of Administration arrange to all duties as chief of Secretary, Vice-Secretary and Junior Secretary at all Ministries and Office of the Secretary, Divisional Majesty, District Inspector, Terror Inspector, Civil Inspector, Assistant Inspector at all villages. At that time period, exclude the branch of general administration and include people police force and prison office branches in the Ministry of Home Affairs.

Old Administrative System of Myanmar was repairing to Colonel Administrative System only. Take duties of works for General Administrative, Development tasks, Rural Development works, Inspection of Literature and Registration works and form the office of General Administrative as Head Office, office of the State/ Divisional and Township, by each other. Objectives of General Administration Department are rule of law, community peace and tranquility, regional development, and to serve the public interest.①

4.4 Myanmar Police Force

Myanmar Police Force is operaing in accordance with the instruction of Ministry of Home Affairs and Headquarters opera of Myanmar Police Force, regarding with security matters, head of the state those who attend the state ceremonies, forums, meetings, ASEAN Summits, SEA Games, tours of the heads of the foreign countries and foreign governmental ministers and Buddhist religious ceremonies, and so, cooperating with other counterpart organisations.

In all towns and villages across the nation, Myanmar Police Force is be-

---

① Ministry of Home Affairs of the Republic of the Union of Myanmar, http:// www.moha.gov.mm, last visited on Apr. 4, 2020.

ing found taking an active part in public-oriented social activities. For the police, not only performing the tasks of prevention and suppression of crimes but also contributing their voluntary labour in social events for the benefit of regional populace can bring about people's trust and reliance. In democratic nations, police forces take the responsibility of maintaining tranquility and rule of law in their respective regions. In doing so, people's trust and reliance is of great necessity, so the system of the people's police force needs reform so that it can stand for the public. The British policing system was introduced in 1885, when the Union of Myanmar became a British colony. Myanmar Police Force was founded in 1889 under the colonial rule as Burma Military Police, Burma Civil Police and Rangoon Town Police. In 1942, Burma Police Force was renamed as Myanmar Police Force, it was learnt. In 1948 when the country gained its independence, the word in Myanmar for 'police' changed from 'palake' to 'ye'. In 1964, it was re-founded as People's Police Force, an independent department under Ministry of Home Affairs, and then renamed as Myanmar Police Force in 1994. It was reorganised on 1 October 1995 and informally became part of Tatmadaw, and it is the law enforcement agency of Myanmar.

Mynamar Police Force was born under the colonial rule but it was found to have changed its system with the changing political systems as public-oriented community policing. In moving on the way of the democratic transmission, police forces had some confrontations with the people. As there were criticisms over those confrontations, reforms were made by conducting training in controlling the mob. Being service personnel performing duties around the clock, Myanmar Police Force may have some weaknesses in contact with people regardless of race and religion. Myanmar Police Force are required to make their concerted efforts to become qualified with capacities and skills in performances of service, organisation, administration and enforcement of rule of law.

In a time when the number of criminals and violators of laws is increasing, it is not an easy task for police forces to perform their duties in accord with rules and law. In addition to the tasks of prevention and suppression of crimes, their performances of maintaining regional peace and stability, enforcing rule of law, preventing the danger of drugs and participating in public-oriented social events must be acknowledged. Once in the past, police were despised and criticised with pejorative words as they used to arrive at crime scenes at belated time. Police routines include crime prevention, search and arrest.

Now that police forces are performing their duties by stand-by watch, sentry and patrol posts around the clock, offences, crimes and criminals can be said to be alleviated. If people participate in preventing and suppressing crimes hand in hand with police forces, regional peace and tranquility can be achieved for sure. Accordingly, in such a period of democratic transition, Myanmar Police Force is practically being found to have changed together with the people. It is expected that Myanmar Police Force can perform the duties of rule of law and sustaining regional tranquility in more modernised ways.①

Myanmar is one of the member states of the United Nations. Myanmar Police Force has been taking its responsibility in harmony with the United Nations Security Council Resolution numbers 1373, 1276 and 1455. Myanmar became a member state of the United Nations Convention against Transnational Organised Crime on 30 March 2004. As a consequence, Myanmar Police Force established the Department against Transnational Crime in September 2004. So cooperation with the international community, especially neighbouring ASEAN countries and other Asian states, has been made up. One police colonel acts as the head of the department activating in suppression of transnational crimes.

The Annual ASEAN Senior Officials Meeting on Transnational organized Crime (SOMTC) and the once-in-every-two-year ASEAN Ministerial Metting on Transnational Crime (AMMTC) are attended by Myanmar with the implementation on what have been decided in regional criminal suppression and prevention. The 9th ASEAN Senior Officials Meeting on Transnational Crime was held on 30 June to 4 July 2009 hosted by Myanmar.

---

① https://www.gnlm.com.mm/myanmar-police-force-rule-law/, last visited on Apr. 4, 2020.

Myanmar Police Force has been cooperating with the relevant government agencies, NGOs, INGOs, UN agencies and other international organisations to combat trafficking in persons issues, especially with the Asia Regional Trafficking in Persons Project (ARTIP) and the member countries of GMS. In accordance with the agreement on cooperation in trafficking in persons with the People's Republic of China, BLOs were established at Muse, Myanmar and Ruili, China in 2007 and also the other 2 BLOs were established at Loijei, Myanmar and Jing feng, China in 2008. MoU on combating trafficking persons between Myanmar and Thailand was signed on 24 April 2009, Myanmar and China on 11 November 2009.①

4.5 Access to Justice and the Role of Court

Section 21 of the 2008 Constitution provides that 'every citizen shall enjoy the right of equality, the right of liberty and the right of justice', while Section 19 lists 3 'judicial principles': the administration of justice independently according to law; the dispensation of justice in open court unless otherwise prohibited by law; and a guarantee in all cases of the right of defence and the right of appeal under law.

In respect of criminal justice specifically, the delegation learned that the Constitution reiterates a provision in the Criminal Procedure Code (CPC) that citizens may not be detained for more than 24 hours without a court's permission. The CPC guarantees a qualified right to silence,② but many common procedural protections, including the presumption of innocence and a rule against double jeopardy are lacking. It also allows judges to extend the 24-hour custody period to 15 days, or 30 days in the case of offences punishable by more than 7 years' imprisonment, while the Constitution itself overrides the 24-hour limit in cases where 'precautionary measures [are] taken for the security of the Union or prevalence of law and order, peace and tran-

① Myanmar Police Force, http://www.aseanapol.org/information/myanmar-police-force, last visited on Jun. 6, 2020.

② A Defendant Need Not Testify, although a Court May Draw Adverse Inferences from such a Failure to Give Evidence: Criminal Procedure Code, Sec. 342.

quility in accord with the law in the interest of the public'.[①]

On 26 September 1988, the State Law and Order Restoration Council promulgated the Judiciary Law and formed the courts at different levels and for the administration of justice in the Union of Myanmar. It was subsequently repealed by the Judiciary Law, 2000 which was promulgated on 27 June 2000 by the State Peace and Development Council, for the promotion of the judiciary, and to revamp the formation of courts. The present judicial system was adopted under the 2008 Constitution and Union Judiciary Law 2010.

The Supreme Court of the Union is the highest organ of the State Judiciary of the Republic of the Union of Myanmar. It is the apex of the court system in Myanmar and exists as an independent entity alongside the legislative and executive branches. The Supreme Court of the Union is the superior court of record and has supervisory powers over all courts in the Union and its decisions are binding upon all courts. A case finally and conclusively adjudicated by the Supreme Court of the Union exercising its original jurisdiction, or a case finally and conclusively adjudicated by the Supreme Court of the Union on the final and conclusive decision of any court may, on being admitted for special appeal by the Special Bench in accordance with the procedures, be heard and adjudicated again by the Special Appellate Bench.[②] The Supreme Court of the Union has the power to issue Writ of Habeas Corpus, Writ of Mandamus, Writ of Prohibition, Writ of Quo Warranto, Writ of Certiorari.[③]

4.6 Union Attorney General's Office

When Myanmar regained her independence in 1948, the Union Attorney General's Office (UAGO) was established under the Constitution of the Union of Burma, 1947 and the Attorney General of the Union Act, 1948. The UAGO continued to exist when the Revolutionary Council took over the

---

① The Constitution of the Republic of the Union of Myanmar, 2008, Sec. 376.

② The Union Judiciary Law, 2010.

③ Constitution of the Republic of the Union of Myanmar, 2008, Sec. 378.

State responsibilities in 1962. When the then administrative mechanism was abolished in 1972, a new one was established and it was vested to carry out the responsibility for prosecution, tendering legal advice, drafting bills and legaltranslation. After that, the Constitution of the Socialist Republic of the Union of Burma was exercised in 1974 and the Council of People's Attorneys was formed. And then, the Attorney General Law 1988 and the Attorney General Law, 2001 were promulgated. These were based on history, experience and practice to meet the needs of the times.

On 28 October 2010, the Attorney General of the Union Law was promulgated in accord with the Constitution of the Republic of the Union of Myanmar and states that 'the President shall, with the approval of the Pyidaungsu Hluttaw, appoint a person from among Hluttaw Representatives or from among those who are not the Hluttaw Representatives who fulfil the qualifications contained in sub-section (a) of section 237 of the Constitution and section 10 of this Law as the Attorney General of the Union to obtain legal advice and assign duties on legal matters' under section 5 of the Attorney General of the Union Law. The Attorney General of the Union is a member of the Union Government and is responsible to the President of the Union.

The only union-level office in Myanmar that can coordinate with the three pillars of the State is the Union Attorney General's Office (UAGO). The significant obligations of the UAGO regarding implementation of international conventions and treaties and its advisory role for the State provided under the Union Attorney General Law 2010 are as follows:[①]

- tendering legal advice to both the Parliament and State or Regional Parliaments;
- tendering legal advice to the executive branch at various levels;
- filing legal cases on behalf of the State to the Court;
- a customary role in drafting bills for national legislation;
- ittee for advising and vetting some legal matters that are to be added

① Section 12 of the Union Attorney General Law (UAGL), 2010. See also the Union Attorney General Office of Myanmar, http://www.oag.gov.mm, last visited on Jun. 20, 2020.

or removed from a bill;

- coordination with and vetting legal advices to relative ministries and organisations if a draft law relates to international conventions and agreements;
- advising on and vetting the draft laws according to the orthography to promulgate the laws smoothly;
- a significant advisory role in signing, implementing, and ratifying international conventions, treaties, contracts and so on.

Nowadays, the Attorney General is a central member of the national-level peace implementation organs.

The duties of the Attorney General of the Union are to perform the duties of member of the Union Government; to submit the unusual situation relating to the legal matters from time to time; to tender legal advice to the President of the Union, the Speaker of the Pyidaungsu Hluttaw or Pyithu Hluttaw or Amyotha Hluttaw, any organisation of the Pyidaungsu level, any Ministry of the Union or Nay Pyi Taw Council; to appear on behalf of the State in applications to issue writs to the Supreme Court of the Union; to prosecute criminal cases; to appear in criminal cases on behalf of the Union including civil case in which the Union is involved as the plaintiff or defendant; to tender legal advice to the Union level organisations on matters relating to international, regional or bilateral or multilateral treaties; to tender legal advice to the Union level organisations on matters relating to memorandums of understanding, memorandums of agreement, local and foreign investment instruments and other instruments; to carry out other duties assigned by the Union Government or any law.

The powers of the Attorney-General of the Union are to determine the duties and powers of the Deputy Attorney-General; to carry out to withdraw the entire case, any charge or any accused in a criminal case; to make decision to close the criminal cases; to give consent in writing under the Code of Civil Procedure in order to institute a suit regarding public charities. The Attorney General of the Union tenders legal advice to the Union level organisations as to whether or not it should be a party to international conventions and regional agreements and on matters relating to bilateral or multilateral

treaties, memorandums of understanding, memorandums of agreement, local and foreign investment instruments and other instruments. The Attorney General of the Union is the Government Attorney General in criminal cases and appears on behalf of the Government in civil cases in which the Government is involved. The Union Attorney General appears, on behalf of the Union, in applications to issue writs to the Supreme Court of the Union relating to citizens, the fundamental rights and duties of the citizens.①

4.7 Anti-corruption Committee

Myanmar knew that rule of law is based on the fight against corruption, so it formed Anti-corruption Commission (ACC). In order to more effectively prevent corruption, the Suppression of Corruption Act was enacted in 1948 in which 6 sections were contained. The Act was amended 4 times. Under Section 4 (2) of the Act, public servants shall be punished with imprisonment up to 7 years and the proceeds of the crime shall be confiscated if they commit 4 kinds of offences prescribed in Section 4 (1) such as receiving gratification habitually other than legal remuneration, receiving valuable things for himself or for any other person in return for his or his senior official's act, receiving valuable thing or money by abusing his position and fraud or misappropriation of trusted property.

Governments have taken measures to combat and prevent corruption. However, corruption exists and some responsible officials disregard the dignity of the State and their reputation by breaking the law and thus corruption becomes widened as a culture in the society. Corruption includes abuse of authority, bribery and willful misconduct, so it is of interest to the general public. It has harmful effects on administration and human rights and also deteriorates the economy, politics and moral ethics. Moreover, it can be an issue of concern if becoming widespread internationally. As global economy is rapidly developing these days, corruption has grown in different form as organised crimes and also transnational crimes. As corruption is committed not only within one country but also in connection with foreign

① Section 13 of the Union Attorney General Law, 2010.

countries, anti-corruption cannot be done by a single country alone.

According to the Transparency International's Corruption Perception Index (CPI), Myanmar ranked 180 in 2011 but in 2015, Myanmar's rank rose to 147. Since the government is endeavouring to develop domestic businesses and also inviting foreign investments for the enhancement of the national economy, it needs to improve the CPI ranking. Myanmar will be enhancing its cooperation in anti-corruption activities with countries within the region and with international organisations as well.

In order to eliminate bribery, the Action Committee against Bribery was formed under the President Office Order 9/2013 dated 8 January 2013. Corruption and bribery could be reported or filed or complained individually and by a group. After scrutinising, complaints required to take departmental action were transferred to the departments concerned for further action and filed where action was not necessary to take. Complaints that needed to be taken action were submitted to higher authorities and investigated in accordance with law and also in cooperation with partnership organisations.

The complaints were preliminarily scrutinised for accuracy and detailed investigation was made based on the findings. Legal action was made if necessary. Action would be taken for fraudulent complaints in accordance with the existing law.

It is found that the Suppression of Corruption Act had only categories of criminal cases and correspond action and there was no relevance to international standards. With the aim to draft a law in line with international standards as prescribed in UNCAC, the Department of Special Investigation initially drafted the anti-corruption bill in 2005 and submitted to the UAGO through the Ministry of Home Affairs for legal remarks. The Anti-bribery Bill drafted by Hluttaw's Bill Committee was submitted to the Hluttaw and publicised in the daily newspapers.

After Anti-bribery law was discussed thoroughly at the Pyidaungsu Hluttaw, the Anti-corruption Law was enacted on 7 August 2013 as Pyidaungsu Hluttaw Law No. 23/2013. It was signed by the President on 17 September 2013. There are 11 chapters and 73 articles in this Law to support rule of law in combating corruption. Under this Law, the Anti-corruption

Commission has been formed with 15 members including the chairman and the secretary under the President's Office Order 6/2014 on 25 February 2014. Its motto is 'Remove Corruption, Promote Prosperity'.

4.8 The Myanmar National Human Rights Commission

It was against this backdrop that the Yangon-based Myanmar National Human Rights Commission (MNHRC) was established by an executive order of President Thein Sein on 5 September 2011, 'with a view to promoting and safeguarding the fundamental rights of citizens'.①

The MNHRC quickly took steps to establish its credibility. An early positive move came in the form of a statement dated 6 October 2011, which announced that it would accept complaints from members of the public.② Concerns have been expressed, however, that the MNHRC remains a tool of the executive, rather than an independent check on government.

This put the body at odds with prevailing interpretations of the Principles Relating to the Status of National Human Rights Institutions (the 'Paris Principles'), the UN-sanctioned statement of good practice, which serves as the basis for collaboration between the OHCHR, the UNDP and at least 60 national human rights institutions.

5. Conclusion

In conclusion, Myanmar has many governmental institutions, such as Ministry of Home Affair, Anti corruption Commission, Union Attorney General's Office and so on. Every organisation cooperates with each other to terminate discrimination and arbitrary enforcement of laws, regardless of ethnicity, gender, religion; supports the rule of law sector with accountability; protects minorities and vulnerable groups, lack of fear to authorities,

---

① Notification No. 34/2011, www.burmalibrary.org/docs11/National_ Human_Rights _ Commission _Formed-NLM2011-09-06.pdf, last visited on Jun. 4, 2020.

② New Light of Myanmar, www. burmalibrary. org/docs14/NHRC-Statement-NLM 2011-10-07.pdf, last visited on Jun. 4, 2020.

lack of access to justice for most of the population, and obeys international human rights standards. Myanmar's rule of law depends on the above-mentioned ministries and they are implementing not only administrative matters but also rule of law sector as legal and institutional base society in accordance with the Myanmar strategic trend. Therefore, every ministry is key to enhancing prevalence of law and order in Myanmar and the international community especially ASEAN, United Nations and neighbouring countries.

At present, the government and people of Myanmar are committed to building a democratic federal union through the promotion of rule of law despite facing multiple daunting challenges. It is believed that the primary responsibility of maintaining and enforcing the rule of law in a country rests with the government and its people. The international community can only support the national efforts through capacity building or other forms of constructive cooperation. Strengthening of rule of law is a linchpin for the maintenance of rule-based international order, and sine qua non for the peace, harmony and development in every nation.

图书在版编目（CIP）数据

中国—东盟法律评论. 第十四辑 / 张晓君主编. --厦门：厦门大学出版社，2023.12
ISBN 978-7-5615-9127-7

Ⅰ. ①中… Ⅱ. ①张… Ⅲ. ①法律-中国、东南亚国家联盟-文集 Ⅳ. ①D92-53②D933-53

中国版本图书馆CIP数据核字(2023)第193576号

责任编辑 李 宁 郑晓曦
美术编辑 李嘉彬
技术编辑 许克华

出版发行 厦门大学出版社
社 址 厦门市软件园二期望海路 39 号
邮政编码 361008
总 机 0592-2181111 0592-2181406(传真)
营销中心 0592-2184458 0592-2181365
网 址 http://www.xmupress.com
邮 箱 xmup@xmupress.com
印 刷 厦门市明亮彩印有限公司

开本 720 mm×1 020 mm 1/16
印张 19.25
插页 3
字数 436 千字
版次 2023 年 12 月第 1 版
印次 2023 年 12 月第 1 次印刷
定价 88.00 元

本书如有印装质量问题请直接寄承印厂调换

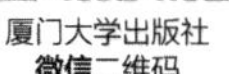
厦门大学出版社
微信二维码

厦门大学出版社
微博二维码